Monkey Puzzle man

By the same author:

Scotland: The Land and its Uses, Chambers Harrap, 1993
Scotland, Land & People: An Inhabited Solitude, Luath Press, 1998
Wild Scotland, Luath Press 1998, revised 2006
Journey into Africa: The Life and Death of Keith Johnston, Scottish Cartographer and Explorer (1844–79), Whittles Publishing, 2004
The Road to Tanganyika: The Diaries of Donald Munro and William McEwan, Kachere Series, 2006
Selim Aga: A Slave's Odyssey, Luath Press, 2007

Monkey Puzzle Man

Archibald Menzies, Plant Hunter

James McCarthy

Whittles Publishing

Published by
Whittles Publishing,
Dunbeath,
Caithness KW6 6EY,
Scotland, UK
www.whittlespublishing.com

ISBN 978-1904445-61-6

Cover: Monkey Puzzle Image, *Araucaria araucana* © David Buchanan.
Cover and frontispiece: Portrait of Archibald Menzies by Eden Upton Eddis, 1836.
(Courtesy of The Linnean Society of London.)

The Sibbald Trust is an independent charitable trust which gives financial support to many different facets of the botanical and horticultural interests of the Royal Botanic Garden Edinburgh.

Design and typesetting by Scotty-Dog Pictures
Printed in Poland by POZKAL

For Jill

Contents

Foreword

This richly detailed account of the life and travels of Archibald Menzies is a most welcome addition to the literature of botanical exploration. Given that a genus of flowering plants, *Menziesia*, was named in his honour, as were over a hundred other species or varieties, it is surprising that he has not previously been the subject of proper biography. Thanks to James McCarthy, we now have a satisfyingly comprehensive account of the life of a Scot who travelled the world as a surgeon naturalist in the Royal Navy. Amongst many other notable contributions, Archibald Menzies pioneered the documentation of the plants of the Pacific Northwest of America. It is frequently remarked upon that Scotland has produced a disproportionately large number of pioneering plant collectors. The Royal Botanic Garden Edinburgh (RBGE) has had a hand, at least, in the lives of many of them. Archibald Menzies and his brother both worked as gardeners at the RBGE when it was situated at its third site, on Leith Walk. He was inspired by the teaching of my most illustrious predecessor as Regius Keeper, John Hope, who was a leading figure in the Scottish Enlightenment.

As a surgeon naturalist, Archibald Menzies led a frequently frustrating double life in which his shipboard duties caring for the crews of the *Prince of Wales* and the *Discovery* dominated over his passion for plants and natural history. Sir Joseph Banks, who had sailed with Captain Cook to Australia on the *Endeavour*, issued Menzies with his instructions for the voyage of the *Discovery*, which included the following requirement: 'When you meet with curious or valuable Plants which you do not think likely to be propagated from seeds in His Majesty's Garden, you are to dig up proper Specimens of them, plant them in the Glass Frame provided for that purpose, and use your utmost endeavours to preserve them alive till your return'. Although even his utmost endeavours were not quite equal to this challenge it is remarkable how many plants he discovered and introduced into cultivation. Without doubt the most distinctive addition to our gardens was the Monkey Puzzle Tree. However, he also discovered one of the most important timber trees, the Douglas Fir. The common name of this tree commemorates David Douglas, who followed in Menzies' footsteps, but its scientific name is, appropriately, *Pseudotsuga menziesii.* Towering examples of this tree flourish in Scotland today. I think that Archibald Menzies would be pleased to discover that centuries after he worked at the RBGE we are still discovering new plants and very much focussed on conserving and protecting the world's conifers through the International Conifer Conservation Programme. His great legacy continues.

Stephen Blackmore FRSE
Regius Keeper, Royal Botanic Garden Edinburgh

Preface

Born in 1754, Archibald Menzies' life spanned a period of rapid expansion in the British Empire based on sea power. He was almost a stereotype of the Scottish boy from a modest rural background, who, starting as a local gardener, succeeded in qualifying as a naval surgeon and subsequently as an official expedition naturalist through two influential patrons, Professor John Hope, Regius Keeper of the Royal Botanic Garden in Edinburgh, and Sir Joseph Banks, President of the Royal Society.

He gained valuable experience as a field botanist while serving as a naval surgeon in the West Indies and on the East Coast of North America. On a private fur-trading expedition to the West Coast of North America in the 1780s, he showed his ability not only as a naturalist but as an observant recorder of native customs, with a capacity for picking up local languages. However, the most significant venture of his career was as the naturalist and subsequently the surgeon to George Vancouver's epic survey of the North American coast, from California to Alaska, in 1791–95, during which he made important collections of plants and birds. He also completed the first ascent of the highest mountains in Hawaii and discovered the Californian Condor.

Because of his ambiguous position on board the *Discovery*, determined by Banks, Menzies had an uneasy relationship with Vancouver, which culminated in Menzies being placed under arrest on the homeward voyage, although the anticipated court martial was pre-empted. Banks himself used Menzies' evidence of Vancouver's intemperate behaviour to undermine the expedition commander, but was unsuccessful in getting Menzies to produce his journal of the voyage before that of Vancouver. Menzies' inability to publish his records timeously undoubtedly limited greater public acknowledgement, although he was held in high regard by other botanists.

Ill-health forced his retirement from the Navy in 1802, but he established a successful medical practice in London and died in 1842 at the age of 88. It is claimed that more plants are named after Menzies than any other collector, many of these and their varieties now popular garden favourites. Equally important, he was the first collector of plants from the North American seaboard, laying down the foundations for botany there, and for the work of subsequent plant hunters. Although he discovered a number of important commercial forest trees from North America, his name is especially associated with *Araucaria* or Monkey Puzzle and the story of its almost accidental collection on his homeward journey with Vancouver.

Acknowledgements

I owe a very special debt of gratitude to Syd House, not only for his considerable encouragement from the start of this work, but also for generously providing all his research notes and a considerable number of images from his collection. The Library at the Royal Botanic Garden Edinburgh (RBGE) has kindly allowed me use of their facilities, while Jane Hutcheon and her staff there have been consistently courteous and helpful. Through their good offices, the Linnean Society of London kindly lent their copy of Menzies' journal of the voyage of the *Discovery*, enabling me to access this most conveniently in Edinburgh. The Society also allowed access to the papers of their first President, James Edward Smith. I have been given invaluable help from the staff at Kew Gardens, the British Natural History Museum (Botany Department), and the British Museum Ethnology Library, where Dr Jonathan King drew my attention to the important Menzies collections and to the National Library of Scotland.

I am indebted to the Strathmartine Trust and to the Edinburgh Botanic Garden Sibbald Trust for financial help which has been much appreciated, and the assistance provided by the Trust's secretary, Ian Hedge, who has also made valuable corrections to the botanical record. In addition, the honorific of a Research Associateship from the RBGE has lent valuable accreditation to the project. Hamish Adamson at that institution together with Dr Keith Whittles of Whittles Publishing have smoothed the path of bringing this work into print very expertly. Thanks are also due to Bob Mitchell for correcting botanical errors in particular and to Erica Schwarz for her meticulous editing. It seems especially appropriate that the Regius Keeper of the RBGE, with which Archibald Menzies had such a close association, should write the foreword, for which I am particularly grateful. Last, but not least, my thanks to my wife for her continuing support.

1

Introduction

In the course of writing this book, I conducted an experiment among a number of colleagues and friends, all reasonably well-informed. Asking the question: 'Do you know anything about Archibald Menzies?' the commonest response was 'Archibald *who*?' Given that Menzies laid the foundations for the development of botany in Northwest America and discovered a number of tree species which have dramatically altered the landscape of the British uplands, this response is sufficient justification for bringing his life before a wider audience.

He is not alone however, for it is only in recent years that the very significant contribution of the Scottish plant hunters of the 18th to 20th centuries to botanical exploration around the globe has been more widely revealed to the public in popular print and through the admirable Plant Collectors' Garden at Pitlochry in Perthshire. Perhaps not too surprisingly, given the importance of the work of the *Discovery* voyage in mapping the western coast of North America in the early 1790s, Menzies is well-known and celebrated there, where several locations are named after the botanical explorer. It is curious however that, in several volumes on plant hunters generally, the name of Archibald Menzies is either overlooked completely, or mentioned only *en passant*.

Serious plant hunting began with William Turner in the mid-16th century, but it was the Tradescants, father and son, who in the early 17th century were responsible for some of the most important introductions into Britain, including lupins, lilies, crocuses and many other plants from North America, Europe and Russia. The Rev. John Banister was sent to North America by the Bishop of London, Dr Henry Compton, in the 1680s and sent back many tree species for the Fulham Palace Garden, including *Abies nigra* (Black Fir), now known as *Picea mariana*, as well as several North American oaks.[1] There was considerable competition between individuals and institutions, since rare species commanded high – and sometimes astronomical – prices. There was much covetousness and greed involved, with the Dutch, for example, jealously guarding 'their' plants by force if necessary, not least their valuable spice sources, such as nutmeg, from the East Indies.

Plants and seeds were of course collected for economic purposes, but exotic species could also be status symbols for wealthy estate owners, sometimes stimulated by the colourful images of previously unknown plants sent back by collectors. The industrial revolution from the mid-18th century onwards created sufficient riches for some to enable them to indulge their pastimes and pursue the aesthetic improvement of their properties. The first half of the 18th century also saw a move away from the excessive formality of previous gardens, allowing for greater creativity in landscaping and planting[2] utilising the new species and varieties which were being brought back by the plant collectors. From 1753 onwards order was brought into the activities of plant collectors through the publication of Carl Linnaeus's *Species Plantarum*, the first systematic classification of the plant kingdom. Antoine Laurent de Jussieu then built on Linnaeus's work to produce a workable classification which is a basis of the system used today.

In plant collecting, Britain was well to the fore, due largely to the established botanical gardens at Kew, Edinburgh and elsewhere, but also to the important patronage of royalty and influential and wealthy landowners, as well as the Horticultural Society, founded in 1804. The gardens at Kew and the great figure of Sir Joseph Banks (1743–1820) – of whom much more later – are indissolubly linked from the last

Sir Joseph Banks by Thomas Phillips, 1809.
(Courtesy of The Linnean Society of London.)

quarter of the 18th century onwards, and it was he more than any other who was responsible for sending British plant collectors, including Archibald Menzies, across the globe. Banks, a wealthy landowner, had distinguished himself as a naturalist on James Cook's epic first voyage round the globe, with his huge collections of exotic specimens, to the extent on his return of almost eclipsing the great navigator.

Banks had the ear of King George III, himself a garden enthusiast, and was the unofficial director of the collections at Kew from 1777. Even by 1768 there were over 3000 plants in cultivation there, including more than 500 species of hardy trees which had been introduced from North America. Much of this was due to Banks' initiatives and interest. He wanted Kew to be supreme, and used the King's name to secure this, constantly referring to 'His Majesty's Botanic Garden' and jealously resisting the competing claims of other European gardens, such as the Jardin du Roi in Paris.

It is said that by the end of his life Banks had introduced some 7000 new species via these illustrious gardens.[3] However, credit must also go to his friend, the Earl of Sandwich, who as First Lord of the Admiralty, and at Banks' urging, agreed to place botanists on board a number of His Majesty's expedition ships. Sir William Chambers, landscaper of Princess Augusta's estate at Kew, in 'Plans of the Gardens and Buildings at Kew 1763', acknowledged 'the assiduity with which all curious productions are collected from every part of the globe', forecasting that 'in a few years, this will be the amplest and best collection of curious plants in Europe'.[4] Kew became the home of the greatest collection of plants, both living and dried, from across the world, and also in time of the international registry of the globe's endangered plant and animal species.

The first plant collector sent out by Banks from Kew was the Scot Francis Masson (1741–1805). It was the collection of some 400 new species by Masson in southern Africa which resulted in Banks proclaiming that Kew now held superiority over every similar establishment in Europe.[5] Banks also later chose David Nelson from Kew to collect and tend, on the instructions of the King, the precious breadfruit from the Pacific to feed plantation slaves. (Nelson had sailed with Captain James Cook on his third voyage, discovering *Eucalyptus* in Tasmania.) Unfortunately Nelson sailed with Captain Bligh on the infamous *Bounty*. At the mutiny Nelson remained loyal to Bligh and died in Timor in 1789. It was left to others to bring back the breadfruit on a subsequent voyage.

It was Peter Good and yet another Scot, Robert Brown, in the *Investigator* in 1801 who did so much to collect Australian plants, although Good died of dysentery in Sydney in 1803.[6] Good's compatriot Allan Cunningham surveyed much of the Australian coast as far as Timor and in 1823 found a pass through the Liverpool Ranges, opening up the previously unknown Darling Downs which were identified as ripe for European settlement. This is a striking illustration of how such plant collectors were explorers in their own right, often being the first to venture into the interior of unknown lands in their search for specimens.

A major challenge for the plant collectors was how to get their material home. There was usually little difficulty with pressed specimens gathered simply for identification,

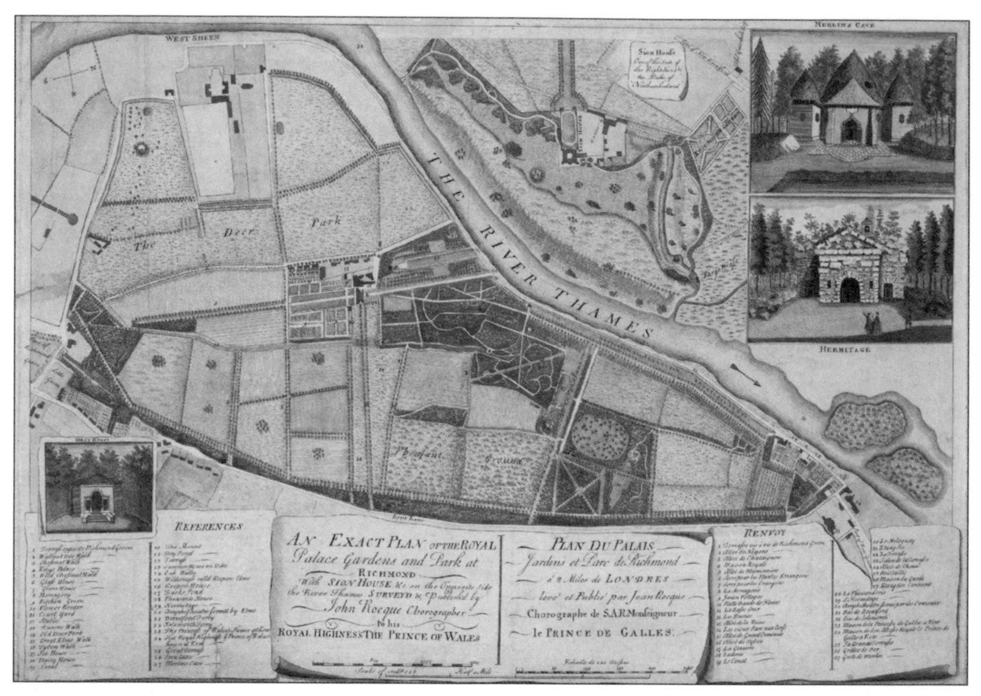

A map of Royal Botanic Gardens, Kew drawn by Jean (possibly John) Rocque for King George II in the 1740s. (Reproduced by kind permission of the Trustees of the Royal Botanic Gardens, Kew, from their archive.)

provided that there was a sufficient supply of drying paper and that humidity or insects did not destroy them. But for seeds which might have to be preserved over many months or even years, this was much more difficult: the transport of live plants over considerable distances could pose an almost insuperable problem. The threat of shipboard vermin eating the plants was a major challenge, while great care was required in aerating, watering, and protecting plants on board. It was John Evelyn (1620–1706), the great forester and landscape gardener, who provided some of the first detailed instructions on the preservation of seeds and live plants. Linnaeus himself was very specific about transported seeds and plants, and gave detailed instructions; there were many experiments in the proper treatment of seeds, such as using mutton fat and beeswax as coatings.[7]

Plant collecting in relatively unknown territories was a risky and hazardous business, and many botanists met an early death. 'Good God, when I consider the melancholy fate of so many of botany's votaries, I am tempted to ask whether men are in their right mind who so desperately risk life and everything else through the love of collecting plants', said Carl Linnaeus in *Glory of the Scientist* (1737). Often exposed to disease in tropical climates, they penetrated into dangerous areas with the risk of being swept away in turbulent rivers, or falling off precipices in their ardent searches for the rare and the beautiful. They were subject to hunger, thirst, and acute exhaustion, when not exposed to frostbite or the predations of hostile local people, often acutely suspicious of their motives. While Menzies was exposed to some of these hazards, he had the relatively secure base of a ship because of his medical duties, and much as he may have wished to, he was rarely given the opportunity of penetrating the interior of countries he visited, other than by boat on channels connected to the sea. Compared with the later hazards faced by his countryman David Douglas, for example, his was a comparatively safe existence.

The question of why these men risked life and limb in their quest for plants is difficult to answer. Few of them were likely to be enriched, unless they were also nurserymen with an outlet for valuable new species. While they might be accorded professional credit by other botanists, they were equally unlikely to achieve fame, let alone fortune. Dependent on their success, they might enhance their prospects from that of a humble gardener, but the hierarchies of their times would usually preclude access to higher social ranks. Although in some cases the motivations remain obscure, amongst almost all of them there appears to have been a genuine curiosity and deep personal and altruistic interest in their subject. This was often allied to a real sense of adventure and desire for exploration of unknown territories at a time when the wider world was beckoning. This was particularly true of Scots of the 18th and 19th centuries.

Menzies' career should be seen in the context of the history of Britain and its empire from the mid-18th century onwards – the so-called 'Second Empire' (see Appendix 1). Britain had, after the successful ending of the Seven Years War with France in 1763, become the dominant world power, largely through military and naval victories. In 1745, the British had taken the strategic French fort of Louisburg in Canada, and with the fall of Quebec in 1759, French power in North America was virtually extinguished. (Neither had the French been able to support the Jacobites in Scotland, who suffered a crushing defeat at Culloden in 1746.) Two years later, with their defeat at Pondicherry, the French had lost their foothold in India, where Clive had already secured Bengal for the British East India Company. Unsurprisingly, conquest and eventual empire acquisition encouraged plant hunting, especially if peace and prosperity ensued. The converse was equally true, with naval warfare in particular placing such activity at a low priority.

But the loss of the American Colonies and their winning of independence by 1783 created a crisis of confidence in Britain's attitude towards overseas territories, resulting in a change to a highly ambivalent attitude towards further colonial acquisitions. Nevertheless, Britain was still the world's greatest sea power with an insatiable interest in overseas trade and raw materials to feed the burgeoning agricultural and industrial revolutions at home. This in turn helped to swell urban populations and a poverty-stricken under-class, many of whom were forced to live on their wits and criminality. The solution was seen by the Establishment to be the export of this problem. Captain

James Cook charted the east coast of Australia in 1769, and just over 10 years later the first convict settlements were established there.

On the African continent, Mungo Park had reached the Niger in 1896, but for over 140 years previously, the west coast had supplied increasing numbers of slaves for the new plantations in the West Indies and the southern states of America, a trade which brought enormous profits to British merchants, protected by Britain's dominance of the seas. It was Britain's mercantile interests there that brought the British Navy to the Caribbean in Menzies' time, specifically to protect the sugar and rum trade, and to enforce the Navigation Acts which required that only British ships could carry cargoes to and from their West Indian possessions. On the other side of North America, Britain became entangled with Spanish interests in the highly lucrative trade in sea otter skins and other furs. Throughout the globe, British explorers, merchants and scientists were not only discovering new lands and resources, but also impacting on native peoples and their cultures.

However, the British were far less interested at this stage in colonial acquisitions than in securing freedom to trade, by establishing trading posts and harbours across the globe, even where others, such as the Spanish on the west coast of America, claimed sovereignty.[8] The competition between European powers in this arena quite ignored, as a matter of course, any indigenous rights of native peoples. In all of these issues of the last quarter of the 18th century, Menzies had his own particular connection, whether as an observer of the decline of French power in Eastern Canada, the use of slaves in the West Indies, and the fur trade off the west coast of Canada, or commenting on the suitability of Western Australia for settlement. In several visits to Tahiti and Hawaii, he was able to see distinct changes in the attitudes of indigenous people as a result of trade and the introduction of firearms.

It was Captain James Cook's earlier historic voyages which laid down the template for subsequent explorations, such as that of Captain George Vancouver (1757–98) on the Northwest coast of America. Having travelled on Cook's second and third great voyages, Vancouver undoubtedly modelled himself on his former mentor and attempted to emulate him. Thomas said of Cook that he was:

> … a master of techniques that enabled him to determine the orientation of a coast, the height of a mountain and the position of a reef – and to transcribe the whole on to a chart. Cook's geography … was mathematical and uncommunicative … . Cook trusted techniques and instruments rather than people who had no particular reason to trust him. He surveyed without asking, because he had been trained to do it that way … but voyaging was never as simple a matter as surveying a passage and putting a line on a chart … . It had effects – on himself, on his crew and on other people – that he could neither anticipate nor control.[9]

Cook's and later ventures of this kind involved 'a mix of motivations, from invasion and dispossession to more humanitarian objectives; encounters with indigenous people entailed both friendship and exploitation, reciprocity and imposition, shared understanding and misrepresentation'. Thomas emphasises that the voyagers and the native peoples not only came from very different worlds, but that these worlds were heterogeneous and changing.[9] All of this was even more true by the time of Vancouver's survey of the Northwest coast of America only a few years later, in which Menzies played his own part.

Menzies was simply one of a legion of Scots, many of comparatively humble origins, who were able to take advantage of Britain's expanding overseas interests, through its dominance of world trade and military power. Michael Fry in *The Scottish Empire* has put it succinctly:

> They were anyway aware that nature's niggardly gifts to their homeland must drive many of them furth of it to earn a livelihood overseas. ... they sought to make themselves useful, to thrive through adventure and enterprise, and to approach other societies not with a desire of conquering, ruling and changing, but of understanding them.[10]

The parish educational system, advocated by John Knox during the Reformation, ensured that many young Scots, including those from rural backgrounds, could obtain a sound basic education, on which, with their characteristic diligence, they could build and make their way in the world. That education focussed strongly not only on the three Rs of 'reading, 'riting and 'rithmatic', but also, notwithstanding a good dose of classics, on the practical sciences in which many Scots have been pre-eminent, including medicine and its foundations of botany. Menzies was perhaps fortunate in being born when he was, passing his formative years during the high point of the Scottish Enlightenment when, not least in the cities of Edinburgh and Glasgow, there was a ferment of intellectual and creative activity, embracing culture, science, philosophy and the practical applications of many new technological discoveries.

In her book *Seeds of Blood and Beauty: Scottish Plant Explorers* Ann Lindsay examines this Scottish connection in some detail and why it was that Scots became pre-eminent in the world of gardening from the 18th century onwards and provided many of the most distinguished plant collectors. 'A handful of Scots ... have hunted out and introduced into the West more plants from around the world than, say, all the European nations combined. Every garden in Britain, and most of our European neighbours as well, contains plants originally brought back to Europe by a Scot.' Although this is a very large claim, Lindsay is able to justify it in her mini-biographies of many of the great Scots plant collectors.

Lindsay ascribes the dominance of these men from the north to a combination of the recognition of their traditional skills, training and what would nowadays be called 'networking'. A number of them, like Menzies, were naval surgeons, who had received a rigorous training in Edinburgh. The medical schools of Glasgow and Edinburgh were valuable sources of botanists at a time when this subject was considered essential for medical men, especially the many naval surgeons who became expedition naturalists. Perhaps even more were practical gardeners, serving their time on the big estates or at the Royal Botanic Garden in Scotland's capital.

In time, landowners throughout Britain demanded Scots gardeners as a matter of course, such was their reputation. This rested not simply on gardening skills, but also on a relatively high level of literacy derived from the Scottish education system, combined with considerable adaptability. The last was often the result of an upbringing on a small Scottish farm or croft, where the young men would have to turn their hand to a wide variety of agricultural tasks in an environment of self-sufficiency.[11] Head gardeners would train their sons and it is hardly surprising that a confraternity developed, with gardeners across the country keeping in touch with one another, alert to any possible employment opportunities.

There was a widespread recognition among the great estates of Britain that the Scots were usually hard-working, and knowledgeable, with a sound practical training, often acquired at such notable institutions as the Royal Botanic Garden in Edinburgh, which had a high reputation. Often that training and experience was handed down from father to sons, so that when an important vacancy occurred, there was a cadre of enthusiastic recruits waiting in the wings. Nor could the Scots avoid the charge of racial nepotism.

The eminent head gardener at the Chelsea Physic Garden from its inception in 1673, John Miller, insisted in employing Scots for any new position. Hardly surprisingly, his son Philip became the director of that garden, and he was to be followed by a succession of able Scots. (Before the establishment of Kew, the Chelsea Physic Garden, owned by the Worshipful Company of Apothecaries, received all new plants arriving in the country and became a hub for gardening institutions throughout the land.)[12] Soon 'gardener' and 'Scotch' became almost synonymous in the great estates of Britain. The novelist George Eliot had commented, 'a gardener [was] Scottish as a French teacher was Parisien'.[13]

Although the Scots gardening 'mafia' had its influence, their reputation was based on real skills which often embraced a very wide range of experience derived from crofting and estate life in the hard northern environment. At a time when botanical and agricultural knowledge was expanding rapidly, the ability to read and keep pace with new information became essential, and the Scots were known for their background education and training, allied to a capacity for learning and an entrepreneurial attitude.[14] Sir Joseph Banks, in seeking suitable candidates for world-wide plant collecting, recognised not only these attributes, but also humility and frugality, which in his battles with a penny-pinching Admiralty commended these budget-conscious Scots to him.

Certainly, those who were selected for overseas expeditions – positions which were much sought after – had to measure up to demanding criteria and were very much an elite. They would have to be considerably more than gardeners or botanists, but have an all-round knowledge of natural history, and as skilled with the gun as with plant-drying. Furthermore, they would be expected to be sufficiently educated to record their observations in a systematic manner and often to be skilled in drawing and painting. They might well be charged with describing the manners and customs of native peoples. On the personal front, they would require to be temperamentally stable to endure close proximity with other voyagers over long periods and sufficiently adaptable to cope with demanding conditions of climate and culture. Physical fitness and stamina was a *sine qua non*. Menzies appears to have fitted this bill admirably.

This was also a time when prestigious institutions such as the Royal Society and the Royal Geographical Society, followed by the Horticultural Society (to gain the epithet 'Royal' 50 years after its establishment in 1804), were becoming increasingly important as centres and nodal points of knowledge for an expanding Empire, barely able to keep up with the flood of information from explorers, surveyors, and scientists with their reports from all quarters of the globe. And at the centre of this nexus were figures such as Sir Joseph Banks, who combined aristocratic and political influence with an intense interest not only in the natural world, but also in its economic potential.

Central to this were plants for both aesthetic and agricultural purposes, including trees, but outside Britain there were also later introductions to other countries, with such well-known examples as rubber, tea, and the cinchona tree used for quinine production.[15] Decorative and useful trees were of special interest to Scottish landowners in their search for new species to beautify their great estates and to provide fast-growing timber for large-scale forestry. Brought up in one of the pre-eminent tree-growing districts of Scotland, with an apprenticeship on a renowned arboricultural estate in Perthshire, Menzies would seem to have been tailor-made to be one of Banks' Empire men. (In his work on Menzies, Justice aptly named an introductory chapter 'For King and Kew'.)[16]

Menzies was not an especially colourful character, and despite an adventurous early life, there is little of the truly dramatic – with possibly one or two exceptions – in his career. In many ways he was the archetypal rural Scot of his time: hard-working and determined, he was nevertheless modest and disinclined to promote himself. But he also had the confidence of his craft behind him, being capable of applying himself rigorously to his subject, so that he made best use of his talents. He appears to have been a quietly engaging personality, with a gift for establishing good relations with native peoples, for example, allied to a curious and enquiring mind, which embraced much more than plant hunting. He is credited with making an important contribution to the ethnological and historical record of the Northwest coast of America, for example.[17]

He was generous in providing both advice and specimens from his collections, and if he had a fault, if such can be described, it was in not looking after his own interests, especially in the matter of pursuing publication of his results and perhaps in too readily giving credit to others. Nevertheless, he appears to have been naturally assiduous in cultivating his mentors and patrons, notably Professor John Hope (1725–86) in Edinburgh and the redoubtable Banks in London, who were key figures in his life and career.

The source material for this biography is widely scattered. There is virtually nothing in the way of family letters, although there is important professional correspondence with Banks, most of this held in the Mitchell Library in Sydney, Australia. Menzies' journal of his voyage in 1787–89 with James Colnett (?1752–1826), assuming he wrote an account, has not been discovered. For this voyage, I have been almost entirely dependent on the recent scholarly work of Robert Galois.

The National Library of Australia in Canberra holds the manuscript of Menzies' journal of his voyage with Vancouver, but the transcript held by the Linnean Society in London has been used in compiling the present biography. This apparently ends in February 1794 (as does the original in the British Library) at the completion of Menzies' ascent of Mauna Loa in Hawaii. Menzies' journal includes a number of reports of boat surveys carried out by other officers in which he himself did not participate, which makes his journal reasonably complete.[18] (C. F. Newcombe transcribed that journal for the period April to October 1792 and published this in the British Columbia Provincial Archives.) It was not until 1993 that Wallace Olson published Menzies' account of his time in Alaska covering the years 1793–94, and he gives a revealing account of the finding of this in the National Library of Australia. Much earlier, in 1920, W. F. Wilson had edited the Menzies journal relating to his time in Hawaii in *Archibald Menzies: Hawaii Nei 128 Years Ago.*

A most important source has been W. K. Lamb's superbly edited *A Voyage of Discovery to the North Pacific Ocean and Around the World 1791–1795 by George Vancouver* (1984) which has many references to Menzies obtained from the journal of the latter, as well as the journals of other officers on this voyage. These include the letters of Thomas Manby now in the Coe Collection of Western Americana in Yale University Library. (This author has freely used excerpts from Lamb's edition of Vancouver's journal.) There is much correspondence in the Brabourne Papers in the Mitchell Library in the State Library of New South Wales in Sydney. The most important relatively recent sources relating to Menzies, primarily as a botanist, are the scientific papers of Galloway and Groves (1987) and Groves (2001) which focus mainly on his voyage with Vancouver, but also include short biographies of the botanist. Apart from these botanical authorities, the very readable work by Clive Justice on the legacy of garden plants left by Menzies has proved especially valuable, not least for his detailed taxonomy and derivation of plants collected by Menzies. Grinnel's paper on the confirmation of the first identification of the Californian Condor appears to be the only one which deals with this discovery by Menzies.

Anderson refers to accounts not only by Menzies, but also by Edward Bell (now in the Turnbull Library, Wellington, New Zealand) and the private journal of Thomas

Manby in the form of letters to a friend. The relationships between these other officers and with Vancouver are well-explored by J. M. Naish (1996). Lisa Rosner's work on medical education at the University of Edinburgh in the 18th and 19th centuries has provided much of the material for this period of Menzies' life, while Keevil's work on Royal Navy medicine is a mine of information on that topic.

There are many other biographies of Vancouver which refer to Menzies, but to this writer's knowledge there has been no comprehensive biography of the botanist until now. It is not difficult to gauge the reasons for this: his own journal of the voyage of the *Discovery* and related correspondence in the early 1790s (and that of Vancouver himself and other officers) is the only substantial record by Menzies himself. His life reached a high point with the termination of that epic journey, when Menzies was barely 40 years of age. Although he spent a further few years in the Navy in the West Indies, the remaining 30 years of his professional life were spent relatively quietly as a successful medical practitioner at home. He retired in 1826 at the age of 72. (See Appendix 2.)

What this work aims to do is to provide the general reader, without a specialist interest in botany, with a reasonably rounded account of the life of a man of many accomplishments whose biographies hitherto have tended to be addendums to Vancouver's historic journey. For this reason, the main references to Menzies' plant collections have been confined to a specific chapter; readers with a more particular interest are referred to the work of Groves and Galloway and Groves above.

Much of Menzies' journal of the Vancouver voyage is taken up with the physical geography of the journey, the traverses of the vessels, and the topography of the country. Given that he was not responsible for surveying *per se*, his attention to this and the weather conditions, etc. is a little surprising, as it inevitably replicates much that Vancouver himself covered in his narrative. (What has to be constantly borne in mind is how such small sailing ships were totally at the mercy of the weather, on which everything depended.) It is also not particularly interesting as biographical material, since it exposes little of Menzies' own reactions, feelings or opinions. For this reason, these somewhat mundane details have largely been omitted, in favour of incidents involving other members of the crew or relations with native peoples, which reveal more of the character of the main subject.

Generally, however, Menzies is reticent on such incidents (other than in his correspondence with Banks) since in some cases they might reflect adversely on his colleagues, notably the commander of the expedition, and he would be aware that his journal might become public property, or at least be read by shipmates. Despite this, and with little to suggest that he is casting himself in the most favourable light, Menzies does come over as being quietly cheerful, making light of considerable difficulties, and prepared to make the best of things. This tends to be confirmed by the accounts of his colleagues who appear to have held him in high regard both as a caring physician and as an agreeable shipboard companion.

The only sour note is struck by one of Vancouver's biographers, Coleman, who implies that the surgeon's mate on the *Chatham*, George Hewett (who like Menzies was educated at the University of Edinburgh), constantly colluded with Menzies in criticising Vancouver. Although Hewett's diary certainly reflects this, there are very few occasions when Menzies does likewise, despite what must have been considerable justification, given Vancouver's reputation and mercurial temperament. It has been suggested that Vancouver's irascibility was due to a hyperthyroid condition known as Grave's disease and that his symptoms, followed by complete exhaustion, showed a progressive development of the illness. On the other hand, one explanation is that his personality derived from his early life experiences, including his mother's early death and his harsh treatment as a teenage midshipman.[19]

Menzies was a diligent and observant diarist, and especially in his comments on encounters with the Spanish (who were at various times officially at war with Britain) and with native peoples appears more sympathetic and generous in his assessments than many of his colleagues. This comes across in the extended quotations which have been included deliberately to reflect this aspect of his personality. (Menzies' often idiosyncratic spellings have been retained, but the longer passages have been sub-divided into paragraphs for readability where appropriate.) What is also clear from this is how much time Menzies dedicated to the writing of his narrative on a daily basis under what must often have been very difficult circumstances of adverse weather and fatigue, not infrequently after exhausting longboat journeys.

Menzies' journal of the voyage of HMS *Discovery* to the Northwest coast of America is mainly chronological and this convention has been followed for the survey of that coast, now largely within Washington, British Columbia and Alaska. It was the custom for vessels to repair to Hawaii during the worst of the winter months for replenishment of food and rest for the crews, and in the case of Vancouver's voyage, time was also spent in California. To avoid repetition and to present a more coherent picture of these lands and their inhabitants, these visits have been consolidated in separate chapters assigned to them. Other than in quotes, the modern names of locations have been used, for example Hawaii for Sandwich Isles 'Owhayee', and Tahiti for 'Otaheite'.

One of the incentives for writing this biography has been to reveal the author's serendipitous connections with Menzies and his travels. My adopted city of Edinburgh, where I have spent the last 40 years, is where Menzies received his training (at the Royal Botanic Garden Edinburgh) and subsequent university education. Apart from a background in forestry education in Aberdeen, Scotland (from which university Menzies was granted an honorary degree in medicine) and a familiarity with his birthplace and early environment through conservation work there, this writer has carried out plant collecting (on Kilimanjaro in East Africa) and spent several months investigating the great coastal forests of British Columbia, Oregon and Washington State in the late 1980s. (Incidentally the author's commissioning regiment, the Black Watch, which Menzies encountered in Nova Scotia, was raised near Menzies' home a few years before Menzies' birth.)[20]

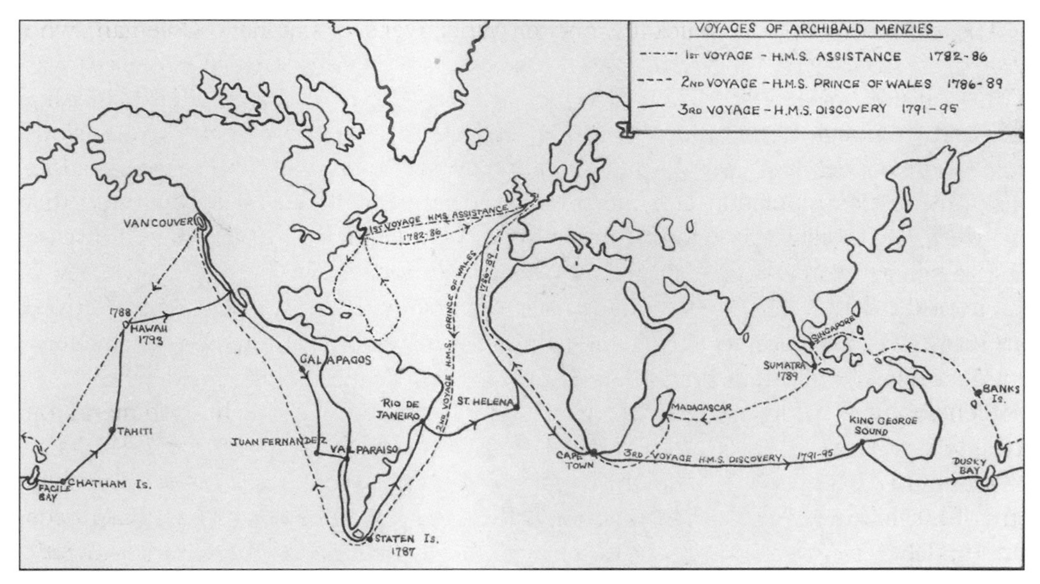

Map showing the voyages of Archibald Menzies,
drawn by J Macqueen Cowan in 1954. (RBGE archive.)

It has not been difficult to empathise with Menzies' enchantment on his first forays into the pristine native woods of Sitka Spruce and Douglas Fir on Vancouver Island, for example, and having seen the great moss-covered trunks of the giant trees in Carmanah reaching to over 100 metres in height, it is easy to understand his wonder. This author had his first sight of the red-barked Pacific Madrone (*Arbutus*), which Menzies discovered, characteristically hanging over the rocky bluffs of Galiano Island, named after the Spanish naval commander whom Menzies met in 1792. In Australia, Menzies' notes on the *Eucalyptus* woodland and *Banksia* species have brought back vibrant memories, while the description of the luxuriant 'ferneries' of the South Island of New Zealand have done likewise. Something of the conditions of voyaging under sail was experienced by the author, albeit replicating the conditions almost 170 years after Menzies' first sea journeys, at a sea training school in the north of Scotland. All of these affinities and experiences have provided a stimulus for writing the story of an eminent Scottish botanist whose name should be more widely known.

NOTES

1. Hepper (1999), 8
2. Ibid., 15
3. Musgrave, Gardner and Musgrave (1998), 35
4. Hepper (1999), 1
5. Ibid., 2
6. Musgrave, Gardner and Musgrave (1998), 116
7. Hepper (1999), 128
8. Lamb's introduction to Vancouver's journal gives a very good history of the conflict between the British and the Spanish leading to the 'Nootka Incident' in 1790.
9. Thomas (2004), xx–xxxiv
10. Fry (2001), 3
11. Lindsay (2005), 8–9
12. The Chelsea Physic Garden was noted for having the first heated greenhouses in England, constructed in 1680, which were a great success and enabled tropical plants to be raised, including the cinchona tree or 'Jesuit's bark' from which quinine was extracted as early as 1685. The Garden played an important role in the development of such crops as tea and cotton. Under Philip Miller it became the most famous garden in Europe for the number and rarity of the species cultivated and in Victorian times had the foremost collection of medicinal plants in Britain. It is still an important resource for pharmaceutical research. (Minter 2000, xii–6)
13. Ibid., 9
14. Ibid., 1–10
15. Musgrave, Gardner and Musgrave (1998), 10
16. Justice (2000), 7
17. King (1994), 35–43
18. Lamb (1993), 241
19. Olson (1993), 7
20. The *Red and White Book of the Clan Menzies* claims that this regiment was founded by Captain Robert Menzies.

2

A Visit to Santiago

On 24 March 1795, on the homeward journey from his epic five-year survey of the Northwest coast of America, Captain George Vancouver sighted the coast of Chile. He was in trouble. With a split main mast of his ship, the *Discovery*, he faced the prospect of rounding Cape Horn and the storms of the South Atlantic. He was also, with 17 cases of scurvy aboard, most anxious to replenish his stocks of green vegetables and fruit. He desperately needed repairs to be undertaken at the only significant port on this coast, Valparaiso, but relations with Spain, who controlled this coast, were tense: he had been instructed by the Admiralty to avoid Spanish ports. To add to his difficulties, his only reference to a route into the bay was a brief note two centuries previously by Richard Hawkins, which merely advised him to look for a great rock or small island to the south of the town for guidance.

In the event, he need not have worried about his reception: he was known to the Governor of the port, Don Lewis Alva, a brother of the Spanish officer with whom Vancouver had conducted amicable negotiations at Nootka, on what is now Vancouver Island.[1] The ship and its company were greeted warmly. After years away from home and civilisation, the men were delighted at the sight of a large town, with its many churches, forts, streets and several ships riding at anchor in the harbour, and relished the prospect of recuperation and some domestic comforts, apart from putting their feet on dry land.

The materials and equipment needed for the repair of the mast required the permission of none less than the Captain-General of Chile, who rejoiced in the name of Don Ambrosio Bernardo O'Higgins de Vallenar – an adventurous Irishman who had been in the British army before entering the service of Spain. He had been promoted after commanding victorious forces against the rebellious Araucanians of southern Chile and was later to become Viceroy of Peru. O'Higgins was apparently more than pleased to assist Vancouver and even invited the captain and his officers to his palace in St. Jago, or Santiago as it now is, some 90 miles from the coast, while the mast was being repaired. Although Vancouver's health was precarious and he would not have relished the long horseback ride, he was beholden to his host to assist in replenishing his ship and in getting essential repairs done. He was not in a position to refuse – such a refusal might well have been taken as a snub at a time of difficult relations with Spain.

Apart from Vancouver, the party of officers included Peter Puget, James Johnstone, Joseph Baker, Joseph Whidbey, William Broughton, Zachary Mudge and the ship's surgeon and naturalist, Archibald Menzies. They were accompanied by two mounted Irish dragoons, serving with the Spanish forces, and a posse of muleteers who drove the mules carrying tents and baggage.[2] After ensuring that the ship's crew were well-provisioned with fresh food and vegetables, the party set off from Valparaiso on what was to become a difficult and uncomfortable journey, particularly for the navymen, who were unaccustomed to riding and had had little exercise aboard ship in the months previously.

The country was harsh and the route was rough. Puget describes one of the dilapidated hovels where they rested as containing only 'a dirty table, a stool, a wretched bed in one corner, and five or six crosses'. Vancouver himself says: 'The land about these miserable hovels was, like the surrounding waste, in a perfect state of nature, without the vestige of any labour having been ever bestowed upon it, not even in the cultivation of a garden.'[3]

After two days' travel, they spent a short and uncomfortable night on the earth floor of one of these mud huts, before the dragoons aroused them for a 3 a.m. start, ostensibly to avoid the mid-day heat. They had a slow pull up the coast range before sighting St. Jago, impressively set against its magnificent backdrop of the snow-capped Andes. Here one of the dragoons was sent off to forewarn O'Higgins of their impending arrival, while the officers attempted to improve their appearance by putting on their somewhat worn best uniforms. To Vancouver's dismay, the dragoons returned with two Spanish officers and five very fine horses, each of their saddles enhanced by gold and silver lace, obviously prepared for a dignified entrance to the capital. The insistence of the Spaniards that spurs be worn for entry into the city almost caused a diplomatic incident, as the British party, not being professional horsemen, were afraid that an unintentional application of the spurs might cause an embarrassing accident. After much argument, with the Spanish insisting that these were *de rigueur* on this occasion, Vancouver and his men were very reluctantly allowed to dispense with the spurs.

After a procession through crowds of gaping onlookers, the party were received by a resplendent guard of honour at the gates to the palace. Here they were welcomed warmly by the Captain-General, who seemed especially pleased to be able to use his mother tongue. A number of ladies arrived, offering nosegays and invitations to supper. On a subsequent evening at a concert and ball given in their honour, the visitors were invited by these ladies, according to Puget, 'to join their party on the cushions: with this we instantly complied'. The officers' ardour may have been dampened, however, by the ladies' 'total neglect of their teeth, which are suffered to become intolerably dirty' and their 'scandalously neglected education'. Vancouver himself was sufficiently observant to note the women's 'under linen garment, the bottom of which, as well as the tassels of their garters, was fringed with lace'. He was less impressed by the bedrooms which were so rubbish-strewn that, according to Puget, 'it would have required a shovel rather than a brush for its removal'. However, a request for a broom produced the astonishing answer that such items were not to be found in St. Jago.[4]

The party spent a total of nine days in the capital, visiting all the main features and being royally entertained in the houses of the most prominent citizens. In a letter to Sir Joseph Banks, Menzies averred: 'We were treated with every mark of attention and friendly hospitality by the President himself, and the principal inhabitants vied with each other in showing us every degree of civility and kindness so that we left Santiago with a very favourable impression of the liberality of the Chilenese and their president.'[5] Apparently, Menzies took advantage of that hospitality at a farewell banquet by pocketing some of the large nuts which were offered for dessert and which were taken back to the ship, to be planted in the frame specially constructed for this purpose. Or did he? Thereby, as they say, hangs a tale …

NOTES

1. Lamb (1984), 1972
2. Ibid., 198
3. Ibid., 1487
4. Ibid., 1495–1501
5. Menzies to Banks, Valparaiso, 28 April 1795. Banks Correspondence 2: 121, Royal Botanic Gardens, Kew

3

'A Lad o' Pairts'

Archibald Menzies was born in the parish of Weem near Aberfeldy in Perthshire early in 1754, a mere nine years after the disastrous rising of 1745 under the Young Pretender, Bonnie Prince Charlie. He was the second son of a large family born to James and Anne Menzies which included five sons and three daughters. The exact location of his birthplace is in some doubt – there are references to Styx House on the southern bank of the River Tay, some five miles west of Aberfeldy. There is still a substantial collection of ruined farm buildings here, marked on modern maps as 'Styx', a little way from the present Kenmore–Aberfeldy road. Although his father had a good position as Head Gardener to Sir Robert Menzies of Menzies, Third Baronet of

The ruined remains of farm buildings marked on modern maps as Styx and possibly Archibald Menzies' birthplace. (Author's collection.)

Nova Scotia, these ruins would indicate an owner of greater standing. Photographs of Styx (Stix) House, apparently still in existence at least into the late 1940s, show a white-washed double-storey house of some prominence. The name Styx is said to derive from the Gaelic *na Suicean* – the Stocks – being a reference to the nearby impressive circle of standing stones known as Croft Moraig.

The Breadalbane country in which young Archibald Menzies was raised, lying on the edge of the Highlands, includes some of the most beautiful landscapes in Scotland, with the rich pastoral straths along the valley bottoms contrasting with the rugged mountains to the north, and with Loch Tay lying only a few miles to the west. The River Tay, the largest river system in Britain, links hills and glens, and some of the finest natural pinewoods in the country clothe the slopes of Glen Lyon and Rannoch, which in the year of Archibald's birth was considered impassable.[1] Today, some of that landscape has been altered by extensive new forestry plantations, but much remains as it would have been in Archibald's time. The huge scattered oaks around Styx probably date from then, as do the larches, first introduced into Scotland by Menzies of Culdares in 1738, which bronze the hillsides in autumn and winter.[2]

The Menzies family were Normans who came to England with William the Conqueror, and the first recorded chief became Chamberlain of Scotland in the 13th century. Archibald's family was probably a sept of the Menzies of Culdares.[3] In 1745

Loch Tay with Ben Lawers in the distance. (Author's collection.)

The Menzies family crest. (Author's collection.)

Sir Robert Menzies' factor, against the wishes of his chief, raised the clan for the Jacobites, but was decisively defeated fighting alongside the Atholl Brigade. This appears not to have been held against the clan chief, even though his wife, a supporter of Prince Charlie, allowed the Pretender to stay two nights at the castle after the retreat from Culloden (J. I. Robertson, *pers. comm.*). Archibald's youth was a time of important changes in agriculture, industry, and indeed a whole way of life in this borderland between Highlands and Lowlands.

Archibald's father would have been a crofter or tenant farmer,[4] with his own patch of relatively fertile land for raising crops of oats, pease, and bere (barley) and the right to graze animals, both cattle and sheep, on the poorer upper pastures. From an early age, the young Menzies became familiar with the daily round of farming tasks and had to undertake the chores of a crofting household, including spreading the old thatch from the cottage roofs, blackened by the peat fires, to provide manure for the fields, the milking of the cattle, and the turning of the hay crop. But the way of life was changing rapidly from a tribal Celtic and essentially feudal system, with its strict fealty to a clan chief, to a more Anglo-Saxon market economy with individual property rights.

Highlands and Lowlands were brought closer together with the improvement of roads and bridges, many built to exercise military control after the 1715 Rising, and the development of industries such as linen weaving, based on the extensive growing of flax, including the building of local lint mills along the Tay Valley. For the first time, a significant proportion of the population worked for wages, migrating from the Highlands to the small townships such as Aberfeldy, the nearest market for Archibald and his family. His parents were neither rich nor poor, but had the security of an income from the laird in addition to the crops and stock which they were able to raise.

In the last quarter of the 18th century the relatively small district of Weem supported over 1000 black cattle and 8000 sheep, but the old tradition of droving stock from Highlands to Lowlands was considerably hindered by the new fenced enclosure of pastures.[5]

Weem, the nearest small hamlet to Styx, was thought of as a Menzies township, with records going back to the 1200s. According to these it was here that Archibald Menzies was baptised on 15 March 1754. The old Kirk, now a mausoleum, is the property of the Menzies Charitable Trust and contains many memorials to members of the clan, while its surrounding burial ground is replete with gravestones bearing the family name. Two miles to the west, the striking turreted greystone Castle Menzies still stands, after considerable alteration and restoration, as a place of pilgrimage for the world-wide diaspora of the Menzies. The association of this territory with the family is indicated by the records showing that in Menzies' father's time, half of the staff employed in the castle grounds were named Menzies.

Castle Menzies near Weem in Perthshire. (Author's collection.)

Weem Kirk, the place of Archibald Menzies' baptism in 1754.
(Courtesy of Robert Brooks.)

By the late 19th century, these grounds had become renowned for some of the largest trees in Scotland, including a Spanish chestnut with a girth at base of over 26 feet, and the largest *Sequoia sempervirens* (Coast Redwood) in Britain, which by 1883 had a girth of 13 feet and 7 inches. The *Arbutus menziesii* (Pacific Madrone) planted here about 1871, a species first discovered by Menzies, was probably the first in Britain.[6] The orchards supported large crops of apples, pears and cherries. There are records of Menzies' father disbursing payment to no fewer than a dozen men for tree planting; he would have crossed from his farm at Styx by the ferry across the River Tay daily to his work on the estate. Menzies was fortunate in being there at a time when the gardens were being re-developed; this included the planting of many new and exotic species of trees, the fashion especially among the richer of the Perthshire landowners who came to be known as the 'planting lairds'. What in the late 18th century must have been one of the finest designed estate gardens in Scotland is now sadly neglected.

Sir Robert must have been of a scientific inclination, as he kept daily records of morning and evening temperatures, barometer readings, and so on, which Menzies would have known about, even if he was not directly involved in their measurement, and this will have enhanced his education in a comprehensive approach to gardening.[7] Later, Menzies became something of a pioneer in marine weather observation. He could not have foreseen that the cliffs above Weem would one day be clothed with the tree species which he himself had discovered, and which were subsequently introduced by his friend David Douglas. An account of the estates of Scotland towards the end of the 19th century, remarking on the fame of the Castle Menzies woods, said:

'Indeed, there is no place in Scotland, far less in Perthshire, where so many gigantic specimens of trees are to be seen in more luxuriant growth and beauty.'[8]

Menzies' family were Presbyterians in the old Scottish tradition, with a strong respect for education. His parents would have been Gaelic speakers in the Perthshire dialect, although they would have understood Scots, and Menzies himself is most likely to have been bilingual, although schooling was strongly orientated towards the learning of English.[9] According to the *Statistical Account* for 1791, 'much attention is paid to their religious instruction; and every violation of moral rectitude is punished with the utmost severity'.[10] If Archibald transgressed, he would have recourse to the 'cooling stane' to sit on outside the school door to relieve the pain of a beating. At least until the mid-19th century, the schoolmaster, paid about £10 a year and appointed by the local Kirk Session, expected each pupil to bring a peat brick for the schoolroom fire, together with a quantity of oats for the mid-day meal.[11] The subjects Menzies was taught would have included the classics, English, arithmetic, and Biblical studies in classes which would have contained a range of ages. The often barefoot children would sit on crude backless benches over a floor of beaten earth.

It seems that all of Menzies' brothers were gardeners and would have worked in the Castle Menzies grounds; one of them, Robert, distinguished himself by becoming a principal gardener at the Royal Botanic Garden Edinburgh (RBGE). Hardly surprisingly, Menzies appears to have developed a genuine interest in wild plants from an early age, having discovered, for example, the rare *Cerastium alpinum* (Alpine Mouse-ear) on the cold high corries of nearby Ben Lawers; this massif on the northern shores of Loch Tay was subsequently renowned for its unique assemblages of arctic-alpine plant species and is now a National Nature Reserve for this reason.[12]

Another brother, James, distinguished himself in quite a different way by joining the United Scotsmen, which started as a local protest against conscription in 1797 and had its centre in Weem. These anti-militia riots against the raising of quotas of fighting men from each parish were put down with great severity.[13] James was charged with treason, but succeeded in evading trial and fled to America where he remained for the rest of his life.[14]

There is no record of how Menzies came to be appointed to the RBGE or exactly when. It seems he may have started there in 1768, when he would have been in his mid-teens; his elder brother William's position there would certainly have helped, and he is most likely to have had a recommendation from Sir Robert Menzies. He was fortunate to be there during the guardianship of the eminent Scottish scientist John Hope, an early disciple of Linnaeus, who even went so far as to erect at his own expense a monument in the Royal Garden to the great Swedish botanist. Hope was responsible for the creation of the new gardens at the top of Leith Walk from 1763 onwards. The garden, originally established in 1670 as a physic or herbal garden by Andrew Balfour and Robert Sibbald, had already moved from its original site near Holyrood Abbey to Trinity Hospital near the present Waverley Station. Hope's new

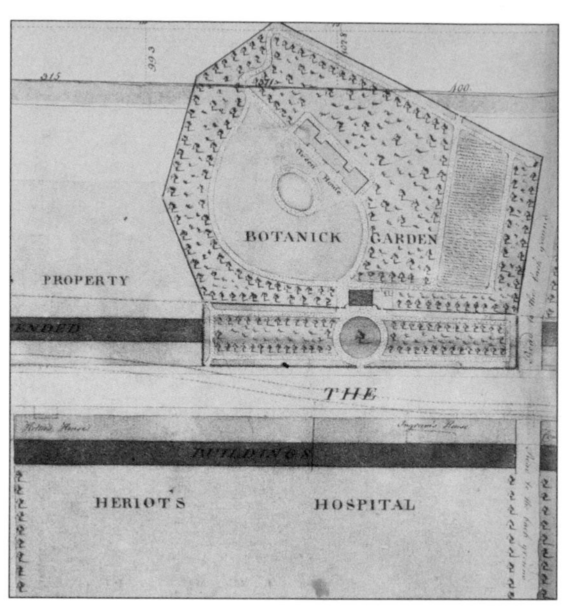

A plan of the Royal Botanic Garden Edinburgh, Leith Walk Garden in the late 18th century. (RBGE archive.)

The only known portrait of John Hope (left) in 1785, speaking to one of his gardeners by the celebrated caricaturist John Kay. (RBGE archive.)

The monument commissioned by John Hope in tribute to Linnaeus, first erected at the Leith Walk Garden and now at the RBGE site in Edinburgh. (RBGE collection.)

> The wages are 4 shillings a week, a share of a bed – sheets and blankets, but neither coal nor Candle; if behaviour unexceptional, when he leaves the garden, for every week he has served, 6 pence more – this in my good will – his attendance in the garden is expected during summer till 8 at night [a similar document refers to another gardener having to attend from 6 in the morning till bedtime if necessary] ... every Sunday in his turn he is to attend upon the garden, Whatever money he receives from them who visit the garden immediately to be paid in to the head gardener. He is not to presume on any account whatever to give away the smallest thing pertaining to the garden without my leave obtained ... he must provide himself in a proper chest for his cloathes and in at least two towels – this is to be observed that he is engaged from week to week. It is proper to acquaint him that he has no prospects of being employed after October next.

A postscript stated that he was not to show the garden to any acquaintance without leave from the head gardener.[23]

Hope had introduced to the garden – ahead of the renowned gardens in Paris – the Linnaean system of nomenclature, which Menzies subsequently depended on in his plant collecting and identification world-wide. Importantly, Menzies would also have learned of the methods of packing seeds and plant material, as Hope had established the first syndicate for importing such material, particularly from North America, which was to be Menzies' most prolific hunting ground. (He himself was to send plants and seeds to Hope and his successor, Dr Daniel Rutherford, who, after Hope's death in 1786, was to remain as Keeper of the RBGE for 33 years.)

Hope also provided well-attended scholarly lectures, primarily for medical students in his position as professor at the University of Edinburgh; this was at a time when the university was just beginning to become pre-eminent as a world centre for medical education. His students not only served as surgeons in the British Navy across the seven seas, but many became dedicated plant collectors, providing their revered professor and the RBGE with seeds and plants from distant quarters of the globe.[24] One of his most distinguished pupils was William Roxburgh, who named and described over 1500 Indian plants and produced high quality drawings of 2500 species, providing the foundation of botany on the sub-continent.

Exactly how the generous Hope enabled Menzies to attend these lectures and provide for his medical education is not known. Most medical students came from the professional classes, presumably because of the cost; poorer students would opt for the ministry, where bursaries were often available.[25] Medical studentship provided the opportunity of upward social mobility, as such education had the purpose of setting up men (there were no women in the profession) in practice. For a physician it was considered necessary to have a liberal education and there was a considerable prejudice against trades or manual work. Social networking was used for introductions to the professors from the student's family and friends, with appropriate invitations to dinner and *soirées*. Although there were no entrance qualifications and matriculation

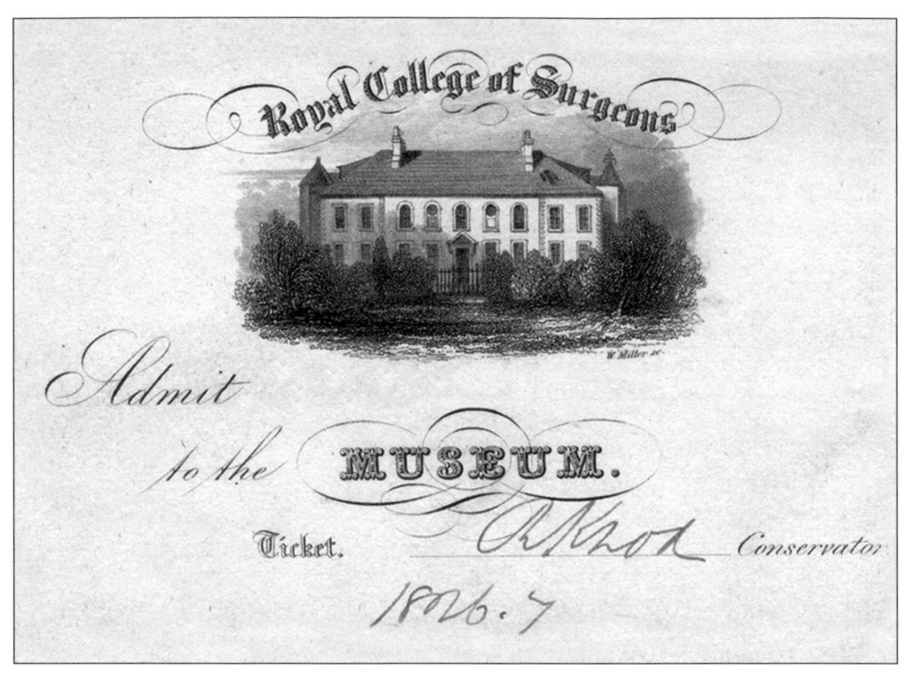

A ticket for the museum of the Old Surgeons Hall, Edinburgh showing the front of the original Surgeons Hall as it would have looked in Menzies' time there as a student. (Courtesy of The Royal College of Surgeons, Edinburgh.)

was not necessary, the payment of fees to the professor was obligatory: it was important for the professor's reputation and remuneration to have his lectures attended by as many students as possible.

Surgery was regarded as an inferior subject, with its emphasis on manual dexterity, and in Menzies' time had only recently become disassociated from barbering. Physicians, on the other hand, were regarded as 'gentlemen', fit for intercourse with polite society, and there was undoubtedly a hierarchy among the students. (The College of Physicians actually refused barber-surgeons to treat disease except when at sea.) The scions of wealthier families could expend up to £500 per winter session to maintain their lifestyles – which might include riding lessons, theatre tickets, foreign travel and even the expense of keeping mistresses – while at the other end of the scale, the poorest would survive on as little as £10, living on the most meagre diet and often skipping meals.[26]

An American student, writing to his brother concerning his expenses and the student hierarchy, said:

> First, the Fine Gentlemen or those who give no application to study, but spend the revenues of Independent Fortunes.

> Secondly, the Gentlemen, or Students of medicine strictly speaking, these live genteely and at the same time apply themselves to study.
>
> Thirdly, the Vulgar, or those who, if they are not indolent, are entirely devoid of anything polite and agreeable. I believe you will not doubt for a moment with which of these orders I ought to associate.[27]

There is a note of one student spending on average six shillings and ninepence weekly, breakfasting on porridge and milk, with a little bread and meat, or bread and milk for dinner, or potatoes and herring, and usually no supper.[28] Aspiring surgeons' assistants would sometimes hire themselves out as apprentices to practising surgeons or apothecaries and receive board and lodging for services, although they might be abused and exploited, as narrated so graphically in Tobias Smollett's *Roderick Random*. As apprentices, they were often indentured at the age of 15 or 16, and were bound for five years to their masters, keeping the shop, cleaning the bandages, compounding medicines, and making up bills. Some more fortunate might live as a member of the family with their professor. A number did not survive their initiation of attending crude surgery for the first time, conducted without anaesthetic, appalled by the whole experience. Charles Darwin fled from one such horrendous amputation being carried out on a child, never to engage with medicine thereafter.

Although Menzies does not appear to have graduated in the conventional sense (he might have had financial difficulties in completing the course) he may have been granted a licence to practise surgery,[29] though there is no official record of this. Such a licence would have been sufficient to qualify him in 1781 for the post of surgeon's mate in the Royal Navy.[30] (Ironically, his birthplace near Aberfeldy is almost as far from the sea as is possible in Scotland.) For such positions, the study of botany was important for the use of medicinal plants, when the naval surgeon was likely to be far from apothecaries. Menzies' unusual knowledge may well have recommended him for that reason for his subsequent naval post, given the low proportion of students who took botany seriously. In Menzies' time, the botany course under Hope was attended by less than a quarter of the students, despite the professor being known to have 'behaved with much good nature to his pupils, doing everything in his power to instruct them'.[31] But one commentator was critical of Hope's successor, Dr Daniel Rutherford:

> … the study of Botany is highly seducing: few who pursue it, reflect that it is only in very slight degree connected with medicine; hence many are led to a wide field of speculation, which although it exhibits some of the most beautiful views in nature, carries off the attention from more profitable pursuits. In studying botany the physiology of plants deserves the principal attention. The long time which Dr. R. employs in explaining the terms of the art, renders the study highly disgusting to the general run of his students, and prevents him from doing sufficient justice to the physiological department of his course … the late Dr. Hope used to

> conclude his course by the exhibition of the exotics, and by a description of their powers in curing diseases, etc. We learn, with much regret, that Dr. R. has hitherto not paid proper attention to so important a part of the course.[32]

It would seem from this that Menzies was fortunate in having Hope as his tutor, but in any case, his experience, both at the Castle Menzies gardens and at the RBGE, would have placed him well in advance of other students, at least in this subject. The same writer above stated:

> ... it is surprising that no private lectures on Botany have ever been proposed. A garden might be hired for a small sum, and there is an excellent field for a man of abilities ... though the botanic garden is maintained at the expense of government, two shillings and sixpence is demanded from the student by the principal gardener: such extortions are shameful.[33]

There was an incentive for such 'extortions', as this income contributed to the head gardener's pay, as indicated in the terms of agreement for John Bell in 1781 whose pay as principal gardener was £25 derived from fees paid by the students and from showing the gardens to visitors – if these did not amount to £25 the difference was to be made up, but the head gardener would be allowed to keep any excess from these sources. If with permission he sold any plant, the money received was to be part of his £25.[34]

The low attendance at these courses may have been due to their being held in summer, when students were out of town. One student, Job Harrison, wrote in 1775:

> Edinburgh is now more filthy and disagreeable than in winter, particularly at night after 11 o'clock, when the inhabitants discharge their daily excrement thro' the windows, and in the morning before the scavengers have cleaned the streets. I am obliged to go through the town every morning to the Botanical Garden, and whenever the morning is hot, and at the same time free from wind, the stench is intolerable.[35]

Apparently Menzies did not take a degree, which was not uncommon at the time. There is no reference to him in the records of the Royal College of Surgeons of Edinburgh. However, licentiates in surgery were awarded after 1770; these required certificates of attendance for a minimum period of three winter sessions in anatomy, chemistry, *materia medica*, principles and practice of surgery, midwifery and practical anatomy, in addition to the student having attended a public hospital for at least a year with a course in clinical surgery. The demand for physicians, surgeons and surgeon's mates was greatly increased by the wars with America and France, and the University of Edinburgh was a popular institution for the training of such personnel between 1777 and 1783, when Menzies entered the service.

NOTES

1. Stewart (1928), 146
2. McDiarmed (1791), xxxiv
3. Balfour (1944), 171
4. Wilson (1920), 199
5. McDiarmed (1791), 802 *et seq.*
6. Hunter (1883), 398–9
7. RBGE mss. Menzies, Sir Robert and Castle Menzies. Miscellaneous Papers 1700–1833, folio 3
8. Hunter (1883), 393
9. McDiarmed (1791), xxix
10. Ibid., 303
11. McKay (1954), 87
12. Hull (2001), 226
13. McKay (1954), 177
14. Lindsay (2005), 142
15. Fletcher and Brown (1970), 57 *et seq.*
16. Morton (1986), 10–11
17. Hope to Banks, 16 July 1783. Banks Correspondence 1: 146, Royal Botanic Gardens, Kew
18. O'Brian (1987), 196
19. Ibid., 154
20. Gascoigne (2004), 691–6
21. Balfour (1944), 171
22. Lindsay (2005), 101
23. National Archives of Scotland GD 253/146/2/12/2 of 28 February 1781. Fletcher and Brown (1970) claim that Robert arrived at the garden in 1789, but this is contradicted by the above document.
24. Naish (1988), 124
25. Rosner (1991), 27–8
26. Ibid., 27–8
27. Lindsay (2005), 112
28. Comrie (1932), 341
29. Groves (1998), 14–15
30. The question of Menzies' qualifications is something of a mystery. The medical matriculation lists for the University of Edinburgh indicate that an Archibald Menzies paid the necessary fees for all of the years 1771–80, but there is no record of his having graduated or that he received a Licentiate Diploma from the Edinburgh College of Surgeons. However, the Dictionary of National Biography claims that he received an Edinburgh MD degree in 1781, which seems most

unlikely (M. Kaufman, pers. comm.). There is no record of him in the Navy List.

31. Rosner (1991), 56
32. Johnston (1792), 13–14
33. Ibid., 43
34. National Archives of Scotland GD 253/146/2/12/2
35. Rosner (1991), 88

4

'A Mere Surgeon'

'But surely,' she cried, 'surely such a fine woman cannot throw herself away on a mere surgeon?'

The Surgeon's Mate – Patrick O'Brian

Despite the demand for military surgeons, it was not always easy to gain a post, particularly in the Navy. It may have been for that reason that in 1778 Menzies took up the position of assistant to a surgeon in Caernarvon in North Wales for a short time, so that he might gain experience. This location is not far distant from Snowdon, famous for its assemblages of arctic-alpine plants, and from the record of his herbarium collection it is clear that Menzies took the opportunity of botanising on this famously rugged mountain. There are no other records of his time there, and by 1782 he had made a successful application to the Navy Board for the post of assistant surgeon in the Royal Navy. Contemporary accounts indicate that this would have consisted of a rather perfunctory oral examination, and he was subsequently appointed to HMS *Nonsuch* under Captain John Truscott.

Although Menzies spent some 18 years in the Navy, apart from the well-documented narrative of his travels with Vancouver in the early 1790s, almost nothing has been written about his day-to-day work as a naval surgeon or the circumstances of that work. However, Menzies served during Nelson's time, and because of this there is considerable information on the subject, notably concerning surgeons in naval engagements.

The pay was meagre, at £100–200 per annum for surgeons and £60–120 for surgeon's mates, the latter undoubtedly being the lowest rung on the medical ladder. An assistant surgeon (or surgeon's mate) in the Navy was required to serve for three years before they could be considered as full surgeons, with the lowest being paid about four shillings a day. A full surgeon, having served 20 years, might expect eighteen shillings a day. During Menzies' time at Edinburgh, the College of Surgeons received its Royal Charter, which enabled students to gain a diploma. Part of this declared that after examination the candidate was found 'sufficiently qualified to act as surgeon's mate in His Majesty's service' – the authority being simply the Royal College of Surgeons of the City of Edinburgh. This diploma conferred no other rights other than to practise surgery, which was not to be confused with a qualification as a Doctor of Medicine.

When Menzies went aboard for the first time, despite having been forewarned, he would have been shocked at the conditions for his work. The surgeon's base and quarters was the cockpit, situated in the forecastle below the hold, and part of the lowest deck. It was usually unlit by any daylight, with some of the poorest ventilation in the ship, and separated from the rest of the vessel simply by wooden screens covered with canvas. Notwithstanding frequent fumigation, officers and men were aware of the peculiar stench that pervaded unventilated ships at this time, and the dampness which seeped into everything unless drying fires were frequently lit. (It is hardly surprising that Menzies later developed chronic asthma.) Tobias Smollett, who had himself experienced life in the Navy as a surgeon's mate, relates in his novel *Roderick Random* how the surgeon's mates were berthed in 'a space as dark as a dungeon' several feet under the waterline with the hold immediately above plus 'an intolerable stench of putrefied cheese and rancid butter'.

These conditions, combined with foul bilge water and the gross overcrowding, contributed to infection, not helped by the lack of hygiene of men, often verminous from their incarceration in shore jails or press-ganged.[1] The extent of overcrowding can be gauged from the fact that Cook's *Endeavour*, in which he made his first global circumnavigation, was a mere 106 feet long by just over 29 feet at its widest, but contained 94 persons and enormous quantities of stores.[2] This constant proximity of men and officers led not unnaturally, after a time at sea, to considerable tensions and irritability.[3] Without refrigeration, food stores decayed rapidly and rats, both dead and alive, were common and were indeed sometimes welcomed as an addition to the diet.[4]

Conditions for both men and officers were made much worse if the hatches were battened down for days on end, as was not unusual in northern latitudes; this was alleviated below decks only if fine weather allowed windsails and ventilators to be operated. The commonest complaint was ulcerated limbs which refused to heal under the damp, airless conditions, while 'gaol fever' or 'ship fever' (typhus), spread by crowded, unhygienic conditions and lice, killed large numbers of sailors. Until

An illustration *The Middle Deck of* The Hector, *Man of War* by Thomas Rowlandson (1756–1827) showing the cramped conditions on board ship during Menzies' time. (Courtesy of the National Maritime Museum, London.)

vaccination was introduced at the end of the 18th century, smallpox was rife. The sailors themselves were often regarded as 'abandoned miscreants, ripe for any mischief or villany' who were kept in some sort of order only by draconian discipline and inhuman punishments. Those who had been press-ganged, frequently on returning merchant ships, were bitter men, brutally cut off from family and home.

The surgeon was responsible for all aspects of the men's health, and the ship's hygiene generally, but he could be considerably aided or hindered by the attitude and interest of the captain, who could over-rule his surgeon if, for example, he asked to put into port to purchase fresh fruit and vegetables to contain scurvy. The surgeon was to find also that the social distinctions which he had encountered at university were replicated on board. He could be denied access to the quarter-deck, considered the exclusive province of commissioned officers.

The midshipmen and upwards were regarded (and regarded themselves) as 'gentlemen' to be treated accordingly and with their own messing arrangements. (In *Roderick Random*, the character Thomson observes: '... as for the captain, he is too much of a gentleman to know a surgeon's mate, even by sight'.) Surgeons, and to an even greater extent surgeon's mates, were not numbered amongst this company. (These distinctions of rank were much greater on the large warships, which could contain upwards of 800 men, than on the much smaller expedition vessels which Menzies was to experience later.)

A physician appointed personally to a flag officer would be in a different category, however. Such was the case of the Scottish MD Sir Gilbert Blane, surgeon and personal physician to the somewhat hypochondriac Admiral Rodney with whom he worked together closely at the Battle of the Saints, in which Menzies was involved.[5] Blane had complete freedom of the quarter-deck and often discussed the health of the men with the officers.[6]

Normally, the surgeon was thought of as an artisan who had certain manual skills, similar to a carpenter or gunner, which were not particularly highly regarded. Blane found that in the fleet assigned to the West Indies the captains often despised their surgeons and neglected their advice to such an extent that he had a set of notes printed (at his own expense) for their guidance on maintaining the health of the sailors. (Blane is regarded as one of the real founders of naval hygiene.) The fact that it was well received may be explained by the social status of Blane as a physician and not a regular naval surgeon. Blane had found that the mortality rate amongst the seamen in the West Indies fleet was one in seven, i.e. 1518 men out of 12,019, which he ascribed to lack of ventilation in the ships, the limited use made of lemon juice (for scurvy) and the plentiful supply of cheap rum on shore, while the hospital accommodation and medical supplies were poor. In May 1781 there were 1077 cases of scurvy alone, which resulted in the highest death rate from all sources.[7] Even as late as 1794, yellow fever afflicted large numbers of the attackers of Martinique, as Lt. Bartholomew James relates:

> In a few days after I arrived at St. Pierre I buried every man belonging to my boat twice, and nearly all of the third boat's crew, in fevers, and, shocking to relate, the Master, Mate, and every man and boy belonging to the *Acorn* transport that I came from England in ... The constant affecting scenes of sudden death was in fact dreadful to behold, and nothing was scarcely to be met but funeral processions in this town of both officers and men.[8]

In the half century before Menzies' appointment there had been a progressive improvement in naval medicine, not least because of the appalling losses of men due to neglect, poor diet and sheer maltreatment, which Tobias Smollett witnessed some 30 years before Menzies took up post. (Smollett had himself been a surgeon's mate on the ill-fated Carthagena expedition against the Spaniards under Sir Challoner Ogle in 1740–41.) Above all, there was a late appreciation that healthy crews won battles: the difference between the French and the British in the engagements in the West Indies in which Menzies was involved amply demonstrated this – British boarding parties frequently found a high proportion of French sailors incapacitated through ill-health, not helped by the practice of retaining corpses for an appropriate Catholic funeral. (On British ships the surgeon was responsible for the disposal of corpses, usually at sea as soon as possible.)

A surgeon's medicine chest of the period, showing some of the instruments and preparations Menzies would have used as a naval surgeon. (Courtesy of the National Maritime Museum, London.)

It was Nelson himself who declared that: 'The greatest thing in all military service is health' and it was claimed that Trafalgar was won because of this. Blane says that after the Battle of the Saints, 'for three weeks after the capture of these ships, the stench resulting from the numbers of wounded men and corpses tainted the air' and that British sailors, on entering the holds of French ships, with their rotting bodies, were 'seized with fever within 24 hours'.[9]

The surgeons were required to provide instruments, and even medicines, at their own expense, inspected to ensure that they came up to standard, although after 1804 this and other gear was supplied by the government.[10] For this, each crew member paid two pence subtracted monthly from his pay. (As with other officers, surgeons had to pay for their mess food.) The instruments themselves resembled nothing so much as a carpenter's tool-kit, with their amputation knives, saws and trepans, bullet forceps, bone nippers and turnscrews.

The surgeon was expected to carefully inspect all new recruits, both for their fitness and for any indication of infectious or contagious disease. (From 1795 to 1805 disease and accidents accounted for 82% of all deaths during the wars with France.)[11] He would supervise the scrubbing of their bodies and the shaving of their heads, while their clothes were either boiled or burnt, to avoid contamination of the other crew members. With the permission of the captain, a general wash day would be prescribed for both bodies and clothes, while the surgeon would be responsible for ensuring that hammocks and bedclothes would be periodically brought on deck for airing and drying. The standard British Navy space allocated for these hammocks and bedding was a mere 14 inches and might be layered, one on top of another.[12]

The sick-berth would be fumigated from time to time by the immersion of red-hot irons in buckets of tar. (On his voyage up the Northwest coast of America, Menzies successfully remonstrated against Captain George Vancouver's practice of keeping fires between decks for ventilation while men in there were lying in fevers in their hammocks.)[13] Any sick men had to report at a given time, when it was the duty of the surgeon to examine them, and wherever possible to anticipate either any contagion or condition which might, like scurvy, break out among the crew generally.

He would also be required to treat men after punishment, and what Menzies thought of the latter is not recorded. A dozen lashes was the norm for most minor offences, but drunkenness, which was very common, earned a sailor 60 lashes, especially if combined with 'insolence'. (The sailors were provided with a gallon of weak beer daily and a half pint of rum.) One seaman received over 700 lashes for theft. Probably the most brutal punishment was 'flogging round the fleet', when the unfortunate was flogged mercilessly in front of the crews of each of the ships that passed by his own vessel – an experience which often resulted in death. A serious flogging resulted in a flayed back resembling raw meat (hence the appellation 'bloody backs' for marines who seemed to come in for more than their fair share of such punishments), which the surgeon might do his best to alleviate.

On the later Vancouver voyage, when Menzies was present as was required of surgeons, the most severe flogging was meted out to a deserter at Monterey who received 144 lashes in two sessions separated by a fortnight, when his back would have only partially healed – no doubt *pour décourager les autres.*[14] (The phrase 'letting the cat out of the bag' refers to the cat o' nine tails, which was kept in a red plush bag by the bosun.) One of the *Discovery*'s officers, Peter Puget, recorded a series of such floggings ordered by Vancouver, which suggests an average of one such punishment every three or four days, which – even for those times – was considered extreme.[15]

The surgeon was also required to train the men in first-aid in anticipation of the wounds from battle, especially in the essential use of the tourniquet, which could be a lifesaver. Usually he was expected to visit the sick and injured twice daily and to keep careful notes on their condition and treatment. In tropical climates, he would dose the men with quinine, in the form of 'bark' in a glass of alcohol. Assistant surgeons would accompany men on shore expeditions to keep a watchful eye on their health, particularly regarding clean water supplies. Even in peacetime, Menzies, as a conscientious medico on board, would have found himself not only fully occupied, but also becoming toughened by the arduous life under sail.

Menzies was on board HMS *Nonsuch* when 50 men died of various diseases on the passage out from England *en route* to the West Indies, exacerbated by foul weather. That ship was part of Rodney's fleet, which won a comprehensive if costly victory at the Battle of the Saints on 12 April 1782 near the coast of Dominica when the French Commander Comte de Grasse was defeated and captured. (De Grasse had been instrumental in the defeat of Cornwallis at Yorktown, a critical battle in the American War of Independence.) In the British fleet 266 men were killed and 810 wounded.[16] Although no record has been found of the direct engagement of the *Nonsuch* in the action at the Saints, it is most likely that it was involved, and if it was, Menzies would have had his baptism of fire as a surgeon, amputating limbs, and treating the horrendous injuries caused by flying shards of wood, not to mention coping with the spread of disease among wounded sailors in the inimical climate, with its heat and humidity.

No previous description could have prepared him for the consequences of the actual engagement itself. In the first few minutes of any battle, up to 20 men or more might be wounded. The after-cockpit was the clearing station and the amputating theatre, while the amputation-tables were often the chests belonging to the normal occupants.[17] These chests were drawn together to form a platform, with a sail thrown over in folds to partly cushion the wounded men. The operations were lit by evil-smelling tallow candles on this platform, with large ship's lanterns attached to the bulkheads. It was a vision of hell as bleeding and dismembered sailors were brought below by their mates, many dying before they got to the surgeons. Half tubs around received the amputated limbs. The short-handed surgeon of the *Ardent* at the Battle of Camperdown reported:

> Ninety wounded men were brought down from the action. The whole cockpit, deck, cabins, wing berths and part of the cable tier, together with my platform and my preparations for dressings were covered with them.
>
> So that for some time they were laid on each other at the foot of the ladder where they were brought down …
>
> Melancholy cries for assistance were addressed to me from every side by wounded and dying, and piteous moans and bewailing from pain and despair. In the midst of these agonising scenes, I was able to preserve myself firm and collected, and embraced in my mind the whole of the situation, to direct my attention where the greatest and most essential services could be performed. Some with wounds, bad indeed and painful, but slight in comparison with the dreadful condition of others, were most vociferous for assistance.[18]

It was a strict and unalterable rule that however serious the injury or otherwise, the wounded were treated in strict rotation as they arrived.[19] With the movement of the ship, the fearsome noise of battle, the roar of cannon and the piteous cries of the men pierced by splinters or shot by ball, Menzies must have wondered whether he could retain his sanity. Even by the standards of the time, the carnage wreaked on both French and British ships in the action at the Saints was unusual.[20]

A contemporary graphite sketch of a surgeon removing a leg in the confines of a busy cockpit of a ship. By an unknown artist. (Courtesy of the National Maritime Museum, London.)

He would come to understand that close-quarter fighting was surprisingly less lethal than engagements conducted at a distance: in the former, the velocity of the cannon balls would carry them clean through the ship, while 'dying' balls smashed masts and spars whose sharp wooden shards could cause the most devastating injuries. While the surgeon was attempting to operate, the recoil of the ship's own large cannons just above the cockpit would shake the vessel to its very timbers. Menzies might have encountered the strange phenomenon of 'wind of ball' whereby a ball passing close to the body, without touching it, could result in serious injury or even death.

Ships' surgeons were renowned for their speed of operation: amputations, including controlling the flow of blood from the arteries, pulling back the muscle to reveal the bone, sawing, ligaturing, etc. were all usually completed in well under two minutes before the man was passed to the surgeon's mate for preparation of the stump. The surgeons knew that, with the effects of loss of blood and shock, any delay was more likely to result in death. There is a written account of one surgeon, without assistants, working frantically from 1 p.m. until 4 a.m. the following morning, treating 90 men. 'So great was my fatigue that I began several amputations under a dread of sinking before I should have severed the blood vessels.'[21]

NOTES

1. Masefield (1971), 73–4
2. Musgrave, Gardner and Musgrave (1998), 16
3. O'Brian (1987), 69
4. Masefield (1971), 75
5. Keevil (1948), 797. By coincidence, Captain George Vancouver, who was to feature largely in Menzies' life a few years later, also fought in that great sea battle which was a crucial turning point in the war with France and which demoralised that country's Navy.
6. Friedenberg (2002), 7
7. Keevil (1957), 131
8. Lewis (1960), 406
9. Keevil (1957), 133–4
10. Lewis (1960), 404
11. Maynard (2003), 76
12. O'Brian (1987), 69
13. Lamb (1984), 212 – Banks n.p., n.d., Brabourne Papers, Mitchell Library, Sydney
14. Coleman (1988), 76
15. Raban (1999), 376
16. Keevil (1957), 133
17. Lewis (1960), 235
18. Keevil (1957), 58–9
19. Masefield (1971), 77
20. Lindsay (2005), 115
21. Keevil (1957), 58

5

Letters from Nova Scotia

Following the Battle of the Saints, Menzies was posted for a short time to HMS *Formidable* before being transferred to HMS *Assistance* on 17 August 1783, which returned to England. In spring 1784, Menzies was again appointed to HMS *Assistance*, to be based at Halifax in Nova Scotia, from where, at the end of the American War of Independence, the ship was patrolling the eastern seaboard of North America and the Caribbean. *En route*, the ship visited Sandy Hook near New York at the beginning of January 1784 and subsequently the islands of Barbados, Dominica, St. Christopher's and Nevis in the West Indies between February and March of the same year, where Menzies collected seeds to be sent to Professor Hope. While at Nova Scotia the ship was designated the flagship of Sir Charles Douglas and was commanded by Captain William Bentinck.

A view of the Nova Scotia coast. (Author's collection.)

The port of Halifax had been established as a fortress in 1749, mainly to counter the French fort at Louisburg, and a naval yard was started in 1758. It was the American Revolution which revived Halifax as a strategic port, and in 1783 the city took in 7000 British Loyalists who had crossed the Upper St. Lawrence as refugee immigrants, many from New England, so that by the mid-1780s the population had doubled. By 1793, the British had lost harbours in New York and Boston in the American War of Independence. Thus Halifax became increasingly important as a key to the control of the West Atlantic, with an accessible harbour and as a colonial *entrepôt*, especially in the wars with France. It was reckoned that the 20-mile wide basin leading to the harbour could contain all of the ships of the British Navy, which used it for refitting and repair facilities and as a naval storage depot.[1]

Menzies served on the *Assistance* from 1783 until 1786, together with his friend, Lt. James Johnstone (who coincidentally was to accompany him on several later voyages). Until 1784 the station was under the command of Sir Andrew Snape Hammond; in that year Henry Duncan took over command. When Menzies landed at Halifax, it was a city of marked contrasts. The American War of Independence had recently ended and a peace treaty had been signed with the French in 1783. General Massey had converted Halifax into a fortress, with its blockhouses, earthworks and trenches, and the military cadres dominated. By the end of the war, there were 14 forts, blockhouses and barracks in and around the town, accommodating nearly 3000 troops.

In addition, as the final base of the British armies and Navy in North America, after the evacuation of New York, a great part of the British army found its way to the city, filling a barracks with some 600–1000 men, together with 25,000 refugees. Every possible accommodation, including churches, was used to overflowing and thousands were under canvas on the Citadel and at Mount Pleasant, indeed anywhere that tents could be pitched. In the winter of 1783–84, while Menzies was there, the condition of many of the refugees was pitiful, with lack of adequate shelter, clothing and food. In January 1784, Governor Parr reported to London:

> I cannot better describe the wretched situation of these people than by enclosing a list of those just arrive in the transport *Clinton*, chiefly women and children, scarcely clothed, utterly destitute, still on board the transport, crowded like a sheep pen, as I am totally unable to find a place for them and we cannot move them by reason of the ice and snow.[2]

Meanwhile, the town was crowded with British soldiers, many Hessians who had fought alongside them, and both American and French prisoners, not to mention Dutch farmers anxious to sell their produce on market days; it was a colourful and polyglot mix of nationalities and conditions of men, among the prettily painted wooden houses of white and yellow.[3] For some, the American war had brought considerable commercial opportunity and prosperity, and the fortunate ones built grand houses and threw lavish parties at the favoured dining and dancing palaces. One British army officer, William Dyott, recalls sumptuous feasts and balls on an almost daily basis. Their lifestyle contrasted with the miserable settlement of loyalist black fugitives at Birch Town outside Halifax.

Not all of the refugees were impoverished, and those who were able to bring their fortunes from the Thirteen Colonies invested in the growing city, often bringing with them their black slaves. They socialised with the British army and Navy officers, with balls, dinners and card parties; this reached its height with the arrival in 1788 of Prince William, one of the wanton sons of George III and then a naval captain. He set new standards in debauchery and licentious behaviour, aped by many of his naval and military entourage ('... he would go into any house where he saw a pretty girl and was perfectly acquainted with every house of a certain description'). When not engaged in drinking and lechery, they amused themselves with duels, cock-fighting, fishing, hunting and coursing hares on the town common.[4]

It is difficult to imagine the serious-minded Menzies in this milieu, but his stay at Halifax does not seem to have been particularly onerous, as he was allowed time and facilities to botanise in various parts of the West Indies and the East Coast. Even by the turn of the century, the interior of Nova Scotia was barely known, with development of small settlements outside Halifax largely confined to the southern and western coasts. The whole of the island had been heavily glaciated, leaving behind much poor rocky soil, while the dense spruce forests and almost impenetrable scrub discouraged clearance on all but the best land with potential for agriculture.[5] The spruce and pine provided an important source of timber for the Navy's ships, and for export to the West Indies, while the sugar maple was tapped for sap for syrup making.

In a letter to his old friend and sponsor Professor Hope, Menzies expresses his pleasure at getting back to plant collecting:

> ... herewith I have sent you a small parcel of seeds of which you have a numerical list enclosed; those marked Sandy-hook were collected near New York, N America the beginning of January past – all the rest were collected during February and March in the islands of Barbadoes-Dominica – St Christopher's and Nevis in the W Indies – as far as I could, I have subjoined their Linnean names, the rest I only numbered, and marked on each the place where they were collected; if these seeds will make any addition to your most valuable collection at the Botainic [sic] Gardens, it will amply recompense my labour and fatigue in collecting them – together with the seeds I have herewith sent some Dry'd specimens collected in a hurry at the same time in the W. Indies.
>
> I arrived here from the W. Indies in the *Assistance* of 50 guns a few days ago and I am charmed with the general appearance of the country which seems to offer a most delightful prospect for Botanical researches as well as other branches of Natural History. I already had two excursions into the woods and I cannot describe

> the pleasure I felt when surrounded with the *Kalmia angustifolia, Andromeda calycantha, Ledum palustre, Gaultheria procumbens, Arbutus uva-ursi, Pinus strobus, P. canadense* and several other beautiful evergreens, which I could not ascertain, besides a vast number of Cryptogamia plants of which you know I am passionately fond.[6]
>
> In this situation the tears trickled down my cheeks in gratitude to you, Sir, who first taught me to enjoy these pleasures which Providence has so conspicuously placed before my eyes, accept of them as the only mark a grateful heart can at present offer. I shall wholly devote my vacant hours to Natural History while I remain on this station and I have no doubt that but I shall be able to send you another parcel of seeds and specimens early in the Autumn – if in this country I can in any other respect serve you, you have a just title to command me, and I shall ever think it my duty to obey ...[7]

This letter has been quoted at some length for a number of reasons. Apart from being the first known professional writing of Menzies, it clearly indicates his real joy at once again being seriously connected with botany and field collecting. If nowadays his effusiveness to Hope may seem excessive, there is nothing to suggest that it is other than a genuine sentiment, reflecting his great admiration for his early mentor. It is also the first record of his sending back from abroad plant material that was to be the *leitmotif*

Gaultheria procumbens
(RBGE collection.)

of his career. On the same day he wrote in similar, if rather more restrained, terms to Sir Joseph Banks.[8] Banks knew Hope, and was destined to become a key figure in Menzies' life. On 22 August 1786, Hope wrote to Banks recommending Menzies.

It is interesting that Menzies, despite being a naturalist, makes no mention of the many animal species to be found in the forests of Nova Scotia, including black bear, wild cat, beaver, moose (4000 were killed in one season during his time there), caribou, otter and many other fur-bearing animals.[9]

At this time, most of Nova Scotia was still a wilderness. Sailing round its attractive if unspectacular 7000 miles of coast, Menzies found innumerable bays and inlets, many of which were to provide good fishing harbours, while the Bay of Fundy demonstrated the highest tidal range in the world. Many species of fish were plentiful, from cod to haddock, salmon, herring, mackerel and flat fish – the fishery kept 10,000 men in employment and was worth at the most conservative estimate £26,000.[10] Everywhere, large pods of right whales surfaced with their spectacular spouts. With the land's varied and ancient geology, including some of the oldest rocks in the world, Menzies would have encountered a landscape not dissimilar to that of the western isles of Scotland; here were low hills, rarely rising above 300 metres, and undulating terrain, often rocky, but with occasional rich pockets of soil in the valleys along the river courses, such as the Annapolis and Cornwallis.

What was different was the almost impenetrable forest and scrub woodland covering much of the land, dominated by several species of spruce, fir, pine and a variety of maples, interspersed with birch, beech, oak and ash. In the lower lying areas of acid soils there were extensive bogs and small lakes, again like so much of the Hebrides where Menzies had botanised. During his time, the economy of Nova Scotia depended on the resources of the forest and the sea. The wandering Indian tribes, with no substantial settlements and reduced to a few thousand, had been decimated by smallpox and were addicted to alcohol, sold to them by unscrupulous fur traders.[11]

It was a rugged country, difficult to penetrate, and most of Menzies' plant collecting would have been restricted to the areas immediately behind the coast wherever he could land safely.

In the autumn of that year he writes again to Hope from Halifax:

> Returned to Halifax after an expedition of 5 weeks in an open boat round the western coasts of Nova Scotia, a journey of some danger and difficulties. Sending a small parcel of seeds and specimens via HM sloop *Bonetta* – some of these new plants not described in 12th.ed. *Linnaeus Syst. Naturae.* When you are at leisure I would be much oblige to you to look them over and give your opinion of them I know your indulgent disposition will readily forgive the mistakes and freely correct the inaccuracies which you will undoubtedly meet with in this investigation so when you are informed that they were examined and described with candlelight in a noisy cockpit which is my station on board – be pleased to clear up my doubts with respect to the *Convallaria*, etc, etc.

He refers also to sending about 40 seeds to Dr William Pitcairn, Sir Joseph Banks, and Mrs Blackburne, a noted amateur botanist from Lancashire.[12]

Again a similar letter was sent to Banks. He was anxious to ensure that Banks received viable seeds of *Arbutus*, but in his letter says:

> Neither in this expedition nor in any of my excursions round Halifax have I met with the *Arbutus acadiensis* nor the genus except *uva ursi* ... I do not however despair meeting with it next summer in Canada or in those parts of Nova Scotia adjacent to that province, when seeds and specimens of it shall be at your service ...
>
> I am happy that my small parcel of seeds arrived safely in England and more so that my humble mite was acceptable to you. [Banks had made fulsome acknowledgement of the first delivery.] Lieut Boys of His Majesty's sloop *Bonetta* with this, will deliver you a small parcel of seeds collected this last summer in Nova Scotia a list of which you have here inclosed ... I have also found a new species of *Kalmia*, in the marshes near Halifax but cannot send you any of the seeds this season they have dropt out of their capsules while I was absent on my last Expedition. As it is reported we go to Canada early next summer, if there is anything in that part of the world which you wish me to attend to, be pleased to acquaint me of it and I shall cheerfully obey your instructions ...[13]

Banks would have been familiar with the coastal flora of the eastern provinces of Canada, and indeed with the problems of collecting from a small ship, as he had spent some seven months with the fisheries protection vessel HMS *Niger* during its survey of the coasts of Labrador and Nova Scotia in 1766; this collection formed the first basis of his subsequent huge herbarium in London.[14,15]

In the summer of 1785 Menzies wrote to Hope:

> I lately received from London the 12th Edition reformed of *Linnaeus Syst. Nat.*, in four volumes and the suppliment to the 13th Edition of his Vegetables, together with your short Genera and Catalogue of Trees and Shrubs for which I return you thanks – in those the beautiful Rhodora is omitted yet I am pretty certain it grew in the open air at the Botanic Gardens where I attended there. I am still left almost in the same predicament with respect to the last Edition of his Vegetables – having only your short genera and Suppliment in addition to my former. I shall with these however renew my researches early next season and I flatter myself with the expectation of being more successful as I become better acquainted with the country. Col. Small, late of the 84th Regiment – a native of the Caledonian mountains – has invited me to spend part of next summer with him in his country seat near Windsor – should we not go to Quebec. This will afford me an opportunity of examining the most fertile part of this province.[16,17]

In January 1786 Menzies acknowledges a letter from Banks thanking him for the last delivery of seeds and apologises for his failure to find either the *Arbutus* or the *Sium nisi*:

> Dr Hope lately sent me out last edition of the *Systema Naturae Vegatibilium* which is a great acquisition to me in my present situation, along with it I had the honour of receiving a Diploma from the Natural History Society of Edinburgh.[18] On account of our being cruising at sea the latter end of last summer I have not been able to collect any seeds – I shall however endeavour to make up for this by carrying home with me next summer live plants of all those which I think worth the trouble.[19]

In the summer of the same year, he wrote to Banks:

> I embrace the opportunity to acquaint you that I have sent to England on 10 May last by Mr George Sayer on His Majesty's Frigate *Mercury* a parcel of seeds containing 56 in number with a letter addressed to you which I sincerely wish may arrive safe. By my letter you will see that the greatest part of these seeds were collected during a short stay of a few days only at New Providence and Abaco, two of the Bahamas Islands the beginning of April last – which I found to be the worst time of the year for my purpose it being the latter end of their dry season so that many of the plants, from which I collected those seeds were not in flower, which rendered it impossible for me to ascertain their names, together with my unavoidable hurry are the only apologies I can offer for sending you this collection in so negligent a manner. Having obtained permission of the Commander in Chief, I set out on this expedition about the middle of March, in full expectation of remaining a month at least at those Islands, and as my sole object was Botany I flattered myself that I should be able in that time to make a collection worthy of your acceptance; but by the first part of this letter you see how far I have been disappointed in my expectations.
>
> Should this small parcel of seeds make any addition to the Noble collection of Plants already at Kew, it will amply recompense all my trouble and add to the pleasure I enjoyed in collecting it. We shall in a few months return to England at which time I shall carry with me from here, live plants of those I have not been able to procure seeds of; and if I am successful in my endeavours you may reasonably expect a part. I have lost all hopes of visiting Canada during this station; notwithstanding it has been my greatest ambition ...[20]

What this correspondence reveals is that despite his strictly naval duties, Menzies was clearly given considerable leeway for his botanical collecting and made very good use of this, despite, as he says, very difficult conditions. It was to be almost 20 years before any further serious botanical work was undertaken in this territory, much of it in the interior by the indefatigable surveyor Titus Smith, commissioned by the authorities to search for potential farmland. In the course of this arduous work, Smith identified most of the 33 tree species native to Nova Scotia, together with some 50 shrubs and no fewer than 100 medicinal plants – a remarkable achievement in the two field seasons of 1801 and 1802. (Even at this early date, Smith records that the population of native beaver had been almost extinguished.)[21]

When Menzies returned to England in 1786, he was formally introduced to Banks by the letter of 22 August to Banks from Professor Hope, who wrote that Menzies had 'paid unremitting attention to his favourite study of botany, and through the indulgence of the Commander-in-Chief had good opportunities afforded to him'. The deference shown by Menzies to both Hope and Banks, perhaps especially the latter, is apparent; given Banks' elevated social position he might even be accused of a degree of sycophancy. Certainly Lindsay's description of Menzies' 'terrier-like ambition' seems apt.[22] Shortly after Menzies' departure for the Northwest coast of America, his great friend and mentor John Hope died, full of honours.[23]

NOTES

1. Hollingsworth (1876), 116–17
2. Raddall (1950), 101–2
3. Jeffery (1907), 30
4. Ibid., 36–57
5. Clark (1965), 298
6. At Port Discovery on 1 May 1792, on only the second landfall on the Northwest coast of America with Vancouver, Menzies was to discover near its northern limit *Arbutus menziesii* or Pacific Madrone. One of the most colourful and attractive of the Pacific coast trees, it was first discovered by the Spanish priest Fra Juan Crespi in 1758 near San Diego, but as the Spanish at this time liked to keep their discoveries secret, Menzies received the credit for its first published description.
7. Menzies to Hope, 30 May 1784. John Hope Collection, National Archives of Scotland, GD 253/145
8. Menzies to Banks, 30 May 1784. Banks Correspondence 1: 163, Royal Botanic Gardens, Kew
9. Hollingsworth (1876), 62–70
10. Ibid., 35–44
11. Ibid., 46–57
12. RBGE mss. Menzies, Sir Robert and Castle Menzies, ff 1
13. Menzies to Banks, 2 November 1784. Banks Correspondence 1: 175, Royal Botanic Gardens, Kew
14. Musgrave, Gardner and Musgrave (1998), 15
15. The reference to Canada refers to the previous French administered provinces outside Nova Scotia.
16. Menzies to Hope, 4 July 1785. John Hope Collection, National Archives of Scotland, GD 253/145
17. The fort at Halifax was an important military garrison and by coincidence it was occupied in Menzies' time there by the 42nd Royal Highland Regiment, raised six

years before his birth near his home at Aberfeldy, and subsequently to become the famous Black Watch. Colonel Small (later Major General) was born in Perthshire not far from Menzies' home district. The second battalion of the 84th regiment, or Royal Highland Emigrants which wore the Black Watch tartan, was commanded by Small based at Halifax, serving as marines. Many took up land grants to settle subsequently in Nova Scotia.

18. Balfour (1944), 17
19. Menzies to Banks, 28 January 1786. Banks Correspondence 1: 221, Royal Botanic Gardens, Kew
20. Menzies to Banks, 8 June 1786. Banks Correspondence 1: 234, Royal Botanic Gardens, Kew
21. Clark (1965), 309
22. Lindsay (2005), 116
23. Keevil (1948), 798

6

'A Tedious Voyage round the Globe'

'I have just the master you need. He sailed with Colnett - you know about Colnett, Aubrey?'

'Why, sir, I believe most officers that attend to their profession are tolerably well acquainted with Captain Colnett and his book,' said Jack.

The Far Side of the World – Patrick O'Brian

In 1785, while Menzies was in Nova Scotia, on the other side of the continent the first fur traders reached the coast of what is now British Columbia and Alaska. Their target was the attractive and harmless sea otter, which had the endearing habit of rearing itself half out of the water and holding up its cubs for the hunters to see. It was to create fortunes for those who hunted for its soft pelt. Its subsequent demise as a species on this coast was inevitable, and apparently no pelt appeared on the London market after 1911 when a single skin was sold for £475.[1] It was also to change the relationships between nations claiming sovereignty over this coast, notably the British and the Spanish, and incidentally, the native North American Indians.

On 29 March 1778, Captain James Cook sailed into Nootka Sound on the west coast of Vancouver Island with his ships HMS *Resolution* and *Discovery*. His detailed account of his third voyage excited great interest, not least for its description of the plentiful sea otter and the value of its fur. In particular, the Chinese at Macao were prepared to pay 120 dollars for a skin in prime condition. (One of Cook's officers, Captain King, reckoned that the crews of the two ships had made the huge sum of 2000 dollars from the sale of furs, the dollar being the Spanish one worth just more than five shillings sterling.) However, well before that, many merchants and sailors had heard of the fortunes to be made from this trade, particularly since the furs could be purchased from the Indians for the equivalent of cheap trinkets. Something like gold fever set in and there was a rush to exploit this fabulous resource.[2]

The most important of the London merchant adventurers was Richard Cadman Etches, of the company of Brooks and Etches, London tea and wine merchants. They had previous experience of the oriental trade and formed a company called 'Associated Merchants Trading to the North West Coast of America'. They also made valuable government connections, and Etches received some encouragement for his proposals

A sea otter, hunted for its fur almost to extinction on the Northwest coast of North America by the early 20th century. (Courtesy of the US National Park Service.)

from the influential Joseph Banks. These were to establish a charter of exclusive trade on the coast of America north of latitude 43 degrees 6 minutes North, a settlement at Nootka Sound (off Vancouver Island), a visit to the Sandwich Isles (Hawaii), the development of whaling, and trade with Japan.[3] In 1785, with the required approval of the East India Company and the South Sea Company, the company fitted out two ships for the sea otter fur trade, under the command of two former naval officers, Porlock and Dixon, who had sailed with Cook on his last voyage.

Two years later, Etches commissioned James Colnett (who had sailed with Vancouver on Cook's *Resolution*) to command the *Prince of Wales* and the *Princess Royal*.[4] Colnett had had a varied and impressive career in the Royal Navy: not surprisingly, his complement of officers and men were largely drawn from that service, and as a result demonstrated a discipline and competence which contrasted with the standards of some of the other commercial traders. (Many of these officers would know one another from other voyages and would be familiar with each other's characters and skills.) After the American War of Independence and before the advent of the Napoleonic Wars, there was a surfeit of naval officers, a number of whom saw the opportunities of making their fortunes in independent commercial trading ventures across the globe.

What these British and American traders (and implicitly their governments) pretended to ignore was the Spanish claim to sovereignty over this coast from the late 15th century onwards. (This conflict was to lead to an impasse, centred on Nootka, in which Menzies was to be caught up in the course of his later voyage with George Vancouver.) The Spanish had established mission stations and garrisons along the whole of the Pacific Coast at San Diego, Monterey, Santa Barbara and San Francisco and a ship-building port at San Blas in California. The peace treaty signed with France and Spain in 1783 opened the door for the fur-trading adventurers who headed for the Northwest as fast as ships could be commissioned and crewed. One of these adventurers was a former Royal Navy officer, John Meares, whose unscrupulous actions led to what became known as the Nootka Sound Incident, a conflict with the Spanish which prompted the British Government in 1791 to send George Vancouver on what was ostensibly a voyage of diplomacy.[5]

Captain James Colnett was an experienced officer who had spent three and a half years under Cook's command, but became embroiled in the Nootka affair largely through the machinations of Meares. It was the possible penetration southwards from Kodiak Island in Alaska by the Russians, who had established a trading post there, which convinced the Spaniards that they had to build a fort at Nootka. It happened that Meares met up with Colnett in Macao and there arranged a partnership involving the Etches Company. Etches was most anxious to establish a trading base at Nootka, after the dismal failure of the Porlock and Dixon expedition (which Etches had financed) to do so. Shortly after his arrival at Nootka, on the west coast of what is now Vancouver Island, having left Meares in China, Colnett had a confrontation with the Spanish commander Estaban Martinez, which resulted in Colnett's arrest and the seizure of his ship, the *Argonaut*, together with two other vessels.[6]

He was sent as a prisoner to the Spanish settlement at San Blas in southern California, but was subsequently released, together with his two ships, on the orders of the Spanish viceroy. Unfortunately, the unscrupulous Meares exploited this situation and, on his return from China, presented a distorted account to the British Parliament of his own treatment at the hands of the Spaniards. Parliament was outraged and demanded restitution for the property – again exaggerated – which Meares claimed had been confiscated. Almost unbelievably, Britain was set to go to war with Spain over the issue, which had largely arisen over the question of sea otter pelts in which the Spaniards were barely interested. However, the Spaniards had had enough of war and agreed a convention on 24 October 1790 which established the basis for a settlement, which in turn opened up the Northwest coast to British and American trade.

In the summer of 1786, Colnett had taken leave from the Navy to command a two-vessel fur-trading expedition under the flag of the Etches Company, and the *Prince of Wales* and the *Princess Royal* sailed out of London for the Northwest coast and Canton in late September of that year. On board was Archibald Menzies. Within a short time of landing in England from Nova Scotia, he had written to Joseph Banks, sending some plants:

> I am informed that there is a Ship, a private adventurer now fitting out at Deptford to go round the world. Should I be so happy as to be appointed surgeon of her, it will at least gratify one of my greatest earthly ambitions, and afford one of the best opportunities of collecting Seeds and other objects of Natural History for you and the rest of my friends ...[7]

A short time later he was to write again:

> I am happy to acquaint you that I am appointed surgeon to an Expedition round the World. There are two vessels going the one a Ship called the *Prince of Wales* and the other a sloop called the *Princess Royal;* and I have care of both vessels. Their general route I am informed is round South America – from thence to the West Coast of North America and by the Japanese islands to China; from thence round the Cape of Good Hope home; and their chief object is the Fur Trade. What I most regret is that we are not allowed to trade or barter for any curiosities. I hope however we are not debarred from picking them up when they come our way.
>
> May I request the favour of a recommendatory letter to Mr. Etches (Principal Director) No 69 Watling Street, if he is known to you, as it may in some measure exempt me from this restriction; especially while my aims in collecting seeds, specimens and other curiosities do not interfere with the object of the Voyage or in the Interest of the Company. As it is expected we are to sail in a few days, I shall impatiently await the return of Post for your final instructions and commissions, which I shall to the utmost of my power carefully obey and execute ...[8]

(Menzies was very much aware that, notwithstanding the general prohibition on crews from bartering on their own account, an ability to offer something in exchange for plants which he might himself not have the opportunity to collect could be important.)

Banks wrote immediately to Etches, and the latter's reply is both complimentary and instructive:

> I was duly honoured by Mr Menzies, to which I feel myself bound to pay every possible attention. I believe you are fully acquainted with the restrictions laid down in the Articles of the former ships, in a young undertaking and of such a nature as the present I presume such restrictions are absolutely necessary, but in the present instance it is my full intention to dispense with them in the case of Mr Menzies, so far as can have any tendency to be beneficial to science in general. I highly approve of his conduct and manners, and as my younger brother (who is part proprietor) is going [on] the voyage, I gave him orders to pay every attention to Mr Menzies and to give him ample latitude in his pursutes, and I have no doubt on his return he will confess having experienced the liberality which your recommendations Sir certainly demands from me ...

Colnett's own description of preparations for his departure indicates some of the difficulties:

I waited on the governor of the Company and after some little conversation the first plan was alter'd and he determin'd on chartering a Ship and purchasing a Smack to accompany her the beginning of August a Ship was pitch'd on and a Smack purchas'd – some doubts arising from the age of the Ship, being thirty six years old, of her ability to make a passage round Cape Horn – she was regularly survey'd by carpenters and pronounc'd fit for the purpose, the command of the Ship was given to me and to be called the *Prince of Wales.* Burthen one hundred and seventy tons pierc'd for fourteen guns, half Frigate built and to carry thirty five hands, officers included. The Smack was to be commanded by Charles Duncan, a Master in the Royal Navy, and to be called the *Princess Royal.* Burthen sixty five tons to carry four two pounders and fifteen hands in all.

Captain Marshall's son, a Lieutenant in the Navy, was to accompany me part of the way (but not with his father's consent) to be landed with fifteen men at New Year's Harbour, Staten Land to carry on a Sea Lion Fishery the articles for this so lumber'd us that the Cabin State Room and Steerage were so full of provisions and stores that we had scarce room to get into our beds, nor was there room left in any part of the Ship for the smallest article to be taken on board ...[9]

The establishment of the seal fishery was in fact another late addition to the objects of the voyage, and involved landing 15 men and their considerable equipment on Isla de los Estados (Staten Island) off Tierra del Fuego, as an addition to the existing Southern Whale Fishery.

A three-year voyage in such tiny ships, including venturing into some of the stormiest seas in the world, leaves little to the imagination, considering what conditions aboard these overloaded ships were like. Duncan was to complain about the lack of essential equipment aboard the *Princess Royal* and its poor sailing qualities; Colnett on several occasions was obliged to leave the smack to make her own way to avoid further delay. He does not mention here the chief mate on the *Prince of Wales*, James Johnstone, another competent Royal Navy man from the Scottish Borders, who had been with Menzies on HMS *Assistance* in Nova Scotia and was to accompany Menzies on the later Vancouver expedition: the two had become good friends.

Menzies wrote to Banks from the Cape Verde Islands, first apologising for not writing from London, due to the hurried departure of the ships:

You must also accept my sincerest thanks for the very friendly manner in which you was pleased to recommend me in your letter at the same time to Mr Etches in consequence of which that gentleman was kind enough to promise me every indulgence the situation of the voyage would permit, and I have no doubt that opportunities will offer to gratify even my most ardent wishes which I must confess are very sanguine; for the west coast of North America presents a new and exciting field for Botanical researches as well as other branches of Natural

> History, and I can assure you that I shall loose [sic] no opportunity in collecting whatever is new, rare or useful in any branch of natural knowledge ...[10]

Prior to his departure, Menzies had had many discussions with the Swedish botanist Jonas Carl Dryander (1748–1810) who was a former pupil of John Hope, and William Aiton (1731–93), the curator of Kew Gardens. He goes on to ask Banks to forward thanks to Dr Dryander for his considerable help in showing him plants, from Alaska and King George's Sound (near to present day Vancouver), contained in Banks' herbarium in his house at 32 Soho Square, London: most of the plants were collected by Banks during his time with Cook's famous expedition on the *Endeavour*. A visitor, the Rev. W. Sheffield, gave a vivid picture of it: 'His house is a perfect museum; every room contains an inestimable treasure. I passed a whole day there in the utmost astonishment, could scarce credit my senses. Had I not been an eye-witness of this immense magazine of curiosities, I could not have thought it possible for him to have made a twentieth part of the collection.' He goes on to describe the enormous assemblage of arms, ornaments and garments of native peoples from all round the world, animals, stuffed birds, insects, and no fewer than 3000 plant specimens.[11]

Banks' collections were made available to any genuinely interested visitors, and he received scientists and others from all over the world, both distinguished and relatively humble. Menzies spent considerable time examining what was then probably the finest collection of dried plant specimens anywhere, presided over by Daniel Carl Solander (1736–88), a Swede and pupil of Linnaeus, who was Banks' devoted friend and curator of this great collection throughout most of his life. It was recognised as a centre of learning; Alphonse P. de Candolle said of it in 1816, 'cette belle bibliothèque de Soho-Square qui est comme la capitale des sciences naturelles'.[12]

Menzies also asked for thanks to be given to William Aiton at Kew who had raised some of the seeds sent from Nova Scotia and whom Menzies asserted as having received him 'with all his usual hospitality and friendship'.[13] He adds:

> I shall use every means in my power to send you the Wintera [Drimys] aromatica from Staten Land or Terra del Fuego, and if we meet with it. I have an excellent opportunity in view. I have nothing further to add, only that we are this far safe and in good spirits for our voyage to Owhyee [Hawaii] etc.[14]

What this correspondence illustrates is not only Menzies' almost boy-like enthusiasm, but also, through the regular correspondence *en route*, his cultivation of his eminent patron, never failing in the courtesies.

After their arrival at Staten Island on 13 January 1787, construction began on the sealing factory. The ships were to stay in this dreary spot for three weeks, departing for Cape Horn on 12 February. During this time they were assailed by heavy rain, gales and hail. Colnett's journal narrates a shore expedition in late January with Menzies and Captain Duncan:

> On Sunday the 28th: being a holiday I went in the boat to the head of the Harbour accompanied with Captain Duncan and the Surgeon [this is one of only two references to Menzies in Colnett's journal] with an intention to walk to the top of a Hill to look for a port which seemed to have an inlet a little to the westward of this. The second mate set out with the Long Boat at the same time on an Expedition to the New Years Isles for birds & seals; it rain'd so hard and blew strong from the WNW they were oblig'd to return ...

Etches describes a rather dreary walk to the summit and contented himself with naming Etches Lagoon before returning to the ship.[15]

During this time Menzies wrote to Banks:

> My last letter to you was from Port Prya- St. Iago. [Cape Verde Islands] I have now the pleasure to acquaint you that Captain Marshall, whom we brought thither with a party of men on a Seal Fishery scheme, has faithfully promised me that he will carry home some plants of the *Wintera aromatica* for you. For this purpose I have planted a few days ago in a tub about twenty small plants of this useful and ornamental tree and directed it to you.
>
> These are intended, if they arrive safe, for you and Dr Hope, and I must request that you will be so good as to forward Dr Hope's by the safest conveyance. This beautiful tree is at present in flower, and everywhere it grows loads the circumnambient air with a most pleasing aromatic odour. As Captain Marshall is to remain here sometimes he has likewise promised to collect some of the seeds and send them herewith to you. I cannot give you the name of the ship in which these are to be carried home as she is not yet arrived, but, should this be necessary you will learn it from the owner, Mr. Etches, No 69 Watling Street.[16]

Unfortunately these plants were lost when Marshall's ship went down.

Colnett himself declares on Staten Island:

> '... the Winter Bark included of which there was a great quantity brought on board. Vegetables were scarce, a little scurvy grass, & some wild Celery ... birch berries were in great plenty, and some few heath and partridge berries.'[17]

Menzies recommended everyone on board to collect wild celery as an antiscorbutic.[18]

The voyage north was delayed by damage to the mast of the *Princess Royal*, and Colnett, observing that he still had an apparently healthy crew, headed directly for Nootka on Vancouver Island, avoiding Hawaii. It is most likely that Menzies would have considered this an error, since by the time they reached Vancouver Island, not having had a sufficient supply of fresh vegetables, most of the crew were seriously sick from scurvy. Even Menzies himself, together with other fit officers, had to attend to the rigging aloft. Colnett describes the situation:

> The Scurvey at this time began to make its appearance amongst us having eleven complaining, a Regimen of diet was prescribed by the doctor and follow'd a pint of Bottled porter was given them in lieu of their Grog [a concoction of rum and water] and every other article that Ship afforded and of service. All our hopes of relief from this fatal disease depended on a fair wind and a quick passage.

When land was sighted in early July, Colnett gave a very vivid picture of their relief:

> … the whole of the coast from the Hills summit to the water's edge was cover'd with trees a pleasing sight to us who had not seen a bush for one and twenty weeks the very thought reviv'd the drooping spirits of those that were able to crawl on deck to see it for no one remained below that was able to get up on their hands and knees and carried. One man who had long been given over (the person spoke of that had receiv'd the hurt in the River) with now the addition of the scurvey and from being the stoutest man outward was reduc'd to bones express'd that he should soon be well again …[19]

Scurvy was a scourge throughout the 18th century. John Meares lost 23 men in the latter stage of his journey up the Northwest coast, through ignorance, since he was unaware of the beneficial properties of spruce beer, the materials for which were readily available. The species used in this area is likely to have been Western Hemlock.[20] The first record of the use of spruce needles combined with molasses to make an antiscorbutic beer is by Cartier in his voyage up the St. Lawrence, where he was introduced to it by local Indians as early as 1535; here the species used was most likely *Thuja occidentalis.*[21] Banks on his travels in the eastern provinces gives the recipe:

> Take a copper [kettle] that contains 12 Gallons fill it as full as the boughs of Black Spruce as will hold pressing them down pretty tight. Fill it up with water. Boil it till the Rind will strip off the spruce boughs which will waste it about one third take them out & add to the water 1 Gallon of Melasses. Let the whole boil till the Melasses are dissolved. Take a half hogshead [a barrel holding 27 gallons] and put in 19 Gallons of water & fill it up with the Essence, work it with Barm [yeast] or Beer Grounds & in less than a week it is fit to drink.[22]

It is thought that the beer brewed on the *Discovery*'s journey had rum added to provide what Banks called 'King Calli'.[23] In the 57-month voyage, not a single man was lost to the scourge of scurvy, almost certainly due to the use of spruce beer and re-provisioning with fresh fruit and vegetables in California and Hawaii. Even today, a form of spruce beer is bottled and sold in Quebec as a spring tonic.

Scurvy resulted in the disablement of more men than all naval actions combined. Under George Anson (1697–1762) two-thirds of the ship's complement died in a crossing of the Pacific. The symptoms of the disease were large spots on the body, swollen legs, putrid gums from gingivitis, and extreme lassitude.[24] There would be severe deterioration of the gums, with gum bleeding, loosening of teeth, painful eating, bruising, and infections which eventually led to death.[25] On 27 October 1792, south of the Columbia River, when he was with the *Discovery*, Menzies reported in his journal:

> ... the Scurvy now began too show itself on some of the people in Spungy Gums swelled legs that pitted on pressure particularly in the evenings, breaking out of old sores & indurated phlegmons that evidently shewed the vitiated state of their constitutions, which was chiefly owing to their being so long upon sea victualling without receiving any permanent refreshment since they left the Sandwich Islands, we may add to this the constant fatigue inseparable from the active service they were employed on during the Summer in distant excursions in open Boats – in navigating the vessel through narrow seas & channels, and besides their other duty at Nootka, the unloading and reloading of the Store ship, which last was performed in wet uncomfortable weather & our late boisterous Gales contributed on the whole not a little to exhaust their vigour, and predispose them to this desponding malady.

By mid-November he was to add:

> ... although the progress of the Scurvy which made its appearance among the people in the passage was in some measure checked by administering various antiscorbutics with which we had been liberally supplied by Government, yet the aid of a fresh vegetable & nourishing diet with the recreation of the Shore was still wanting to eradicate the disease & restore health among us.

It is interesting, if hardly surprising, that here Menzies recognises that the cooped-up conditions of shipboard life for any lengthy period were not conducive to good health. Captain Cook was so concerned for the welfare of his men that he instituted a regime of hygiene and good diet, and it was he who set the standard that was followed by the officers such as Colnett, Johnstone and Vancouver. Cook fed his men with sauerkraut, portable soup (in blocks) and malt, but also obtained fresh vegetables wherever he could. He succeeded in getting his conservative sailors to accept this by feeding these items to his officers first. Joseph Banks found on his first voyage with Cook that lemon juice corrected the symptoms of scurvy very quickly.[26] The root cause of the problem, i.e. lack of vegetables and fruit, was not recognised until the middle of the 18th century: Dr John Lind published his treatise on the subject in 1753, but it was not until 1795 that the Royal Navy took consistent measures to combat the disease.[27]

By the beginning of the 19th century, some 50,000 gallons of lemon juice were being consumed by the service against scurvy. The affliction was a particular concern for Menzies throughout his career at sea, and it is clear that he gave great attention to its abatement, so that during his time as a surgeon on board not a single life appears to have been lost from this source. Apart from scurvy, the usual poor diet contributed greatly to the chronic constipation which most sailors of the time suffered from. Another all-too-common medical problem was ruptured hernias caused by heavy hauling, working the windlasses, and lifting heavy weights which were all part of the daily routines of navymen.

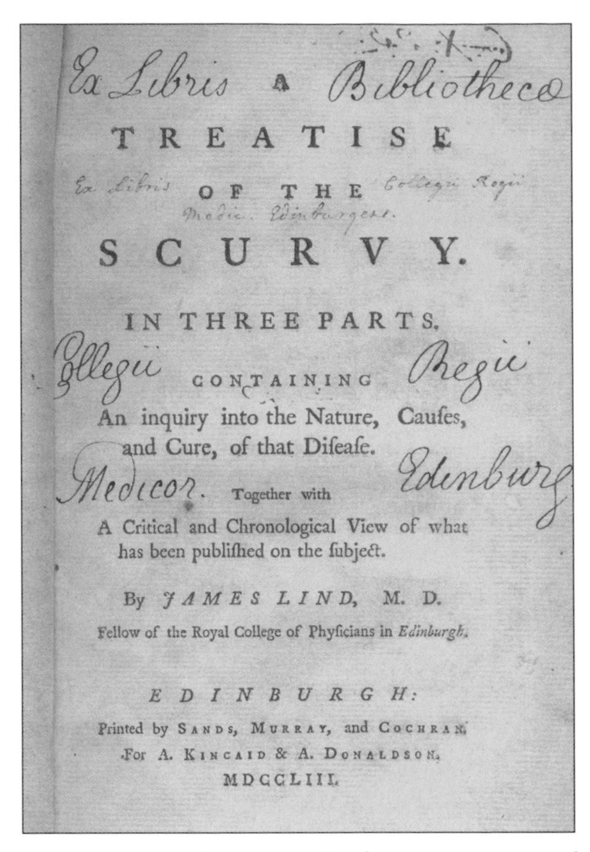
Ex Libris A Bibliotheca

TREATISE

OF THE

SCURVY.

IN THREE PARTS.

Collegii CONTAINING Regii

An inquiry into the Nature, Cauſes, and Cure, of that Diſeaſe.

Medicor. Together with Edinburg

A Critical and Chronological View of what has been publiſhed on the ſubject.

By JAMES LIND, M. D.

Fellow of the Royal College of Phyſicians in *Edinburgh*.

EDINBURGH:

Printed by SANDS, MURRAY, and COCHRAN.

For A. KINCAID & A. DONALDSON.

MDCCLIII.

The title page of Dr Lind's influential work of 1753, *A Treatise of the Scurvy.* (Courtesy of the Royal College of Physicians of Edinburgh.)

From Nootka, Colnett made trading journeys mainly for otter skins as far north as Mount Fairweather in Alaska, and spent two winters in the Sandwich Isles (Hawaii); when Menzies returned to the Northwest coast and Hawaii with Vancouver in 1791–95, he was remembered from his previous visits and welcomed. Apart from Colnett himself, another officer, Andrew Bracey Taylor, third mate on the *Prince of Wales*, also kept a journal. Whereas Colnett's journal is understandably concerned with official log entries, that of Taylor often contains the more interesting accounts, with considerable detail on the appearance of the natives, their arms, ornaments, etc. Much original survey work was also carried out, mainly by Menzies' friend James Johnstone in small boat expeditions, which Menzies frequently accompanied on plant collecting forays.

Not long after their arrival, both Colnett and Taylor reported serious thieving by the local Indians.[28] Taylor says that one Indian caught was flogged with 30 lashes:

> ... he was regularly seized up hands and feet, but not without some difficulty as he was a powerful man. He bore his punishment without much complaint, though the blood sued copiously from his back, till towards the conclusion of his flogging, when the pain produced the usual effect. Had this man been kept out of the Ship, he could not have attempted to steal, so that I conceive we were equally culpable.[29]

This last comment is remarkable for its time, but the incident resulted in the practice of strictly controlling local access to the vessels. In his journal Colnett refers to this constant problem:

> Their Women might be reckon'd handsome when wash'd clear of paint, having very regular features some colour in their Cheeks & a pleasing and very agreeable countenance; but this must be confined to the Younger sort & not the Ladies with the plate in under their lip, for that gives them a most horrid aspect, as to their Chastity it may be compared to those of the Sandwich and Friendly Isles, their favours purchas'd at a very easy rate, but this I do not think a very common failing of theirs; when we first arrived among them Iron was very scarce, & they had no Skins to purchase it of us, they robbed us of every hook & Thimble out of rigging they could come at but still their wants were great, they soon found out that their Women were the next thing coveted to their Furs, and the Men and parents, whom they are under great subjection to readily barter'd them, we soon found many Ladies desirous of disposing of themselves & the numbers so increas'd that they had no purchaser.

(Taylor states that one chief's wife was very offended that no attention had been paid to her daughter despite her beauty.)[30]

However, much more serious was the incident which occurred on 12 October at Taylor Island between St. James and Anchorage: the *Prince of Wales* foundered seriously on a rock with potentially dire consequences – the situation was so bad that even the bosun, a very experienced man, was in tears (as were many of the crew), and there was a real fear that they would lose the vessel entirely. Taylor comments: 'I think I may venture to assert that the brain of every Man in the Tent, not at work at that moment, [was] thinking how he might contrive to get to Old England.' In very difficult weather conditions the *Prince of Wales* was eventually repaired – during which time the longboat with essential provisions (10 casks of beef and pork) was stolen by Tsimshian Indians. By the time the Indians were tracked down and dispersed by musket fire they had partially destroyed the boat.

The whole incident was blamed on the advice of Captain Duncan, commander of the *Princess Royal*, and the crew demanded that he be prevented from giving orders, which Colnett refused.[31] The Indians continued successfully to harass the ships, and there was one fight, on 20 October while the *Princess Royal* was still grounded and disabled, in which a woman and a man were killed. Arrows were fired by the Indians and grape shot from the ships' guns had to be deployed to disperse them.[32] It was not until 15 November, a whole month after the ship had been disabled, that the *Princess Royal* was fully repaired. The whole incident, which could have ended the expedition there and then, was a near disaster and contributed to a marked deterioration in relations with the Tsimshian Indians.[33]

The practice was followed of retiring to Hawaii for the worst of the northern winter months. Here the ships' complement could recuperate, obtain fresh food, and repair vessels. Following Cook's relatively recent murder in Hawaii, there was considerable tension between the islanders and the ships' crews, exacerbated by internecine warfare between different local clans vying for power. Taylor tells of one chief bringing a shirt of Captain Cook's which he said Cook had been killed in – it had blood in several places – saying that he was present when it happened and how it happened – but some doubt was expressed about this.[34] On their second visit to Hawaii, Colnett encountered a native who, in his words:

> ... was the man Captain Cook fired the Small Shot at, and shew'd us several marks which he said it left, also told us he gave him the blow which occasion'd his Death, producing a shirt mark'd IC No 6: which he said was the one he fell in and came to his share, and he had made it a present to the King of the Isles, it had some dark coloured marks as if stain'd with Blood and near the waist a Hole as if made by a Pahia or weapon resembling a Dagger ...[35]

Europeans had contributed to the unsettled condition of the islands by selling arms and ammunition to different groups. Their trading created jealousies between the tribes, resulting in the chiefs strictly controlling access to the Europeans by force or using the taboo system. The seamen were constantly on the alert against thievery and even attacks to capture ships and goods: as early as 6 January 1788 the crew of the *Prince of Wales* felt obliged to use firearms against the natives for the first time. At Wimea Bay, between them both ships killed between five and fourteen islanders, with others wounded.[36]

According to Taylor, Menzies had a particular female companion, Nahoupaio, sister of the friendly Chief Matua.[37] On 23 February 1788, in one of the two references to his surgeon in his journal, Colnett says that Menzies 'had taken a good deal of pains to make himself acquainted with the language',[38] which made him particularly useful, and no doubt enhanced his relationship with Nahoupaio. On 5 March Taylor remarked:

> Several of the Females who came off were our old acquaintances who were on Board while at anchor in the Bay with ye Seamen among others was Nahoupaio, Sister to Matua who had ever been strongly attached to ye Physician of ye Squadron & tis not improbable but her presence was ye principal cause of our being favour'd in ye company of many of ye other Females.

Taylor goes on to say that the women were more than keen to come aboard and make free with the sailors.[39] More crucially, Menzies' facility with the language enabled him to confirm from a Hawaiian dancer that the Hawaiians intended to attack and take both the ships, and to weaken the crew previously with poison, after they had successfully cut the anchor cable.

It is not difficult to imagine that after months at sea in exclusively male company, the crews of such ships, sometimes away from home for years, yearned for female company. They had heard of, and sometimes experienced, the availability and open sexuality of the attractive women of such island groups as Tahiti and Hawaii. While some captains understood this and were indulgent, others such as Vancouver were aware of the problems this could create, and that these were not confined to the spread of venereal disease. Female services rendered often had to be paid for in the form of cloth, nails, fishing hooks, etc. at the same time as the ship was using these trade goods to obtain necessary supplies of fresh food and water. With oversupply of ships' goods including 'leakage' via individual entrepreneurs, prices for foodstuffs could rapidly escalate.

Vancouver and others wisely put embargoes on shore leave – much to the frustration of sailors and officers alike – until the ships were satisfactorily provisioned, and even then, restrictions were imposed. Desertions were not uncommon. Something of the attitudes towards women is reflected in Taylor's comments on an Indian couple on their second voyage to the Northwest coast:

> ... we had a woman alongside with a fine child she appeared about 30 years of age of a comely countenance and good features long Dark hair a handsome nose and Dark Eyes we considered her the Belle of ye Coast & only she and her husband a dapper little fellow was in the canoe her chastity was attempted without success, but we had instances to the contrary in others.[40]

In Hawaii Taylor notes: 'Seamen catching the venereal very fast and Dumbring gave us to understand we had injured several girls residing to windward. Obser'd many Men in a most frightful state with the Dry Pox. Discharging from all parts of ye Body.' Eventually, the women were 'tabooed' and according to Taylor:

> ... every man nearly at the time was furnished with a lass for the night, but this alarm caused an immediate stir. The Girls said they must go on Shore or their Fathers wou'd be kill'd. The Seamen were unwilling to part with their Girls but the poor Girls fears prevailed & most of them jumped overboard instantly. This did not however seem to affect the whole, for others came on board out of other Canoes careless of ye Taboo.

Taylor indicates that those who jumped overboard, seeing their rivals, returned.[41]

The commonly used portrait of Menzies as a relatively old man shows a handsome face of some nobility, deep-set eyes and a high forehead. In his younger years he would have been good-looking and his arduous plant hunting ashore across a variety of terrains would have kept him fit and lithe, quite capable of climbing the rigging as he was required when scurvy hit the ships before their first arrival at Nootka. Beyond that, he had the distinct advantage of being able to familiarise himself with native languages both on the Northwest coast and in Hawaii. Coupled with his intense enthusiasm for plants and an innocent desire to ask questions about their characteristics and uses, which was usually the province of native womenfolk, it is not surprising if some of them were attracted to this gentle-mannered surgeon who might be asked to treat their ailments.

While botanising near Nootka, Menzies was usually accompanied quite voluntarily by the wife of the younger brother of the important Chief Maquinna, probably for his protection or because she was fascinated by his plant collecting, which was usually done by Indian women for food: they had a great store of knowledge about the edibility and culinary possibility of many roots, bulbs and seed. Whether she was helping him in this or had been deputed to keep an eye on Menzies is not known, but there can be no doubt about the welcome he gave her several years later when they met up again on the voyage of the *Discovery*.

On the morning of 16 January 1788, in Hawaii, the ship was surrounded by nearly a thousand natives all armed with every appearance of hostility. Colnett reckoned that his ships were not feared and the very large natives were contemptuous of the British crews. Some attempted to board, forcing the ship to set sail. The reception was quite different when they reached Chief Matua's district, where they had good relations with this friendly chief's people.[42]

On 5 February, Taylor reports that Menzies and others were received very politely by the chief who asked them to strip to show the whiteness of their skins, which were much admired.[43] Later however Taylor records the sloop firing for no apparent good reason at two natives on swimming boards and castigates this uncivilised behaviour, which resulted in the sloop being 'tabooed'. Captain Duncan seems to have excused this, to Taylor's disgust. Taylor, who appears to be sensitive to native custom, also criticises Colnett for not going ashore to provide the traditional greetings to the chiefs whom he ignored.[44]

Later Colnett tells of yet another native attack:

> Three Canoes stay'd alongside for some time & in one of them Poheva The Chief that had been at the death of Captain Cook, a heavy fireing from the *Princess Royal* hastened their departure; but some of the Crew flew to whatever arms were in their reach & fired a great Gun & musket. I desired them to desist which was immediately comply'd with, but a man was kill'd in Poheva's Canoe instead of him.[45]

Duncan did in fact kill a considerable number of natives whom he thought were after his anchor – Taylor thinks about 20 were killed or wounded. The natives certainly stole an anchor and Colnett had to enter into negotiations over 15 days to bribe for its return, giving arms, powder, iron, etc. The chief apparently wanted both arms and a member of the crew to impress potential invaders and rivals. Ironically the crew member who had been taken ashore as a hostage decided to stay of his own accord, having become enamoured of the chief's daughter.[46] Captain Duncan and the crew of the *Princess Royal* do not appear to have exercised much discipline, and in general the behaviour of the crews compared unfavourably with that of the crews on the later Royal Navy expedition under the tight command of George Vancouver.

In March 1788 the trading expedition left Hawaii for the Northwest coast, anchoring at Macleod Bay, Montague Harbour in Prince William Sound on the 27th of that month, having had very bad weather *en route* which necessitated extensive repairs to their ships.[47] With these old timber boats, there was a constant battle to prevent rotting of wooden hulls and much time was taken up with running repairs to masts, spars, rudders, etc.

Generally Colnett found the Indian propensity for thieving just as frustrating as on his previous visit to this coast, but he considered the Sitka Tlingit Indians between Cross Cape and Cape Edgecombe honest and friendly. (Taylor says 'nothing cou'd exceed their civility considering they were savages'.) However, he revealed his distaste for unnecessary violence in reporting an incident where a sailmaker shot an Indian who had stolen his fishing line: '... but it was done with a degree of cruelty, for he fired twice. I was not on deck myself or would have endeavour'd to prevent it, & those whose busyness it was in my absence, looked on with the greatest unconcern.'[48]

The boats stayed on this coast trading for skins as far north as Prince William Sound until November, when they retired to Hawaii. They returned by the middle of March, but Colnett appears to have collected relatively few pelts.[49] Taylor reports from the area in the Queen Charlotte Isles where Captain Dixon had purchased 500 skins in four hours: '... the Natives had scarcely Skins to cover them and were far in every respect inferior to our friends on the side of ye isle we did not even get a supply of fish ... comparatively speaking we were starving in the midst of plenty'.[50] For Colnett and his sponsor Richard Etches this was the greatest disappointment of the voyage – Colnett attributes it to the successful trading of another vessel in the same area.[51,52]

After re-victualling in Hawaii for most of September 1788, the ships sailed west to Canton. Here they spent several weeks, selling off their furs – some 2000 skins at a value of just over £21,000 – and taking aboard tea and silk.[53] Colnett decided to proceed to Macao, to await another ship for further trade on the Northwest coast of America, eventually joining forces with John Meares. For the homeward journey of the *Prince of Wales* he gave command to James Johnstone. The ship stopped at Sumatra in February 1789, and at the south end of that island Menzies collected plant specimens, forwarding both dried specimens and seeds to Kew; these included six new genera and a fine collection of lichen and Musci.[54] It appears that on this voyage Menzies also collected in Singapore, Martinique and Madagascar *en route* to the Cape of Good Hope.[55]

Menzies arrived in England on 14 July 1789, and immediately wrote to Banks announcing their safe arrival:

> … after a tedious voyage round the globe of nearly three years during which time the officers and Crews of both vessels continued pretty healthy, notwithstanding the sudden and many vicissitudes of climate … we have lost only one man during the whole voyage, who died about 20 days ago, of a lingering disease he contracted in China, in consequence of intemperance. On the west side of north America in a remote corner inland, I saw the Natives have a short warlike weapon of solid brass – somewhat in the shape of a New Zealand Pata-patoo, about fifteen inches long; it had a short handle with a round knob at the end and the blade was of an oval form, thick in the middle but becoming gradually thinner towards the edges and embellished on one side with an Escutcheon inscribing Jos: Banks Esq, The natives put a very high value on it, for they would not part with it for very considerable offers. The inscription and Escutional embellishments were nearly worn off by their great attention in keeping it clean. On which I beg leave to remark that the inscription etc on such durable tokens left among savages ought to be deeply impressed. Announce the date when and if possible the place were [sic] left, for it remains to be determined through what intermediate conveyance the above instrument has reached the place as I am almost certain we were the first Europeans with whom the Natives ever had any direct communication.
>
> To commemorate this discovery I have given your name to a cluster of Islands round where we was then at anchor and in the course of a few days I hope I shall have the honour of pointing out to you their situation and extent on a Chart I have made of the coast – as also presenting you with a few momentoes from that and other parts of it …[56]

In all of this, Menzies appears very much aware 'on which side his bread was buttered' as far as Banks was concerned, though the naming of locations throughout the globe to honour their patrons or other eminent persons was common practice.

He also wrote to Banks on articles that would be most useful for trading:

> At Nootka we found Copper the article most sought after & in this we were deficient, having little or none aboard. At Prince William's Sound the natives preferred Iron & put very little value on or anything else – they were so overstocked with Beads as to ornament their Dogs with them. At Queen Charlotte's Isles and Banks Isles, Iron, Cloth, Beads with Brass and Copper trinkets answered best. At Cape Edgecombe, Iron Frying-pans – Tin Kettles – Pewter basons and beads formed the chief articles of Trade. Ornamental lofty caps with Brass or Copper would be good presents for the Chiefs and Warriors.[57]

The sheer variety of trade goods eventually supplied is mind-boggling: axes, hatchets, adzes, chisels, hammers, nails, various saws, files, rasps, gimlets, pocket knives, spades, shovels, pick axes, sickles and augers, with a large quantity of bar iron, brass and copper sheets, kettles, goblets, bracelets, buttons, thimbles, frying pans, pewter pots, spoons, not to mention scissors, needles, thread, scarlet cloth (which proved immensely popular), linen, red caps, earrings, and various colours of beads; Menzies also added 'Scotch Tartan or parti-coloured blankets, Daggers and Old bayonets and Muskets and other fire Arms with Powder & balls'. Given his views on arming natives, the latter is rather surprising. To this Banks added 1000 'Medals of H. Majesty' to mark the expedition's passage, which were not provided.[58]

Menzies also recommended that two blacksmiths and a forge be sent, to fashion those metal articles most sought after by the different tribes of Indians. This advice proved particularly useful to George Vancouver on his voyage along this coast accompanied by Menzies in 1791–95, but it also reflected the diversity of native cultures and the frustration of Europeans in understanding how to deal with this sheer variety.

Menzies honoured his promise to send botanical material to the Royal Botanic Garden Edinburgh and introduced himself to Hope's successor, Professor Rutherford, in a letter of 12 September 1789, referring to the seeds and the location of their collection. He also mentioned Rutherford's predecessor, Dr Hope, saying of him: '... in him I have lost my best and only friend whose sincere attachment and disinterested kindness towards me I shall ever venerate with a grateful remembrance'.[59] Rutherford was obviously pleased with the material, and in his reply Menzies refers to having the use of Banks' house, library and herbarium in London to help identify the seeds to be sent to Edinburgh, and also promises to send plants for Rutherford's herbarium.

Menzies goes on to say:

> The Gardener which you have engaged for the Botanic Garden is my Brother – he has been with me here these 10 days and we have already visited many of the great collections of plants in the vicinity of this metropolis and be assured that during his short stay no opportunity will be lost that may contribute to this improvement for I shall exert my utmost endeavours to render his correspondence here as extensive and respectable as possible as I conceive it may contribute much to the interest of the Botanic Garden.

He also mentions that he has introduced his brother to Dr Pitcairn and Mr Aiton at Kew.[60]

During the rest of 1789 Menzies worked in Banks' London library and herbarium, where he met James Edward Smith (1759–1828), first President of the Linnean Society. Smith had purchased the whole of the library and herbarium of Linnaeus for 1000 guineas and had it sent to his London home.[61] He had attended the University of Edinburgh, and like Menzies, had been a pupil of John Hope, who had awarded him a medal for the best collection of native Scottish plants. In 1820 Menzies encouraged Smith to apply for the post of Professor of Botany at the University of Edinburgh, reckoning that the garden would be worth £10–12,000 per year, '... and no doubt an able

Prof. would make that of it' (presumably in receipts from visitors). In the event, Smith took up the post of Professor of Botany at Glasgow University.[62]

In the course of the voyage, Menzies had sent more than a hundred specimens to Banks, accompanying each with an exact description of the locality where he found it, its identity where he was able to establish this, and its habitat; these specimens eventually found their way to the British Museum.[63] He was becoming recognised as an able professional botanist. In 1790 he was made a Fellow of the Linnean Society, and he was sometimes incorrectly referred to as the 'Father' of this august confraternity. At the end of that year he received his warrant as a surgeon.[64]

The fur-trading voyage of James Colnett in the years 1786–89 has been largely overshadowed by the immensely successful later voyage of George Vancouver along the same Northwest coast of America, which Menzies also accompanied. However, Colnett's travels made a very significant contribution to Vancouver's success, since he had access to Colnett's journals, and equally importantly to his charts, many of them made by James Johnstone on his small boat sorties. Johnstone may also have been the original source of an anonymous 'chart of the coast' that Menzies had constructed by the time he arrived back in England. Colnett and his officers made interesting and important ethnographic observations and are credited with making some of the very first European contacts with a wide variety of tribes. For his part Menzies was the first serious natural history explorer of this region, and the voyage provided a foundation for his subsequent scientific work with Vancouver.

The considerable achievements of the Colnett voyage, which were so important to the success of Vancouver's official government-sponsored expedition, may well have been overshadowed by Colnett's subsequent and unfortunate association with John Meares and the notorious 'Nootka Incident' of 1789–90 which Vancouver himself was sent to resolve.

There is no record of a journal kept by Menzies on the voyage, although it is difficult to believe he did not write one.[65] Despite the term 'tedious', Menzies had obviously developed a taste for adventurous travel, and had been especially drawn to the Northwest coast of America, whose ruggedness so much reminded him of his native Scotland. He took the very next opportunity of revisiting the region.

NOTES

1. Balfour (1944), 172
2. Naish (1996), 7
3. Galois (2004), 7
4. There is a fine short biography of Colnett in Galloway and Groves (1987), 37.
5. See Naish (1996), 11 *et seq.* for further on Meares.
6. Olson (1993), 4

7. Menzies to Banks, 21 August 1786. Banks Correspondence, Royal Botanic Gardens, Kew
8. Menzies to Banks, 7 September 1786. Banks Correspondence 1: 243, Royal Botanic Gardens, Kew
9. James Colnett 1786–1789. *A Voyage to the NW Side of America. Journal of the Prince of Wales.* National Archives, London, ADM 55/146
10. Menzies to Banks, 16 November 1786. Banks Correspondence 1: 249, Royal Botanic Gardens, Kew
11. O'Brian (1987), 168
12. Keevil (1948), 798
13. Banks Correspondence Transcripts, British Museum (Natural History), London
14. Menzies to Banks, 16 November 1786. Banks Correspondence 1: 249, Royal Botanic Gardens, Kew
15. James Colnett 1786–1789. *A Voyage to the NW Side of America. Journal of the Prince of Wales.* National Archives, London, ADM 55/146
16. Menzies to Banks, 11 February 1787. Banks Correspondence 1: 259, Royal Botanic Gardens, Kew
17. Galois (2004) says (332 note 50) referring to Winter Bark: 'Drimys winteri, commonly used in the eighteenth century as an antiscorbutic.'
18. Ibid., 89
19. James Colnett 1786–1789. *A Voyage to the NW Side of America. Journal of the Prince of Wales.* National Archives, London, ADM 55/146
20. Balfour (1944), 172
21. Justice (2000), 14
22. Lysacht (1971), 120
23. Justice (2000), 13
24. Keevil (1957), 292
25. Naish (1996), 54
26. Keevil (1957), 309–11
27. Ibid., 302
28. Galois (2004), 107–10
29. Ibid., 133
30. Ibid., 134
31. Ibid., 150
32. Ibid., 157
33. Ibid., 164
34. Ibid., 188
35. On a subsequent visit, the Hawaiians expressed great sorrow at the killing of Cook.
36. Galois (2004), 62–3
37. Ibid., 61
38. Ibid., 189

39. Ibid., 195
40. Ibid., 239
41. Ibid., 186
42. Ibid., 178–9
43. Ibid., 366 note 57
44. Ibid., 187
45. Ibid., 192
46. Ibid., 195 *et seq.*
47. Ibid., 204
48. Ibid., 224
49. Ibid., 230–3
50. Ibid., 242–3
51. Ibid., 244
52. There is a claim however of Menzies securing 200 otter skins in one purchase (Balfour 1944, 172).
53. Ibid., 18
54. RBGE mss. Folder 2 of 4, Edinburgh
55. Cowan (1954), 119–227
56. Menzies to Banks, 14 July 1789. Banks Correspondence 1: 356, Royal Botanic Gardens, Kew
57. Galois (2004), 60
58. Lamb (1984), 40
59. Menzies to Rutherford, Edinburgh, 12 September. Archives, RBGE
60. Menzies to Rutherford, 19 October 1789. Archives, RBGE
61. Naish (1988), 440
62. Dawson, W. R. (1934), Smith Correspondence, 22 January 1820, Catalogue 24: 41, Linnean Society, London
63. Keevil (1948), 798
64. Ibid., 799
65. Galois (2004), 66–70

7

'A Particular Desire for Traversing Unknown Regions'

Following the success of Cook's voyage 10 years earlier the British Government decided in 1790 to send yet another expedition round the world, with three objectives. The first was to confirm the existence of what is now known as Antarctica; the second was to find the so-called North West Passage to the Orient via North America (thus linking the Pacific and Atlantic Oceans) which Cook had searched for; and the final one was to accept from the Spanish the settlement of Nootka which had been agreed between Britain and Spain. The terms of this agreement allowed the British to trade along the Northwest coast and to use Nootka as an anchorage and base.[1] In addition, the expedition was to return via the west coast of South America and to survey that territory.[2]

Captain George Vancouver was appointed to command the expedition which comprised the ship *Discovery* and its tender, *Chatham*. *Discovery* was a newly-built sloop of 330 tons, and just under 100 feet in length, while *Chatham* was only 131 tons.[3] The complement of the *Discovery* was 100 including 16 marines, while that of the *Chatham* was 38, with eight marines. (This establishment was very similar to that of Cook's last two voyages, but much had been learned from the deficiencies experienced with stores.) In addition, a supply ship, the *Daedalus*, was commissioned to rendezvous with the expedition at the Cape of Good Hope, in the event only catching up with *Discovery* at San Francisco in October 1793.[4]

On the question of discipline and order, Vancouver would almost certainly have followed the practice of his admired mentor, Cook, in observing standard Royal Navy routines, as if on a man of war. This involved absolute punctuality in the division of the day's work, punctuated by bells and the bosun's pipe: the upper decks would be swabbed down at dawn, the hands piped to breakfast at eight bells, while the lower decks were cleared; at 12 bells, noon was formally reported and the officer of the watch was advised of the latitude, which was conveyed to the captain, for the traditional beginning of the nautical day, with its succession of timed operations. It did not take long for the new seamen to recognise that this ordered routine was to be their lot for the duration of the voyage, and perhaps eventually for them to take a pride in its observance. Apart from providing additional security, the precision drilling of the marines obviously gave a useful impression of organised discipline to native peoples.

After his own experience as a scientist on the first Cook voyage, Joseph Banks had successfully persuaded the British Government that to maximise the opportunities of such expeditions a competent naturalist should be included among the personnel. He himself had been accompanied by two naturalists, two artists, two footmen and two black servants. He was constantly promoting the cause of agricultural development overseas and he saw exploration and commerce as quite complementary. Much plant collecting under his aegis was for imperial purposes, specifically colonial trade, particularly in the tropics, in such commodities as cocoa, cotton, sugar, coffee, etc.[5] Several times Menzies refers to bringing in plants and animals for the improvement of local agriculture.

Banks did not accompany Cook on his second voyage, however, as Cook refused his outrageous demands to have a complete additional deck built and to accommodate a small orchestra![6] But Banks was by this time in a very good position to influence who should become the naturalist on the voyage of the *Discovery*, since he had not only the ear of the King, but also powerful friends both at Kew and at the Admiralty (notably the Earl of Chatham, the First Lord of the Admiralty, and William Grenville, the Secretary of State). Reading the correspondence between these various eminences one gains a sense of how powerful and close this 'old boys' club' was in all such matters.

After being given an indication that he was likely to be invited to join the expedition, Menzies was dismayed by the lengthy delay in confirmation of his appointment. Captain Henry Roberts, who had sailed on the last two of Cook's expeditions, had originally been given command of the expedition, but this plan was changed and the waiting made Menzies desperate, as apparent from a letter to Banks:

> Captain Roberts is to have another vessel, and to go out in the Spring [1790] – but he could not say whether I was to go with him, or in the *Discovery* – I need not observe the necessity of obtaining this information soon, that if I go in the latter, I may have some time to equip for the voyage ...[7]

By good fortune, Menzies had received his warrant as a Royal Navy surgeon (as distinct from his previous rank as assistant surgeon) on 13 December 1790.[8] In a fever of uncertainty, he had to wait a year from first intimation of his appointment as naturalist under Roberts to confirmation of his role as surgeon/naturalist aboard the *Discovery*. He wrote to Banks in almost ecstatic terms:

> From the first moment I had the honour to be your correspondent I found within me a particular desire of traversing unknown regions in quest of my favourite pursuit, and fondly looked for the enjoyment of that indulgence under your kind tuition and patronage ... I need not therefore tell you, Sir Joseph, how ready I am to undertake your instructions whatever they may be; or how cheerfully I will exert, on every occasion my utmost endeavours to the completion of their object; and what pleasure I shall enjoy in transmitting to you from time to time, an Epitome of our proceedings by a faithful and diligent correspondence.

> I know well I have been already on many occasions extremely troublesome to you, which I hope you will attribute in some measure to my long and tedious state of suspense more intolerable than the hardship and fatigue of traversing the wildest Desert: but be assured I will not fail now to exert the only means in my power to repay in some measure your disinterested attention and friendship towards me by a diligent and persevering zeal in the promotion of that Science which you so liberally and indefatigably patronise ...[9]

Even given the language often deployed at this time, this letter borders on obsequiousness to his patron. Banks, while respecting Menzies as a competent naturalist, in all likelihood simply saw him as the best man for the job to achieve his own aspirations. Banks had quite clear ideas on the sort of person who would be most suitable, and valued personal integrity and loyalty to Kew and to himself as much as professional skills, including humility and civility. He preferred bachelors for their single-minded dedication – and required them not to get above their social station as servants. When Banks wanted a collector for HMS *Nautilus*'s survey of the West African coast he had in mind a gardener: '... active and healthy, able to write a good hand and willing to write down such observations as he may make. Whenever he lands he should have a little idea of botany and be well acquainted with the manner of gathering and drying specimens and be able to give some idea of the soil, whether sandy, loamy, clayey, boggy, etc.'[10]

Banks demanded a great deal from his collectors, not least Menzies with his medical training and previous collecting experience: when surveying new lands, he would be required to make notes on habitats which were to accompany the despatch of plants, for example.

In addition to his collection of plant specimens, Menzies was expected, in quite detailed instructions, to assess a territory's suitability for settlers, fauna, social life and crafts of natives, etc., and was urged to seek coal deposits and minerals with commercial applications[11] (see Appendix 3). With the great loss of transported plants, much attention was to be given to packaging – for example using damp moss in cut-down casks with drain holes.[12] Menzies followed these instructions precisely, with dated chronological entries in his journal, though there was not always an entry for each day.[13] However, the instruction to Menzies to deliver his journal direct to the Secretary of State, and not, as was normal practice, to the captain of his vessel in the first instance, was to cause serious dissension. Banks' instructions, deliberately conveyed through Admiralty orders, gave Vancouver no room for manoeuvre and were to sow the seeds of an unseemly breakdown in relations between the captain and the surgeon towards the end of the voyage.

Banks warned that the daily routine of tending plants took precedence over the collector's personal comfort – he enjoined David Nelson not to allow even an hour's negligence to threaten his collections and 'to guard yourself against all temptations of idleness or liquor'.[14] Banks was also almost obsessively protective of the reputation of

Kew Gardens and its exclusivity, so much so that if any collectors on authorised expeditions disposed of plants to commercial nurserymen or others, it was considered a cardinal sin.[15] Banks regarded a Scottish education with particular favour because it inculcated the habits of industry, attention and frugality.[16]

These collectors would certainly have to be frugal on an average pay of £150 a year, which is what Menzies was paid.[17] He was already £200 in debt as a result of a long period of unemployment, and complained to Banks about the large amount of cash – some £90 – he was required to pay for his stores, including liquor, to enable him to join the gunroom mess.[18] There was an unfortunate dispute as to whether he would be allowed, as an 'inferior' officer, to mess with the commissioned officers, a reflection of the relatively lowly status accorded to surgeons and scientists at that time. Eventually Vancouver was able to report to the Admiralty that an agreement had been reached with Menzies' messmates on this issue, but the failure to reach a more equitable settlement regarding expenses remained a sore point with Menzies.[19]

Banks continued:

> In all places where you can procure a friendly intercourse with the natives you are to make careful enquiry into their manners, customs, ceremonies, religion, language, manufacture, and every other thing in your opinion likely to interest mankind. And if you find the abominable custom of eating human flesh, which they are said to practice, to be really in use among them, you are, if you can do it with safety and propriety, to be present at some of their horrid repasts in order to bear witness to the existence of a practice all but incredible to the inhabitants of civilised countries, and discover, if you can, the original motives of a custom for which it seems impossible to suggest any probable cause ...[20]

If Menzies got too close to the practice, he could of course end up as the main item on the menu! However, Lord Evan Nepean (1751–1822), who was Secretary to the Admiralty from 1795, wrote to Banks on 24 February 1791 indicating that Lord William Grenville, Secretary of State, thought the instructions to Menzies should be signed by Banks himself and that on the question of cannibalism, this should not be included in official instructions, but would be more appropriate in a private letter, indicating official sensitivity on this matter.[21]

Cannibalism, the last taboo, fascinated and repelled Europeans and much ink was expended in relation to the practice. Regarding the Maoris, Banks wrote:

> It is now a long time since I have mentioned their Custom of Eating human flesh, as I was loth a long time ago to believe that any human beings could have among them so brutal a custom. I am now however convinced and shall here give a short account of what we have heard from the Indians concerning it ... looking carelessly upon one of these [provision baskets] we by accident observed two bones, pretty clean pick'd, which as appeared upon examination were undoubtedly human bones.

Banks cross-examined the natives to obtain their confirmation that these were the bones of their enemies killed in battle: 'The horrour that appeared in the countenances of the seamen on hearing this discourse which was immediately translated for the good of the company is better conceived than described.'[22] One could of course compare the barbarity of this with, for example, that experienced by those British seamen subject to 'flogging round the fleet' by their masters, a practice which frequently ended in a slow death, but which was largely accepted as just by these same apparently horrified seamen.

One instruction from Banks which was to have important consequences was that any records maintained or collections made by Menzies were to be handed over to the Home Department, and on the day following, Lord Grenville forwarded a copy of what was to become a crucial letter to the Admiralty.[23]

George Vancouver was a Norfolk man, of Dutch extraction. Born in 1758, he grew up in King's Lynn and would have absorbed all its historic seafaring traditions. His first

A portrait thought to be of George Vancouver by an unknown artist.
(Courtesy of the National Portrait Gallery, London.)

experience of life at sea was as a 14-year-old midshipman on board Captain Cook's *Resolution*, and he was present at the fighting which accompanied his leader's murder in Hawaii.

He would of course have been aware of Banks' activities – and autocratic demands – on Cook's first voyage and seems to have developed an antipathy to the King's advisor. He was known to have an uncertain temper, and Banks was to warn Menzies to note any occasions of obstructive behaviour by Vancouver which could be used in evidence against him. Banks had a tense encounter with Vancouver who strongly objected to the plant cases on his deck; as Lamb observes, Banks was apt to assume that if he took an interest in a project this gave him the right to interfere.[24] Menzies claims, probably correctly, that he never heard what Vancouver's objections to his appointment were.

> How Vancouver will behave to you is more than I can guess, unless I was to judge by his conduct towards me – which is not such as I am used to judge from persons in his situation. As it would be highly imprudent in him to throw any obstacle in the way of your duty, I trust he will have too much good sense to obstruct it.[25]

Vancouver's subsequent attitude towards Menzies, whom he came to respect as a surgeon, is likely to have been influenced by seeing the botanist as Banks' man more than anything else. Banks had used his considerable influence to have Menzies appointed as a naturalist to the expedition: for some reason Vancouver objected to his appointment as a surgeon, but eventually agreed to have him as supernumerary naturalist and botanist. Why Vancouver should have resisted Menzies being appointed as a surgeon and botanist is puzzling, but Vancouver would have been wary of Banks, with his considerable standing in society and in the scientific world, especially after his resounding success as a result of the first Cook voyage. Banks was a personal friend of King George and very rich – there may have been a form of inverse snobbery on Vancouver's part, but being a traditional seaman, he would certainly have resented any usurpation of his position as naval commander and any undermining of his right to control anyone on his ship.

In addition the captain had many other problems to contend with before the ships set sail, not least of which was the need to find replacements for those deserters – some 16 from the *Discovery* and five from the *Chatham* – who had been enticed by the prospect of war with France and the possibility of sharing in compensation for the capture of 'prize' enemy ships. Unfortunately many of these replacements had to be discarded as unfit for the sort of service that an arduous three-year voyage demanded.[26]

It would not have helped the relationship that Banks had persuaded the Admiralty to issue instructions on the facilities to be afforded to Menzies, including the care of a plant frame, a boat and working parties as required, fresh water for his plants, trade goods for the botanist's use, etc.; all such instructions were labelled 'secret' and were not made known to Menzies. Vancouver soon found out that Menzies, under Banks' patronage, was a 'protected person'. Crucially Menzies was to report to Banks and not to the commander of the expedition.[27] He was also supplied with a 'Botanist's Lieutenant' in J. Ewing. (Kew Gardens were quite willing to recompense seamen who looked after plants on a voyage.)

The official surgeon on the *Discovery* was Alexander Purvis Cranstoun, supported by three surgeon's mates, George Hewett, Adam Mill and John Mears, while the accompanying tender had William Walker and William Nicholl as doctors. With so many medical men to care for a complement of 140 men, Menzies would have seemed to be superfluous as a surgeon and was expected to carry out only naturalist duties. This would turn out not to be the case, as Cranstoun had to be sent home as medically unfit shortly after the expedition's first arrival at Nootka.

Menzies was at this point officially confirmed as surgeon, but it is clear that he had undertaken surgeon's duties from an early stage in the voyage, including attending on Vancouver who himself had precarious health, and who preferred to be treated by him rather than Cranstoun, an indication of his confidence in him. In Menzies' own words, he had 'constantly prescribed for Capt. Vancouver since we left England'. This official appointment must have added considerably to his workload, as he would now have been responsible for all health matters for the whole crew. At the end of the voyage, and notwithstanding their disagreements, Vancouver was to declare in his journal that Menzies 'fulfilled his task quite admirably'.[28] Banks went further to state that shortly after leaving Tenerife, 'Menzies saved Vancouver's life by putting him on a diet when he thought himself within a few days of his dissolution'.[29]

Menzies was given detailed instructions on how to gather, store, and bring back seeds and dried specimens, all of which were to be packed in paper packages labelled with date and place of collection, together with notes on soils and climate of the collection locality. He was to give the commander ample warning of requirements of water for his plants, which were to be brought back alive in a plant frame.[30] Given the problems that this so-called 'plant hutch' was to create, it is worth detailing its construction.

It was a seven foot by thirteen foot box, with three-foot high sides consisting of a sill or curb with four sliding light windows, and alternating wood panels with paired shutters. The top of the hutch was of four removable wood gratings similar to a ship's hatch covers, supported by and fitted onto two longitudinal beams. Inside there was a bench which held rows of clay pots by the rims and several ten-inch deep trays along with openings in the centre of the bench so that a person could stand in it and tend the plants. It was quite a sophisticated shelter, with its moveable glass panes and shutters, which allowed both air and sun to reach the plants but were also capable of being closed in inclement weather.[31]

Banks was convinced of the need for small glasshouses or 'plant cabins'[32] but this was to become a real bone of contention right from the start, and towards the end of the expedition became the cause of a serious rift between Vancouver and Menzies. Vancouver was infuriated by the Admiralty's instruction, on Banks' stipulation, that such a 'plant hutch', which Banks had designed, was to be located on his hallowed quarter-deck. Banks would have been persuaded of the necessity of this from his experience on the *Endeavour* voyage, when a storm resulted in the loss of all his boxes of seeds and plants.[33] In Vancouver's eyes it must have been seen as an excrescence on a space which was the purlieu of himself and his commissioned officers. Vancouver had noted with approval that Cook had won a battle with Banks over the question of the latter's subsequent demands. When Menzies had his appointment to the *Discovery* confirmed by the King, he was told that he would receive his instructions from Banks. He wrote to Banks on 8 October 1789:

> I am therefore anxious that you may be in town before any considerable progress is made in the Outfit of the Vessel, in order that a suitable place may be constructed for bringing home the plants in safety, as also for preserving the seeds and specimens which may be collected during the Voyage. There is a young Boy with whose fidelity and disposition I am already acquainted with and whom I would wish to take with me as a servant if you think it will be allowed – if not – I must provide otherwise for him. I conclude by returning you my sincerest thanks for the very friendly part you have already taken in my behalf; and shall omit no opportunity in exerting my utmost endeavours to merit your approbation ...[34]

On 24 February 1790 Menzies wrote a very worried letter to Banks from Portsmouth expressing his anxiety about the completion of the frame being built on the quarter-deck – it was a long way from being finished, and Menzies complained: 'I have not yet heard anything about the glass (50 panes)', and went on to suggest by the tone of his letter that he had little confidence in Vancouver's will to complete it – the first indication of strain between the two men. Nevertheless, Vancouver in his journal of the voyage wrote:

> Botany, however, was an object of scientific enquiry with which no one of us was much acquainted; but as in expeditions of a similar nature, the most valuable opportunities had been afforded for adding to the general stock of botanical information, Mr. Archibald Menzies, a surgeon in the Royal Navy, who had before visited the Pacific Ocean in one of the vessels employed in the fur trade, was appointed for the specific purpose of making such researches, and had, doubtless, given sufficient proof of his abilities, to qualify him for the station it was intended he should fill. For the purpose of preserving such new or uncommon plants as might deem worthy of a place amongst His Majesty's very valuable collection of exotics at Kew, a glazed frame was erected on the after part of the quarter-deck, for the reception of those he might have an opportunity of collecting.[35]

The young boy referred to in the earlier letter above is likely to have been Tooworero, then aged about 16, who had been taken from Hawaii at his own request by Captain Duncan of the *Princess Royal* on the previous Colnett voyage. In China, Tooworero was transferred to the *Prince of Wales*, then commanded by Johnstone, who was to become master of the *Chatham*. (He and another young boy were the first Hawaiians

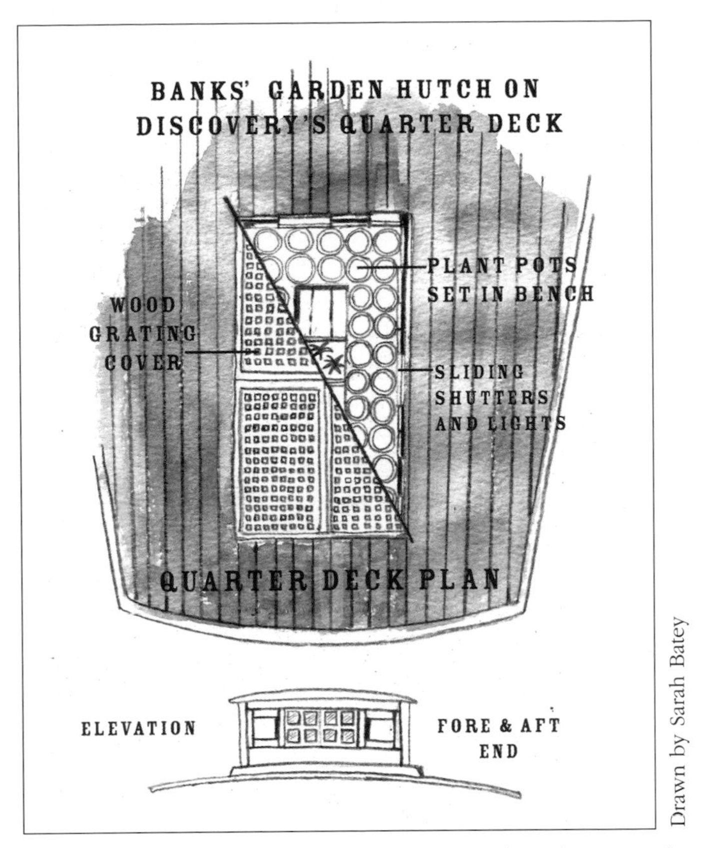

Drawn by Sarah Batey

Plans of Banks' plant hutch on the quarter-deck of *Discovery*, based upon a drawing by Clive L. Justice from his work *Mr Menzies' Garden Legacy: Plant Collecting on the Northwest Coast*. (Redrawn with kind permission of Clive L. Justice.)

to land in England.) Johnstone had looked after the boy in England and had even sent him to school in Plymouth: he could apparently copy and became an accomplished draughtsman. On the *Discovery*, Menzies lent him his cabin for the journey to Portsmouth where Menzies was to join the ship. Banks and other prominent men had interested themselves in his welfare and they hoped that on his return to the islands his seafaring skills would be of some use to his countrymen and his knowledge of English a help to visiting ships.[36] He was later to prove his usefulness on the Northwest coast, primarily in detecting pilfering by the Indians there, but was to get into serious trouble with Vancouver at Tahiti on the outward journey.

> I have this day received my instructions by a Messenger which is just arrived from the Admiralty & while I report myself ready to undertake them as far as may lay in my power I cannot help lamenting the situation in which they place me in; – by not being empowered to ask for a boat at any time from ye ship or the least

assistance Whatever – by not being impowered to claim the least Article of Trade to carry my instructions into execution in uncivilised countries – and by being instructed contrary to my expectations to deliver up on my return whatever collection I may make of Animals, Minerals & Curiosities without having that liberal Outfit which might enable me to procure & collect them to advantage for my Employers and credit to myself. – but the Captain is perhaps instructed to aid and assist me in each of these particulars – how am I to know that? It would not surely be inconsistant with the service to let me have a copy of that part of his instructions which relates to myself, that I might know what latitude I was to have. For the present I have not the least authority to apply to him in any instance whatever – and what is more distressing I shall be oblige probably to go to Sea in this Situation before I can receive an explanation on the Subject but be that as it may I again assure you that no part of my endeavours shall be wanting to accomplish the object of my Mission as far as may lay in my own power & shall confidently look up to you & you alone, on my return, for that liberal indulgence which my situation may merit.

We now only await the arrival of the *Chatham* which is hourly expected from Portsmouth to join us, and then we shall bid Adieu – a long Adieu to the English shore. I have the honour to Subscribe myself with due respect

Sir Joseph, Your most Obed.t & most Hum.ble Servant
Archibald Menzies.[37]

This letter was written only 10 days before the ships sailed for the Northwest coast of America and is quite at variance with the instructions which Banks issued to Menzies in December 1790. It is assumed that some wires had got crossed between Banks and the Admiralty which must have subsequently been resolved, as Menzies did receive at least some of the assistance he sought, although Captain Vancouver did not reveal to him what these instructions were. The letter also demonstrates that not only did Menzies appreciate very well, from his experience with the Colnett voyage, what was needed, for example in using trade goods to acquire 'curiosities', but also that he was quite capable of expressing his views in a forthright manner when required, while reassuring his patron on his determination to faithfully carry out the tasks assigned to him. The instructions Vancouver received in a letter from the Admiralty on 8 March are quite clear on the assistance required to be provided for achieving some of the most important 'Objects of the Expedition', including for example not allowing any ship's animals to enter the plant frame.[38]

On 31 March 1791, on the eve of his departure from Falmouth, Menzies wrote a farewell letter to his mother and brother William. In this, he agrees that his brother should take over the house and farm at Styx 'for his long and faithful services' and care of his mother, until Menzies himself should be able to take on that duty. He also indicated that should anything happen to him on this voyage he believed that 'my station now in the Royal Navy will entitle her to a yearly pension from Government during her life', ending 'Farewell – a long farewell!' To his mother, he says that he has sent a will in her favour to his executor, sending her meantime four guineas via his brother Robert, and promising to send more before his return. He wishes her good health and happiness in very affectionate terms, sending also his good wishes for his brothers and sisters, signing himself 'your dutiful son'.

From his previous experience, Menzies was obviously well aware of the potential hazards of such an expedition and felt therefore that he should formally settle his affairs.

At the same time, Menzies wrote to Olof Swartz (1760–1818) in Stockholm, a pupil of Linnaeus's son, letting him know of his imminent departure and thanking him profusely for a packet of cryptogamic plants, which Menzies says are

> … inestimable treasures! No gift, could I receive that would render me equally happy on the commencement of the New Year … You have Sir placed in my herbarium so many momentoes of your liberality and kindness as will ever keep you dear in my remembrance to whatever quarter of the Globe providence orders

My Dear Mother

I have this day sent My Will in your favour, to my Cousin Mr John Walker No 21 Berkeley Square London, whom I have appointed Executor, as he is better acquainted with the present situation of my Affairs than any one else – My Brother Robert has upwards of 4 Guineas of of mine in his hand which I have directed him to send to you, and if we are likely to remain long on the Voyage, I will write home to my Agent to supply you with more before my return – as I am now upon the eve of leaving England, offer my love and affection to all my Brother & Sisters – & May the guardian hand of Divine Providence long – long continue its protection towards you, & grant you the full enjoyment of Health in this life, and happiness in that which is to come hereafter, will ever be the sincere prayer of Dear Mother Your dutiful Son

AMenzies

Adieu!

A facsimile of a letter from Menzies, bidding his mother farewell before embarking on his voyage with HMS *Discovery*. (RBGE archive.)

> my lot. You may therefore rest assured that it is my greatest ambition to be able to make you a suitable return on my arrival in England ...[39]

At Falmouth, Menzies describes a visit by Lord Camelford and his son, the Honourable Thomas Pitt (later after the death of his father usually referred to as Lord Camelford), who was to join the voyage:

> Early on the morning of the thirteenth we were favoured with a visit from Lord Camelford accompanied by his only son the Honourable Thomas who notwithstanding the unparalleled hardships he suffered in his late perilous situation on board His Majesty's ship *Guardian* off the Cape of Good Hope, was now again to encounter the boisterous elements & accompany us in our long Voyage – thus despising the comforts of ease and affluence this young nobleman embarks at a very early period in his life, to acquire that necessary degree of knowledge & experience in the practical parts of his profession, which cannot fail of rendering him an exemplary ornament to the British Navy.[40]

Menzies was not to know of course that the subsequent behaviour of this young scion of the British aristocracy and Captain Vancouver's reaction was to virtually end the latter's career. However, Pitt was only the most prominent of a whole group of young 'gentlemen' from the upper classes whose acceptance on board had been engineered by their influential relatives and friends, from the Honourable Charles Stuart, son of Lord Bute, to Thomas Manby, friend of Marquess Townshend. There were no fewer than 15 of these aspiring patricians, whose supporters saw such a voyage as part of their education, the maritime equivalent of the Grand Tour, which would provide them with dining-out stories for a long time to come. Few of them had serious naval experience and they depended on the skills of regular officers. Some of them would prove to be a thorn in their captain's flesh, who, from his relatively humble origins, deeply resented their supercilious condescension towards him. It is clear that, by the end of the voyage, discipline was maintained only by rank and that in many respects the community aboard the *Discovery* mirrored in an extreme form the social hierarchies prevalent in England at that time.

NOTES

1. Groves (1998), 73
2. Lamb (1984), 43
3. Ibid., 36
4. Ibid., 38
5. Desmond (1995), 122–4
6. Naish (1996), 83
7. Menzies to Banks, 1790. Banks Collection MSPN 1: 16, Sutro Library, San Francisco

8. Keevil (1948), 799
9. Menzies to Banks, 1 March 1791. Banks Correspondence 2: 34, Royal Botanic Gardens, Kew
10. Banks to Aiton, 29 August 1785. Hyde Collection, Somerville, New Jersey, in Desmond (1995), 113–14
11. Banks Papers, Mitchell Library, Sydney; Naish (1996), 495–507
12. Desmond (1995), 117
13. Groves (1998), 75
14. Desmond (1995), 118. Banks to David Nelson, 1787. Copies of the letters of Sir Joseph Banks, British Museum (Natural History)
15. Ibid., 16
16. Ibid., 114
17. Ibid., 115
18. Naish (1996), 83
19. Keevil (1948), 800
20. McNab (1908), vol. 1, 115–19
21. British Museum (Natural History). Add. MS. 33979.80
22. Quoted in Thomas (2004), 105–6
23. Keevil (1948), 799
24. Lamb (1993), 232
25. Banks to Menzies, 10 August 1791. Brabourne Papers, Mitchell Library, Sydney
26. Lindsay (2005), 124
27. Lamb (1984), 31
28. Ibid., 181
29. Notes by Sir Joseph Banks: Dawson Turner Collection 10(1): 83–6, British Museum (Natural History), London
30. Naish (1996), 57
31. Justice (2000), 17
32. Desmond (1995), 121
33. O'Brian (1987), 58
34. Menzies to Banks, 8 October 1789. Banks Correspondence 1: 362, Royal Botanic Gardens, Kew
35. Vancouver, G., *A Voyage of Discovery to the North Pacific Ocean 1798*, 3 vols, London, in Keevil (1948), 800
36. Naish (1996), 81
37. Brabourne Papers, Mitchell Library, Sydney
38. National Archives, ADM 2/1344
39. Menzies to Swartz, 12 March 1791. Swartz Correspondence, Carl Gustav von Brinkman Collection, Trolle Ljungby Castle, Bäckascog, Sweden, in Galloway and Groves (1987), 16
40. Menzies Journal, 14 March 1791

8

'Every Situation Afforded to my Mind Something New or Rare'

The *Discovery* sailed on 1 April 1791. Menzies kept himself busy during the first stage of the voyage by making measurements of sea temperatures at different depths, recording the barometric pressures at the same time – he saw himself as a general scientist determined to learn as much as possible about the nature of the seas and lands over which he was to travel. Throughout this outward voyage, he was assiduous in describing any new species of fishes or birds, or indeed any natural phenomena, and kept copious notes on the weather. It is clear from his detailed descriptions of, for example, parasitic worms in the innards of fish caught, that he was a trained and acute all-round natural history observer, in addition to being a botanist. On Madeira, he collected plants at no little risk on the steep, unstable slopes of the mountains.[1]

The first port of call on the journey southwards was at Tenerife, where an incident occurred which could have had serious repercussions. For good reason this was omitted from Vancouver's official log, but Menzies relates this in a letter to Banks:

> In the afternoon the Midshipman who went on shore for the liberty-men had a scuffle with the *Chatham*'s people on the wharf which induced the Spanish Sentinels to interpose and one of them had his Musket wrenched out of his hands by one of our Marines, upon which he immediately ran to alarm the guard, at this time Capt.V- & some of the officers came down to the water side and were endeavouring to get the people into the boat, when the Spanish guards arrived, accompanied by a numerous mob, and began to knock down our men and officers without distinctions. Capt.V- was thrown from the wharf into the sea & luckily taken up by our boat without being much hurt, the attack then became so general that the Hble. Mr Pitt and some others jumped into the Sea and swam to the boat to save their lives. Mr. Baker, 3rd Lieutenant of the *Discovery*, who was indeed the only Officer armed and in full uniform, and had never shown the least sign to draw upon them was knocked in the head in several places & wounded. Many of the Men were likewise bruised & wounded in several places, but none I believe dangerously … That the quarrel originated with our people is, I think, pretty evident from every information I can collect, but that the Spanish guard acted very unbecoming Soldiers will not, I think require much examination.[2] In this incident Lt. Whidbey had a miraculous

> escape from death when, two soldiers charged at him with fixed bayonets which he avoided by stepping a little to one side, when the bayonets struck the nearby wall with such force that they broke.[3]

At Santa Cruz in Tenerife, Menzies went botanising, although it was too hot and dry for plant collecting. Menzies took Tooworero with him on his first expedition. Scrambling over dangerous arid cliffs to obtain specimens of *Euphorbia canariensis*, they were tormented by thirst – but Menzies was pleased with the new plants.[4] On 3 May Menzies rode with Tooworero to the more fertile parts of the island near Laguna where they met a dromedary caravan taking supplies to the port: Tooworero was terrified, running into the bushes until they had passed.

On leaving Tenerife Vancouver became ill and he came to rely increasingly on Menzies for his medical treatment.[5] Menzies busied himself with his oceanographic and zoological studies, examining the stomachs of several sharks and bonitos, and describing in detail the sucking fish and parasites he found in them. He noted all the birds he saw and changes in the weather. Always active and ingenious, he experimented with a machine to blow air into the water that was collected in the awnings to get rid of its bad taste. He was scathing about the Navy diehards who resisted his suggested improvements in the operation of the traditional ventilator for purifying water. He was particularly intrigued to find that, just south of the Tropic of Capricorn, the air temperature was lower than that of the surface water.

When the ships arrived at the Cape of Good Hope, they found no fewer than 17 ships of many nations already anchored there, including three convict ships: the Dutch had established a profitable trade in provisioning vessels. It was here that the *Discovery* took on 18 months' supplies while the *Chatham* took on 15 months. However, dysentery, derived from a Dutch vessel, broke out on both ships and on 7 September, *en route* to Australia, one marine died.[6]

Menzies had met up with the Scottish botanist Francis Masson in South Africa – he wrote to Banks recommending Masson as the best person to accompany Captain Roberts, who was initially assigned to command the *Discovery* expedition, as naturalist. Lamb claimed that 'Francis Masson, the botanist, then making his second visit to South Africa to gather plants for the Royal Botanic Gardens at Kew, had accompanied Menzies on some of his own excursions there'.[7] The expedition spent five weeks in South Africa and Menzies reported to Banks that although the country was 'apparently dreary' it was for him 'richer than any Garden, in the vast variety of vegetable productions'.[8] Menzies was delighted with the South African landscape, writing to Banks: 'I am so charmed by the romantic appearance of the mountains which now surround me that I promise myself some pleasant excursions.'[9,10]

However, the outbreak of dysentery on the expedition ships almost certainly curtailed Menzies' botanising, although he refers, in his letter to Banks, to Masson accompanying him on some of his excursions up Table Mountain and around False

Bay, but adds that he did little collecting assuming that Masson, 'whose study it had been for many years', had 'already collected everything new and rare'.[11]

Just before they sailed he wrote again to Banks:

> ... whether I traversed the sandy scorching plains or clambered up the craggy ridges of mountains every situation afforded to my mind something new or rare, for even many genera with which I was acquainted but by name here presented themselves to my view in full perfection ... In these excursions the Cryptogamia Class was not neglected for I have made some new additions to it by several species.

This was the first mention of Menzies' special love for a group which made his name – nowadays he is regarded as a pioneer in lichenology. Such was his collecting enthusiasm that he began to run short of paper for drying his collections and asked for more to be sent by the *Daedalus.*

During his five weeks in South Africa, Menzies also met up with the Scots botanist and soldier William Paterson, who had made important plant collections from his adventurous journeys into the interior. While the *Discovery* and the *Chatham* (as well as Paterson's ship the *Gorgon*, which was to take him to Australia where he eventually assumed the Lieutenant-Governorship of New South Wales) were waiting for favourable winds to take them north-eastwards, Menzies and Paterson, together with his wife, took the opportunity of visiting a small sandy bay to collect shells. Menzies describes a hazardous landing:

> We landed about two miles to the eastward of Messenberg [Muizenberg] or the half way house, & were not in a little danger from the high surf which broke at least a quarter of a mile from the beach & incessantly rolled in upon it. When we entered this surf we were carried with great velocity towards the shore till a wave rose the stern of the boat so high that the steering oar lost its influence, and the boat turned broadside to the next wave which came roaring on and had very nearly in one moment ingulphed us all in its foams, but the timely dexterity of Mr Melville, Master of the *Britannia* got her head again towards the shore on which we soon after landed safe & very grateful for our miraculous escape. The calmness with which Mrs. Paterson bore this pending danger bespoke a presence of mind armed with more fortitude and resignation than fall to the lot of many of her sex, indeed her eagerness on this occasion in a favourite pursuit seemed to bid defiance to all hardships & difficulties, and the same laudable zeal will I doubt not enable her & her husband to complete the object of their wishes in a valuable collection of the natural produce of New South Wales, in accomplishing which I heartily wish them that success which their merits so richly deserve.[12]

However, this adventure was hastily terminated when they realised that the wind was now coming favourably from the north and all the ships were getting under way. In Menzies' words:

> We immediately relinquish'd our plan & hastened towards the boat which we found ready at the place appointed to receive us, and got on board the *Admiral Barrington* just in the nick of time ... and soon after joind the *Discovery* for both she & our consort were by this time under sail & advanced beyond the Roman Rock.

It is not difficult to imagine Vancouver at this time pacing the quarter-deck impatiently wondering what his single-minded naturalist was up to. (Later, on the last visit to Hawaii, he was to be infuriated by a similar incident.) Paterson went on to send to Banks an illustrated account of the botany of Norfolk Island, where he was initially put in charge of a detachment of soldiers guarding this notorious penal settlement, while his very likeable wife became renowned as a devoted worker on behalf of women and children there.

After they had left the Cape *en route* to New Holland [Australia] a violent storm resulted in ankle-deep water between the decks and in the cabins. The surgeon had what was described as a 'paralytic stroke' and many aboard were very ill, with the death of one marine from dysentery.[13] On 10 September, at Vancouver's request, Menzies took charge of the sick bay.[14] In a letter to Banks later from Monterey, Menzies writes that they reached King George's Sound, near the present city of Albany and from where Vancouver surveyed some 350 miles of coastline:

> On 26 September we made the coast of New Holland ... we remained here about a fortnight, which gave me the opportunity to examine the country in various excursions around the Sound making a copious collection of its vegetable productions particularly the genus Banksia which were there very numerous. The climate is very favourable the soil tho' light is good and fertile, particularly inland, where the country is chiefly covered with wood, diversified with pasturage and gently rising hills of very moderate height, well watered by small rivulets – whatever grows at the Cape of Good Hope will flourish here with equal ease in short it is a delightful country and well worth a more particular investigation by Government, on account of its nearness and access to our settlements in India.[15]

Menzies was delighted and almost overwhelmed by the sheer variety of flowering plants which he found, many of which were not listed in his edition of Linnaeus. He reported many as new discoveries, notably the noble, clean-trunked *Eucalyptus marginata* which was found in great abundance, the Holly-leafed Banksia and various mimosas – all these plants and shrubs which according to Vancouver 'afforded Mr. Menzies much entertainment and Employment'.[16]

Menzies also describes many species of birds, including pelicans, hawks, eagles, ducks, shags, penguins, gulls, curlews, and the iconic black swan of Australia. Although he observed whales, seals, some snakes and various reptiles, his only encounter with a mammal was a dead kangaroo. The crew also found a plentiful supply of oysters and an abundance of wild celery, which was a well-known antiscorbutic.[17] However, the party did not encounter any native people, although they found recently deserted huts in a very miserable village: there was plenty of evidence of extensive fires which Menzies conjectured about at length, but eventually attributed to human activity.[18]

At Green Island, Vancouver, in typical imperial mode, 'took possession' of all land seen north-westward of the cape on behalf of the King and named the anchorage King George the Third's Sound, i.e. King George's Sound. In his letter to Banks,[19] Menzies says that he is '... making a copious collection particularly of the genus *Banksia*'.[20] Although they passed virtually within sight of Van Dieman's Land [Tasmania] no landing was made there.

If Menzies was delighted with his discoveries in Australia, he was entranced by his explorations at Dusky Sound in New Zealand, which the ships reached on 2 November and where they remained for almost three weeks. (The bay was first discovered and named by Cook in March 1770 and Vancouver had visited the area with Cook in 1773.) The sound is a complex series of branches and inlets, interspersed with islands, providing calm waters and deep anchorages.

Entering the bay, Menzies' first impression was also of wild and romantic scenery, with steep cliffs contrasting with 'the calm serenity of the evening and the wild hideous noise of a heavy surf dashing incessantly against the rocks of a cavernous shore'. Later

Dusky Sound, New Zealand from an oil painting by Jonathan White.
(Courtesy of Jonathan White.)

he was to say: '... the birds entertained us with their wild concert'. He lost no time in starting to botanise and found tall New Zealand Spruce suitable for masts and spars, which the crews cut for repairs. Here he discovered large trees of *Drimys aromatica* which he had found on Staten Island years before, and also encountered a

> ... vast variety of ferns and mosses I have never seen before ... They are the two tribes of plants of which I am particularly fond, therefore no one can conceive the pleasure I enjoyed unless placed under similar circumstances ...
>
> I returned on board in the afternoon loaded with my treasures, & had sufficient to employ me in examining & arranging for the following day ... I was particularly entertained among a vast variety of Cryptogamic plants, especially my favourites the Musci, of which I made a tolerable good collection, and shall be able to add some new species to that natural order, and I think even a new Genus from thence approaching near the *Jungermanni.*[21]

Of these ferns and mosses, the eminent botanist Sir J. E. Smith later said they represented perhaps the richest collection of *Jungermanniae* that was ever made by one person.[22,23]

Seaforth Valley, a painting by Jonathan White.
(Courtesy of Jonathan White.)

Menzies made himself useful in other ways by locating *Leptospermum scoparium* (New Zealand Tea) which was used as an ingredient for brewing beer, and apparently greatly improved its palatability: he found an abundance of this plant in the upper woods. Here he also collected New Zealand Flax for growing at Kew. The shore parties amused themselves by shooting geese and ducks, but also a number of parrots which are likely to have been the endemic New Zealand kakas, now endangered. At one point the officers felt moved to drink to Captain Cook's health and the accuracy of his survey of Broughton Arm, one of the inlets debouching into Dusky Sound. Menzies himself ensured that he followed Banks' instructions by compiling a very competent general description of the country, its landscape, soils, vegetation and climate, with his own commentary on the reasons for the lack of a native population, in addition to enumerating the very many species of seabirds, including albatross, terns, shearwaters and petrels of several kinds. The record made by Menzies during his relatively short time at Dusky Sound testifies not only to his powers of observation, but also to his sheer enthusiasm for his work as a naturalist.[24]

NOTES

1. Menzies Journal, 17 April 1791
2. Menzies to Banks, Tenerife, 5 May 1791. Banks Papers, Mitchell Library, Sydney
3. Lamb (1984), 314
4. Naish (1996), 97
5. Ibid., 98–9
6. Anderson (1960), 50–1
7. Lamb (1984), 28
8. Ibid. quoting Menzies to Banks, 10 August 1791. Brabourne Papers, Mitchell Library, Sydney
9. Naish (1996), 100
10. The Cape region, with its uniquely diversified environments and climatic regimes, is probably the richest 'floral kingdom' in the world, with over 9000 vascular plants: Table Mountain alone has more plant species than in the whole of the United Kingdom, and new species are constantly being found (Moll 2006, 278–95). No wonder that Menzies was overwhelmed by its botanical riches.
11. Menzies to Banks, 10 August 1791. Brabourne Papers ix: 79, Mitchell Library, Sydney
12. Menzies Journal, 17 August 1791
13. Lamb (1984), 1635
14. Menzies Journal, 10 September 1791
15. Menzies to Banks, Monterey, 1–14 January 1793. Banks Correspondence, Dawson Turner Transcripts, British Museum (Natural History), London

16. Lamb (1984), 351
17. Menzies Journal, 30 September 1791
18. Ibid., 29 August 1791
19. Menzies to Banks, Monterey 1–14 January 1793
20. Menzies is credited with discovering five species of *Banksia*, a genus unique to Australia: *B. attenuata* (Slender or Candlestick Banksia), *B. grandis* (Giant Banksia), *B. praemorsa* (Cut-leaf Banksia), *B. verticillata* (Albany Banksia), and *Banksia menziesii*, which was named after him. The last has spectacular red and yellow flowers and today occurs only along the coast from Perth northwards. *Banksia verticillata* is very rare, occurring only in small populations around Albany. There are now known to be 58 species of Banksia in this region. (A *Banksia* is incorporated in the logo of the Australian National Botanic Gardens, Canberra.) He also discovered *Hakea oleifolia, Melaleuca diosmifolia* and *Eucalyptus marginata.* (Cavanah 1990, 278–81; George (n.d.), 10)
21. Menzies to Banks, Monterey, 1–14 January 1793
22. Balfour (1944), 173
23. *Jungermanniae* is now part of the plant group Jungermanniales or hepatics, which includes the lichens.
24. McNab (1908), vol. II, 483–95

9

'Precipices so Hideous & Full of Danger'

Tahiti was the first port of call on the voyage where the expedition encountered a substantial native population. Captain Cook first visited in the *Endeavour* in 1768 and twice again in the mid-1770s. The islands subsequently became notorious for the mutiny on board HMS *Bounty* under Captain Bligh in 1787. With its easy living and complaisant women, Tahiti became a byword for the ultimate in sybaritic tropical life.

At Rapa Island, just off the main island of Tahiti, the natives, while open and friendly when they had overcome their fear of the white visitors, saw their goods as ripe for plunder. Menzies narrates this vividly:

> The belaying pins on the quarterdeck, the hook and eyes about the guns & rigging & everything about the Forge particularly attracted their roving eyes and hands which incessantly moved about with the utmost rapidity. One of them seeing an Anchor laying on the forecastle attempted to take it up with the same strength he would apply to a piece of timber of an equal bulk & appeared much surprised when he could not move it.[1]

The Tahitians had developed to a high art the skill of stealing metal, as had been discovered by early voyagers, notably by Cook on the *Endeavour*. Relying previously on primitive tools of wood, stone and shells, they greatly prized any metal tools, such as axes, which they saw were far superior to their own implements. And of course, armaments made of metal conveyed enormous power and prestige: on the *Endeavour* voyage, one of the most serious incidents occurred when a marine killed an islander for running off with a musket.[2]

Perhaps because of this, and the knowledge of the temptations likely to arise on both sides, Vancouver became anxious and on his guard, no doubt from his previous experience of Hawaii. He was also determined not to repeat Bligh's mistake and allow the men too much licence ashore, especially that they not be allowed to trade except through the captain – such trading could cause mayhem with prices and violence. Only those who had a duty ashore were allowed on the island. This control of the men, not excluding the officers, was bitterly resented. In particular Vancouver was insistent that his men should not sleep ashore, although women were allowed on board. (According to Lt. Manby, when this happened 'love … , Kisses, and delight were the recompense each tar experienced for traversing many thousands of miles'.) He was

A woodcut illustration showing Tahitian vegetation with the mountains where Menzies botanised in the background. From *Iorana! A Tahitian Journal* by Robert Gibbings. (Duckworth, 1932.)

also determined to prevent pilfering of stores for trade and when Thomas Pitt offered an iron barrel hoop to one young girl, Vancouver sentenced him to be flogged with two dozen lashes, tied to a gun in the main cabin, which was a great humiliation to the young and petulant aristocrat. It had considerable repercussions on Vancouver's return to England.[3]

At this time, Menzies very amusingly describes an encounter between a native and a mirror:

> ... seeing himself reflected in a large mirror in the Cabin began making a yelling noise dancing & capering before it for several minutes & seeing all his actions so well mimicked, that he could not anyways outdo his imitator he approached it with a blow which had not his hand been withheld would in a moment have brought down the whole fabric, but when he afterwards coolly felt the glass & found it a smooth solid surface, he then attempted to insinuate his hand behind it, imagining no doubt that the Buffooner must be standing at the back of it.

Overall, Vancouver's relations with the islanders were good, particularly with the old king Pomarre ['Pomurrey'], and the various chiefs appeared to respect and admire him: Vancouver spent much time socialising and exchanging presents with the chiefs of the island. One of his great successes was a spectacular fireworks display combined with a performance of drilling by the ships' marines. Pomarre had developed a taste for alcohol and on one occasion on board the *Discovery* drank a whole bottle of undiluted brandy, and four strong men were required to hold him down. But Vancouver was nothing if not a disciplinarian, both with his own men and with the islanders. When two of the latter were caught in some petty thieving, he had no compunction about ordering two dozen lashes each in front of the chiefs and assembled population, capped by the humiliating shaving of their heads: like all native peoples, they were horrified by the flogging.

Vancouver's tactics seemed to be successful until at least the last week of his stay, but by then the first serious tensions after nine months away from England began to arise.

He was incensed when the youth Tooworero disappeared with stolen goods including arms, perhaps with the connivance of Pomarre, whose daughter Tooworero was

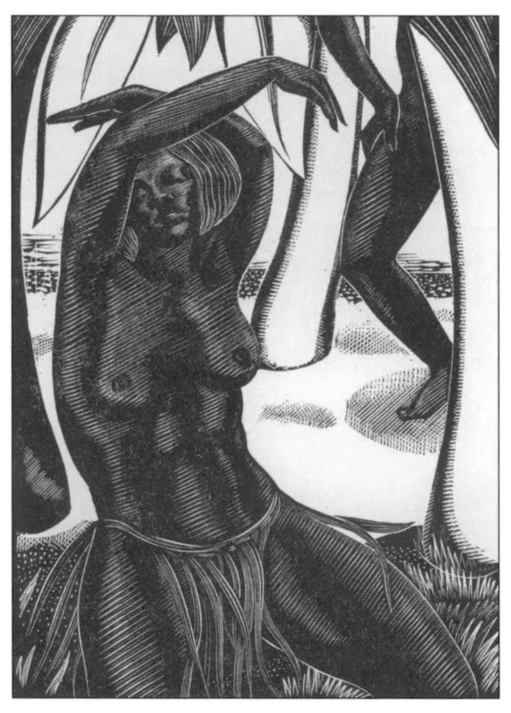

Another woodcut illustration showing one of the possible pleasures awaiting the sailors on Tahiti after their long voyage. From *Iorana! A Tahitian Journal* by Robert Gibbings. (Duckworth, 1932.)

enamoured of, to such an extent that he wanted to stay in Tahiti rather than be taken back to his Hawaiian homeland. Vancouver was so angry that the king became very afraid at the temper displayed by the captain. At one point Vancouver actually tried to capture some of the royal canoes but was prevented by a hail of stones. Eventually Pomarre returned with Tooworero and Vancouver forgave him – but not Tooworero.

Although Vancouver had effectively maintained discipline it was probably from about this time that a cabal formed against him, including Hewett, the surgeon's mate of the *Chatham*. Menzies thought Vancouver had grossly over-reacted to the thefts and considered Tooworero's treatment harsh – he was removed from the gunroom where he had had the privilege of messing since leaving England and was left with virtually no clothes – and Vancouver made himself look ridiculous in the eyes of his crew.[4] According to Naish, however, Menzies does not seem to have understood Vancouver's obsessive nature nor his sense of insecurity, or to have an understanding of the weight of responsibility which Vancouver carried, and his determination to avoid the mistakes of Bligh.

On 18 January 1792 Menzies went on a botanical expedition and found himself in serious difficulty:

> ... here the natives pointed out to us on the left hand side a high cliff from the top of which they said a path went up the Mountains, but this rock appeared to us inaccessible till we saw one of the Natives scramble up with great alertness & on gaining the summit he made a rope he had about his middle fast to a tree & threw the end of it down the rock by means of which the rest hauld themselves up one after another & we managed to mount by the same conveyance though I must say not without risque & difficulty ... from the top of this rock we began our ascent by a very steep narrow path where we could only follow one another through thick woods & sometimes along the verge of precipices so hideous & full of danger that a slip or false step would in a moment prove of fatal consequences. At other times we crossed chasms and valleys with great labour and fatigue ... I collected a number of plants which I had not before seen, by sending the Natives here and there off the path in different directions, who brought to me branches of every plant they saw either in flower or fruit or seeds.

Encountering yet another valley to be crossed 'we were now quite disheartened & here threw ourselves down upon the ground almost exhausted with fatigue, while some of the Natives went on, to kindle a fire and prepare these huts for our reception'. However, heavy rainfall forced the party to return before the valley they had first ascended became flooded. On the now very slippery paths '... we were in the utmost danger of sliding down chasms or precipices dreadful to behold & frequently obliged to lower ourselves by ropes fastened to trees or held by the Natives'. It was only with the aid of the natives, whom Menzies commended heartily, that they were able to cross the main river, which they had to do at least 20 times before they reached safety.

10

'The Red-faced Man who cut off the Limbs of Men'

From his visits to Hawaii with Colnett, Menzies was familiar with the islands, and in the course of the voyage of the *Discovery* he was to make a further three visits, the first of these *en route* to the Northwest coast of America in March 1792. Hawaii by this time had established itself as a convenient winter base for provisioning and repairs, and incidentally, to allow the crews some rest and recreation after the rigours of their survey work in the northern latitudes. For their part, the natives increasingly recognised the ships as sources for barter, and Menzies noticed some changes on his return to the islands.

Vancouver established good relations with the most important personage in the archipelago – Chief Kamehameha. Apparently born propitiously in 1758 at the same time as Halley's Comet was seen in the skies, Kamehameha had been raised in the royal court of his uncle. He was given a prominent religious position and the important guardianship of the Hawaiian god of war, and himself became a successful warrior chief, eventually overcoming the chiefs of all the other islands. He did this through the power of firearms obtained from western ships, and the training of his soldiers by westerners; by 1810 he became the acknowledged king of the whole of Hawaii, vigorously defending its traditions and culture until he died in 1819.

One of the most significant of the changes noted by Menzies and others was that the islanders were no longer afraid of firearms and frequently demanded these in exchange for goods and services – they had after all been successful in obtaining weapons from the fur traders in the past. The acquisition of firearms not only conferred prestige, but also gave a chief a distinct military advantage in the intertribal warfare which seemed to be a constant in the islands. They were puzzled therefore when Vancouver refused their requests, but he rather cleverly explained this away by claiming that the British King had 'tabooed' such arms as far as His Majesty's Navy was concerned. (The 'taboo' was well understood by the Hawaiians, who were subject to various forms of this complete restriction, whether to place or activity on the order of chiefs, being the basis of their law.)

On his second visit with Vancouver early in 1793 Menzies declared his regret that the natives had not been 'kept without the use of those destructive weapons that have been so industriously dispersed amongst them and which serve to stir up their minds with a desire for conquest, ruin and destruction to their fellow creatures'. He foresaw

A split cone of the female *Araucaria araucana* [Monkey Puzzle]. The seed, often eaten as nuts, is seen to the right of the picture. Was it these nuts that Menzies pocketed at the farewell banquet in Santiago in 1795? (RBGE collection.)

Loch Ness with Ben Nevis in the background. Menzies was commissioned as a young student by Professor Hope to collect plants from the Scottish Highlands, such as on Ben Nevis, for the eminent English botanists Dr John Fothergill and Dr William Pitcairn. (Author's collection.)

Cerastium alpinum [Alpine Mouse-ear], a rare plant identified by Menzies during his early botanising around the high corries above Loch Tay. (RBGE collection.)

Model of a Royal Navy lieutenant dressed in the uniform as it would have been in Menzies' period of service, carrying a quadrant, the predecessor of the sextant. (Courtesy of the National Maritime Museum, London.)

Black bear were plentiful around the heavily wooded forests of Nova Scotia and hunted extensively in Menzies' time there with HMS *Assistance* in the 1780s. (Courtesy of the US National Park Service.)

A modern day image of timber being worked on Vancouver Island, a haven for the scurvy stricken HMS *Prince of Wales* in 1787, causing Captain Colnett to log in his journal, 'the whole of the coast ... was cover'd with trees a pleasing sight to us who had not seen a bush for one and twenty weeks'. (Author's collection.)

Eucalyptus marginata [Jarrah], valued for its fine timber and discovered by Menzies for the first time at 'New Holland', present day Australia, in 1791, on his voyage with HMS *Discovery*. (RBGE collection.)

A plantation of *Citrus grandis* [shaddock trees]. Tahitian guides pointed out trees 12 metres high near Matavi Bay to Menzies in 1792, planted by Sir Joseph Banks in 1789. (Courtesy of Craig Elevitch of Agroforestry.Net.)

A painting showing Chief Kamehameha in a canoe, sailing out to meet Captain Cook on arrival in Hawaii in 1789. (Courtesy of Syd House.)

Cibotium (Dicksonia) menziesii, a large Hawaiian tree fern named in honour of Menzies. (Courtesy of Forest and Kim Starr, USGS.)

Left: A Hawaiian volcano crater. Between January and February 1794 Menzies explored and botanised most of the 10 distinct climatic zones on Hawaii, described later by Twain as 'all the climates of the world at a single glance of an eye'. (Courtesy of Syd House.)

Right: Menzies is credited with being the first collector of Californian birds, describing for the first time the Californian Condor and the California Quail, seen here. (Courtesy of the British Columbia Provincial Museum.)

Left: Arbutus menziesii [Pacific Madrone], overlooking Discovery Bay, in present day Washington State. First recorded by Menzies in 1792 as he botanised along the Northwest Coast. (Courtesy of Ross Hamilton.)

Rhododendron macrophyllum [Pacific Rhododendron], discovered by Menzies in 1792 and now adopted as the state flower of Washington State. (RBGE collection.)

Cornus canadensis [Dwarf Dogwood or Bunchberry], a prolific plant with edible berries, identified by Menzies during his survey of the Northwest Coast of North America. (Courtesy of Syd House.)

Cornus nuttalli [Pacific Dogwood], discovered by Menzies in Admiralty Inlet in May 1792. It was later to become the first plant species to be protected by British Columbia law. (RBGE collection.)

A carved Native American house post. Menzies marvelled at the size and intricacy of the carvings of these poles as he encountered them along the coast of Queen Charlotte's Sound. (Author's collection.)

Alaskan Reflections. In 1794 HMS *Discovery* undertook its third and most northerly survey of the Northwest Coast of North America, reaching the inhospitable but beautiful landscapes of Alaska. (Courtesy of the US National Park Service.)

A mature *Araucaria araucana* on the Glasshouse Lawn at RBGE. (RBGE collection.)

The statue of Chief Kamehameha at Kapaau, Hawaii. (Courtesy of Syd House.)

a day when the natives would 'become more daring and insolent in their behaviour, more exorbitant in their demands for refreshments, and by their overpowering numbers and stratagems, will become too formidable for any single vessel to encounter or venture amongst them'.[1] Although in one sense Menzies is right, it also reflects an imperial attitude about who should or should not have access to power through arms. There was considerable animosity between the various chiefs and jockeying for Vancouver's favours, while the whole question of mutual presents could induce resentment if they were not seen as equitable – gifts given to Tooworero were seized by jealous chiefs.

Menzies also noted that, compared with his previous visits with Colnett in 1787 and 1788, the Hawaiians had 'added to their former stock of vegetables, greens, musk and water melons, which they rear to such perfection and plenty that we had a daily supply of each'.[2] Menzies himself provided over a hundred seedlings of orange and vine which he had grown for Tooworero to take back to his homeland. Later Menzies was to find orange trees thriving at relatively high altitude from material he had brought in 1786. He also presented the islanders with the best Imperial cabbage seeds from Kew, having been impressed by the quality of the savoys that they sent to the ships.

At one stage, he proposed sugar-growing without the abhorrent slave labour system practised in the West Indies, and forecast that this could be an important island industry: by the first quarter of the 20th century, sugar was being exported to a value of 75 million dollars, making fortunes for the sugar barons.[3] On a later visit in 1793, both sheep and cattle were landed – a previous attempt at breeding cattle had failed, in Menzies' view because it was necessary to use young animals which could more readily habituate to the local environment.[4] The ships apparently did not make a dent in the islands' stock of hogs, despite having had no fewer than 1000 of these animals during the 1794 visit alone, according to Menzies.[5]

Menzies detailed many of the customs, religious observances, agricultural practices and habits of the various islands that he visited, establishing a baseline of anthropological observations which were to prove invaluable to later researchers (quite apart from his important natural history records). Here is some of his detailed description of women making *kappa* or bark cloth:

> The women were no less assiduously employed in collecting and manufacturing the bark of a shrubby species of nettle which grew wild in the woods, for making a kind of coarse russet cloth, and which they prepared and dyed as follows: The inner bark being separated from the long twigs, the exterior rind was made into small bundles and a certain quantity of a particular kind of fern, a species of *Adiantum*, mixed with it. Both were wrapped up together in the leaves of plantains, or the *Dracaena ferrea* [Cordyline species]. A number of these bundles being in the manner got ready, an oven is made by digging a hole in the ground where they are put, intermixed with hot stones and covered up with green leaves in the same manner as they dress or bake their victuals. By this heating or sweating process, the fern imparts a reddish brown colour to the bark, which is afterwards beat out into cloth.[6]

Throughout their three separate visits to Hawaii between 1792 and 1794, relations between the British ships and the islanders – notwithstanding the murder of Captain Cook in February 1779 which the Hawaiians professed to deeply regret – were generally good. Menzies records on 3 March 1793 how Vancouver and several officers were invited to view, with Kamehameha and his queen Ka'ahumanu, the spot where the illustrious voyager was killed, and were given a minute description of Cook's end in the presence of his killer. It was for all of them a most emotional and poignant occasion, but also one of reconciliation which apparently moved the whole company deeply.

The most serious and fatal encounter in Vancouver's voyage, which Vancouver only learnt about many months later when he was at Nootka on the Northwest coast, happened to the supply ship, the *Daedalus*. In this incident Lt. Richard Hergest, Mr Gooch and a seaman were killed in what seemed to be a petty dispute in the course of water collecting. On his return to Hawaii early in 1793, Vancouver was determined that the murderers be punished. On the island of Oahu, three natives were identified by the chiefs as the murderers of Lt. Hergest and were called aboard the *Discovery* on the pretext of considering their pearls for purchase. Here they were put in chains, and on the following morning Vancouver was obliged to watch while the alleged killers were executed by their chiefs in canoes by pistol shot.[7] Vancouver was punctilious in assuring the chiefs and the people that, justice having been done, this was the end of the matter and that he wanted a complete reconciliation with the islanders.

Vancouver knew he had to maintain good relations with the chiefs. Kamehameha was the most important and the most co-operative, almost certainly in order to maintain his prestige and power against other warring chiefs. He was the greatest of the warrior chiefs of Hawaii, and was eventually to unite the islands for the first time under his kingship. He was a formidable figure, both physically and in his authoritative persona, ruthless in his ambition, but also good-natured. Kamehameha and Vancouver recognised each other's rank, respecting the other's authority,[8] and a remarkably empathetic relationship was to develop between the two men.[9] Vancouver went so far as to authorise the building by the ships' artificers of a schooner, which Kamehameha dearly desired.

Menzies provides an interesting comment on this key figure in Hawaiian history when he says: 'We were pleased to find that this great chief's manners and countenance were now very different to what we were led to expect from the report given of him in Cook's voyage by those who visited these islands fourteen years ago.' He goes on to delineate Kamehameha:

> Kamehameha is now about forty years of age, stout and well made. He walks erect, firm and graceful, with a dignity of deportment well becoming his quality and high station. His countenance, though not mild, is by no means displeasing. His lineaments are strong and expressive and form a perfect index of the emotions of the mind than we find among the generality of his countrymen. In our broken conversation with him, he possessed a quickness of comprehension that surprised us, and in his behaviour, he was open, affable, and free, which much attached us to him even in this first visit.[10]

This description says as much about Menzies as about his subject: a sharpness of observation and understanding of character, allied to a warm basic human empathy towards someone from a totally different culture, reflecting on Menzies' own openness and freedom from preconception. In this and other ways, Menzies exhibits a number of the traits which exemplified the Scottish Enlightenment of his time.

On Vancouver's arrival in late January 1793 on his second visit to the islands, Kamehameha received him impressively in a double-hulled canoe propelled by 46 rowers. Menzies described the scene, which must have been a most impressive sight:

> ... Tamaiha-maiha [Kamehameha] came in great state from the shore accompanied by a number of double canoes that stopped at a little distance from our Stern while the King in his canoe was paddled with great rapidity round both Vessels, which occasioned no little hurry & confusion among the Canoes that surrounded us to open an avenue for him, numbers of them were overturned & some of them nearly run over. He stood upright in the middle of the Canoe with a Fan in his hand & was gracefully robed in a beautiful long cloak of yellow feathers; his underdress

> consisted of a loose Gown of printed Cotton girded on with a sash which he said had been given to him by Captain Cook.
>
> Having in this manner performed a large circuit round both Vessels, he stopped astern of us, and arranged the Canoes that came off with him on his right hand, in a line abreast, in which order he led them along side the *Discovery*, and on his coming on board, he first presented a variety of feathered Caps and Helmets to Captain Vancouver, and then taking him by the hand to the Gang-way, he told him there were ten Canoes loaded with Hogs for him, and desired that he would order his people to take them on board: This was done with such a princely air of dignity, that it instantaneously riveted our admiration, as the manner of presenting & the magnitude of the present far exceeded anything of the kind we had seen before or experienced in the Voyage.[11]

Later, with great ceremony, Kamehameha was to present Vancouver with just such an elaborate feathered robe which he emphasised was to be worn by none other than King George, since it was the only one of its kind on the islands, according to Menzies,[12] and was made from some 20,000 of the single tiny bright yellow thigh feathers of the Kauai O'o bird (*Moho braccatus*).[13] (The finest of these cloaks was estimated to be worth 100,000 dollars.)

On a later expedition, Menzies explained how these valuable feathers were obtained:

> ... feathers are in great estimation, it is with them that a large portion of the Rents are annually paid to the Chiefs by the lower class of people, who thus employ themselves by catching the Birds with Bird-lime, which they do by spreading a little of it here & there on the boughs & placing two or three red berries near it which the Birds are very fond of, & as they perch to eat them they are entangled with the Bird-lime, but the natives are very cautious of not exterminating the Birds by killing all that are in this manner caught, many of them after being stripped of their most valuable Feathers are again set at liberty, and run the chance of being fleeced in the same way next year.[14]

This use of birdlime to capture birds seems to be an ancient practice in many countries, although they are usually captured for their flesh. No other account is known of this tradition for harvesting on a sustainable basis for conservation.

In return for this most generous welcoming gift, Vancouver presented Kamehameha with four cows, two ewes and a ram.

> ... when landed, [they] ran up and down the country in the wildest manner to the no small dread & terror of the natives, who fled from them with the utmost speed in every direction, which was not at all surprising as they were the first Animals of the kind they had ever seen prancing about their Country in a state so lively and vigorous, for though the Bull and Cow which were landed in a sickly state a

few days before might in some measure have lessened their curiosity, yet when they received these with the loudest acclamations of joy, & we sincerely wished that they may in due time increase & multiply so as to prove useful to the natives of these Islands as well as to the future Navigators that may touch here for refreshments.[15]

The progeny of these animals in time became semi-wild and provided an important resource; one was also responsible for the death of Menzies' colleague David Douglas (1799–1834) when it gored him to death after he had fallen into a pit dug as a trap for the beast.

The generous Menzies thought that Vancouver too often put himself on the wrong side of the chiefs by being somewhat mean with his gifts to them and noted that Tooworero, on his departure, was much more successful in getting generous gifts from the *Chatham* than from the *Discovery*. Lieutenant Manby noted the huge chief's appetite at the feast laid on for his visitors when, almost unbelievably, he consumed two large fish, a large bowl of poi, a small pig, and an entire baked dog! Later he laid on a very realistic, but dangerous, sham battle in which he himself participated boisterously, catching spears with great dexterity and throwing them back. In the final charge using spears 15–18 feet long, one spearman was killed and his body carried off in triumph by the victorious team.[16]

Meanwhile, Vancouver was hatching a strategy for persuading Kamehameha to cede Hawaii to Britain, a move which he thought would not only provide a very convenient staging post for British vessels, but also prevent it falling to either the French or the Spanish.[17] (Menzies notes this attempt to persuade Kamehameha on 5 March 1793, when he was present with Vancouver and the chief in Vancouver's cabin, but interestingly, Vancouver omits this from his journal.)[18] Although Vancouver went out of his way to get the agreement of the friendly chiefs, including laying on a spectacular fireworks display, he could not accede to their stipulation that one of the British ships should remain behind to protect them from their enemies.

Something seems to have been agreed on 25 February 1794, but it was almost certainly interpreted differently by Kamehameha who did not envisage surrendering sovereignty or annexation, as opposed to protection. (Vancouver did have a signal and surprising success in re-uniting Kamehameha with his estranged and favourite wife Ka'ahumanu by very discreetly arranging a surprise meeting between them on board the *Discovery* in February 1794, which Vancouver describes very touchingly, and which resulted in general public rejoicing.)[19]

Later that month, Menzies journeyed into the interior of Maui, using John Smith, an Englishman who was from an American ship going to the Northwest for furs and had become a Hawaiian chief, as an interpreter and general overseer of the expedition. (Because of his status, Smith was not allowed to drink or eat anything that had not first been consecrated and reacted intemperately to the attention paid to him, which

Queen Ka'ahumanu, favourite wife of Kamehameha.
Drawn by an unknown artist of the time.

Menzies tried to calm.) On the upper slopes, Menzies marvelled at the sophistication of the cultivations, which produced excellent vegetables, carefully husbanded, and where the plantations needed no security because of the traditional laws respecting property and produce. Here too he was delighted to find in good health the young orange trees which Tooworero had distributed amongst different owners.

Despite suffering frustration at the lack of plants in flower, Menzies found a number of interesting species on this expedition, including what he named as *Rumex gigantea* (i.e. *Rumex giganteus*), a dock which under suitable conditions can grow to over 30 feet. (He was later to be delighted to find that William Aiton had successfully raised fine plants of this species from seeds which Menzies had sent.) He also encountered the sweet root named by him as *Dracaena ferrea*, which had a variety of uses including its leaves for the thatching of huts and the making of skirts, but is now better known as *Cordyline*, varieties of which are now common garden plants because of their attractive spear-shaped burgundy-coloured leaves. Later, Menzies was to claim that the best fish he had ever eaten was wrapped in the leaves of this plant and cooked over hot stones.

At the end of this short expedition Menzies was unstinting in his praise for the honesty and hospitality of the local people, who apparently anticipated their every wish, including providing a refreshing massage (*roomee*) at the end of a particularly fatiguing day, 'an operation which we found on these occasions very lulling and pleasing when gently performed'. In his words: '… in no instance did any of them betray the confidence reposed in them'.[20]

Menzies commented on the distance travelled over rough ground in the heat of the day by natives for water for the ships, well satisfied with a few nails:

> … a settlement established in these Islands would in this way procure indefatigable labourers at a very ease rate, and how far preferable this would be to that disgraceful mode of Slavery by which we still continue to cultivate our West Indian Islands, in short it might well be worth the attention of Government to make the

The taro plant, the root of which is used to make *poi* – a dish of cultural significance for Hawaiians. (Courtesy of Syd House.)

> experiment and settle these Islands by Planters from the West Indies – men of humanity industry & experienced abilities in the exercise of their art would here in a short time be enabled to manufacture Sugar & Rum from luxuriant Fields of Cane equal if not superior to the produce of our West India Plantations & that too without slavery – by merely cherishing that tractable principle of industry and labour in the inhabitants they might gradually be led on to perform every duty belonging to a plantation with the greatest ease and cheerfulness & at very little expense, which would certainly be much more satisfactory to their Employers and the World at large than if they groand under the galling yoke of slavery which God forbid they ever should.[21]

Here Menzies appears to be somewhat disingenuous, although expressing utilitarian views not very different from many others of his time. Under the cloak of anti-slavery, he seems to be attracted primarily by the prospect of cheap and willing labour, to be paid a pittance for the profit of landowners and their shareholders back home. It is very much of a piece with the imperial ideal, which was accomplished not by Britain, but by the USA. In the 19th century it secured its mainland sugar markets by the establishment of vast plantations of this and other crops such as pineapple in Hawaii, worked mainly by immigrants from the Far East.

Vancouver was very much attracted by Hawaii, compared with the Northwest coast of America, most of which he considered repellent in its dreariness, and he wrote much more about the islands' people and their politics, whereas his northern descriptions are largely confined to the topographical.[22] This was enhanced by the fact that from their past voyages, together with Menzies and several other officers, he became relatively proficient in the local language. Menzies put this to good use, and made some of the earliest observations of Hawaiian customs. For example, he discovered that the various taboos were far from arbitrary and were regulated by phases of the moon which were used as a form of calendar. Nevertheless, no doubt with Cook's demise very much in mind, the anxious Vancouver remained on his guard during his periods in Hawaii. At one point Vancouver was convinced that local fires were the prelude to an attack:

> This alarmed Captain Vancouver ... so firm was he of this opinion, that, on our joining our party, he could not help expressing his mind to the surrounding multitude with such menacing threats that they became alarmed in their turn by a general desertion from our encampment, excepting the chiefs above mentioned, who still remained with us, and to do them justice, used every means in their power to convince him to the contrary, by saying that the fire had been kindled to burn down the old shrivelled grass and low vegetables, and for no other purpose whatsoever, which I believe was literally the case, as I recollected well that the same fields were burnt down in the same manner when I was here a few years ago.[23]

Going ashore Vancouver suspected the natives of deliberately upsetting his canoe, when he almost drowned – it was Menzies who proved his fears unfounded when he deliberately spent a night ashore in a native village. On another occasion, Menzies gives fulsome praise to the honesty of the islanders when they retrieved valuable arms and other items which had been accidentally lost in the surf when a canoe capsized the previous evening.

One other chief who was kindly disposed to the British was the intelligent Taio [Kaeo]: both Vancouver and Menzies had known him from previous voyages (Vancouver with Cook and Menzies with Colnett). Menzies was to say: 'In him I was happy to meet an old friend to whose hospitality and kind offices I had formerly been under many obligations at a time when it was not in my power to repay him with any adequate return.' So Menzies exposed all his treasures from which the chief chose a red cloth and 'then touched Vancouver's heart by producing a lock of the young midshipman's hair which he had carefully tended for 14 years'.[24]

Menzies received a similar welcome from the old chief Enemoo who had met him on a previous voyage.[25] Nevertheless, Vancouver's uncertain temper sometimes got the better of him, even in the presence of chiefs, who fled his ship in fear when he flew into an intemperate rage over a piece of ribbon purloined by one of the visiting women: Menzies much regretted this, since they had been so well treated by the chiefs and local people. However, even Menzies, usually emphasising the best sides of the local people, had to admit to deep disappointment when it was found that one of the visiting chiefs had been guilty of some last minute pilfering on their departure from Hawaii, and came to the conclusion that their honesty up to this point had perhaps been due to dread of punishment rather than anything else.

Vancouver was later to acknowledge the general honesty and friendliness of the natives of the main island of Attowai [Kaui].[26] However, commenting on the extreme licentiousness of the women of Attowai, he claimed to be '... pestered and disgusted with the obscene importunities of the women', a feature of Kauai at the time, apparently encouraged by their menfolk.[27] This was even against the standards of other Pacific islands he had known, and he considered that this was new, resulting from increased European visitation.[28] It was incidentally on Kaui on 26 March 1793 that Menzies recorded the largest canoe – some 60 feet long – he had ever seen, apparently made from pine which could only have come from the American mainland.[29]

As in Tahiti, Vancouver attempted to curtail fraternisation, to the frustration of his sex-starved sailors, but apparently not to very good effect, according to the energetic Lt. Manby, referring to his dalliance with one of the chief's wives: 'Two hours I revelled in extatic enjoyment.' Later one of the 'Queens' appeared in the dark in a canoe with some presents for Manby: 'After staying with me two hours, she again took a sorrowful adieu and left the Ship with a heavy heart.'[30]

Menzies, who was apparently not immune to the charms of the island women, reported that 'Women came in numbers, not only in canoes but on swimming boards with no other intention than of tendering their persons to anyone that would choose to have them, and those who were unsuccessful in their aim went away chiding us for our want of gallantry'.[31] Later after the women had been forbidden by the chiefs to visit, he said: 'The women were still tabooed, at least none of them durst come off in any of the canoes, but to evade this part of the restriction, they swam off to the ship in great numbers, and the sailors had the humanity and gallantry to take them in as they came alongside, and in the society of the honest tars, they found an asylum of freedom more congenial to their disposition and native simplicity.'[32] However, on a visit to the chief Kahowmotoo, Menzies is less than chivalrous in his description of the womenfolk:

> The party paraded with the marines as escort to the chief's residence, where we found his Wife, Mother & two Sisters seated on a Mat under a canopy erected before the house, & if size & corpulency are here necessary qualifications of dignity, these Ladies were certainly entitled to the highest rank, for four stouter & more masculine Dames could hardly be met with anywhere.[33]

Towards the end of 1793 on their last visit to Hawaii, Vancouver appeared out of sorts: he was much preoccupied with the political situation in the islands, and his failure to secure British sovereignty over them. Relations between himself and a number of the officers were strained. Given their close relationship, the final leave-taking between Vancouver and Kamehameha was emotional, but not without some sourness. On 1 March 1794, Menzies writes to Banks:

> Kamehameha asked Captain Vancouver at parting, to add to his other presents as much red cloth as would make him a Maro, a thing in great estimation at this time among the Chiefs, and would not require above half a yard of cloth; this was refused him, from what motives we know not, and he left the ship apparently in a huff. On his way to the shore he went with the Queen and John Young to take leave of his friends aboard the *Chatham*, where he complained of Captain Vancouver's stinginess & told the story in a manner that induced the Commander of the Vessel [Puget] to present him with the last piece of red cloth he had. The refusal of a trifle of this kind, on such an occasion, cannot be viewed in a favourable light, when we reflect on the boundless generosity of this worthy prince towards us, his zeal and perseverance in our favor, his studious care at all times to preserve a good understanding between us and his people, his ready compliance to all our requests, his hospitality and kind protection to all those whose duty or desire of recreation, led them to traverse the country.

This last panegyric is largely true, even if Menzies is 'over-egging the pudding' somewhat, although he was particularly indebted to Kamehameha for his considerable assistance on his mountain expeditions. Vancouver was known for his meanness, even in Tahiti, but his refusal seems irrational, especially as on parting, the chief had given a hundred fat hogs and a huge quantity of vegetables. However, Vancouver's behaviour may have been due to the illness which was to become increasingly evident later.

One of Menzies' ambitions was to climb the highest mountain in Hawaii, Mauna Kea (13,796 ft/4295 m) and its sister peak, Mauna Loa (13,679 ft/4169 m) with a view to collecting plants at various altitudes. (The latter has a claim to be the largest single mountain on earth, covering 75,000 cubic kilometres, and with a total height of 17 kilometres, if the undersea portion is included.) He accomplished this towards the end of the last visit to Hawaii. There are in fact some 10 distinctive zones on Hawaii, and Mauna Loa has all of them, from lowland scrub to alpine stone desert. (Mark Twain was later to say of Hawaii that it had 'all the climates of the world at a single glance of an eye'.)

By way of practice, Menzies tackled the lesser nearby mountain of Mauna Hualalai (8271 ft), starting out on 17 January 1794. He was accompanied by Swaine, one of the *Discovery*'s lieutenants, and several midshipmen, together with an American, a Mr Howell from China. He carried with him a portable barometer, given to him as a present by Colonel Gordon at the Cape of Good Hope, in order to ascertain the height of the mountain. (He had taken the precaution of arranging for the *Discovery*'s barometer to be read at two-hour intervals in order to calibrate his own.)

Menzies, ever the 'canny Scot', devised a means of shedding the very many 'hangers on' from the villagers – there were more than 20 porters to carry the provisions alone, which apart from yams, coconuts, etc. included live hogs and poultry – who assisted the party:

> As I observed that we were accompanied by a number of idlers, who were unwilling to burden themselves, I took the opportunity, as the party arrived upon the summit, to mark all those who were well loaded, by tying a piece of variegated tape round the arm of each, as a badge of distinction, telling them, at the same time, that on producing these badges, when we returned to the ship, they should be well paid for their service, while those who brought up small loads would receive but little. This induced several of the idlers to return to the plantations for loads, and as they arrived with them each had a similar badge; but if any of them, after this, misbehaved, or was not sufficiently careful of what was entrusted to his charge, he was discarded, by taking his badge from him; this produced an emulation amongst them, which had a wonderfully good effect during the remainder of our excursion.[34]

After crossing scorching lava fields, they came to rich plantations and vegetable fields where they stayed at a high village. (At one stage Menzies was to comment on a cleverly constructed aqueduct for irrigation: 'It was built in so neat and artful a manner as would do no discredit to more scientific builders.') On the following morning, Menzies tells of inspiring views not only of the mountain above, but also of the panorama of the woods and sea below. Entering dense woods, Menzies botanised along the way, employing natives on either side of the wood-cutters' path to bring him specimens of any plants or bushes in flower. (His frustration at not finding many plants in bloom is reflected in his *cri de cœur*: '... I could not help considering my situation as the most vexatious and tantalising that a scrutinising Botanist could ever be placed in ...'.[35]

He was scrupulous in abiding by the villagers' strictures on not disturbing the many sacred places which had been tabooed, considering that these sites were just as important to the natives as any European shrines. By mid-morning, after a steep and rugged climb through alpine scrub, Menzies reached the summit of Mauna Hualalai and was rewarded by spectacular views, which he described romantically:

> The whole western side of Hawaii lay beneath us with its indented shore. Bays, villages, plantations and forests depicted as it were like a map upon the vast sheet of extended ocean before us, while fleecy clouds hovering at a distance appeared like an immense extent of frozen country with towering mountains and steep valleys of softest shades, every moment varying their aerial shapes and situations, and presenting the most beautiful prospects of picturesque scenery over which the eye could eagerly wander without weariness, and continue imparting to the mind new felt pleasures.[36]

The party stayed for two days around the summit, and Menzies, with the aid of his portable barometer, calculated the height of the mountain at 8062 feet above sea level. He botanised vigorously:

> In my rambles I collected every plant I met with, either in flower, fruit, or seed, which, I was sorry to find, did not amount to a very numerous catalogue, on account of the very dormant state of the vegetation in these upper regions at this season of the year: but, from the variety I saw of small plants and low shrubs, in appearance quite new to me, I consider this peak as a very interesting tract for a botanist to explore ...[37]

He was not to know that the island would become known for more orchid plants than anywhere else on earth. One of the two indigenous tree species which he encountered, and was the first to record, was the koa (*Acacia koa* var. *hawaiiensis*) which reached 70 feet in height. Despite frequently missing the flowering season, Menzies has some 19 plants from Hawaii named after him. One of these was the very stately *Cibotium* (*Dicksonia*) *menziesii*, the huge Hawaiian tree fern which can reach a height of well over 30 feet. It bears on its fronds a silky fibre called *pulu* locally used to stuff quilts and which was exported for this purpose in large quantities between 1850 and 1870.[38]

He also observed the Hawaiian Goose or *nene* which has recently made a comeback from the brink of extinction and is now the state bird, and the Hawaiian Crow which has been reduced to only 12 birds inhabiting this mountain massif. The return journey by a different inland route over extremely difficult lava boulders, when the party suffered from painful feet and great thirst, proved arduous. This did not deter them from, on 22 January, making an attempt on the snow-capped Mauna Loa. The natives were proved right in their reluctance to go forward, when the party encountered both dense scrub and dangerously fragile lava underfoot, forcing them to abort this attempt.

They spent a night at a village among what Menzies described as '... the most exuberant fields of the esculent vegetables of these islands, which for industry of cultivation and agricultural improvements could scarcely be exceeded in any country in the world ...'.[39] He then goes into rhapsodies about the entertainment provided by a young itinerant professional dancer:

> Every joint of her limbs, every finger of her hand, every muscle of her body, partook unitedly of the varied sympathetic impulses, while the motion of her eyes transferring their transient glances and the harmony of her features were beyond the power of description ... If we might judge of her merits from the specimen we had just seen of her acting, we think she was possessed of natural powers to entertain even in a more refined country.[40]

On the advice of the chief Kamehameha, the second attempt on Mauna Loa was made from the south side, involving a longer sea passage in canoes. Menzies was flattered by having a reliable chief, Luhea, to oversee the expedition and on this occasion was accompanied by Third Lieutenant Joseph Baker, and midshipmen George McKenzie and Thomas Heddington. It was to prove probably the most demanding and fatiguing of any of the expeditions that the botanist ever undertook. The coastal journey itself was not without incident. At one particularly barren fishing village, the Europeans were astonished at the skill of the canoemen in landing in huge surf amongst precipitous cliffs with the greatest accuracy. Later, they were equally amazed to see naked young women catapulting themselves off a 30-foot cliff into the turbulent sea, clambering back up the jagged rocks to repeat the performance many times.

The overland journey started on 10 February. *En route* to the base of the mountains, the party passed through a number of populous villages, with Menzies again commenting on the industriousness and economy with which the villagers laid out and managed their crops, with intricate irrigation and fallowing. Among the party were a number of local women which Menzies appreciated:

> After taking our meal, the priests consecrated our shade by planting taboo sticks round it. This deprived us entirely of the society of the ladies, for though they sat down on our mat before breakfast and were very chatty and cheering, yet nothing would induce them to approach it after these rods were stuck up; such is the powerful influence of priest craft among these people.[41]

What this also suggests was that there was no significant language barrier between the party and their followers: given that the latter probably had little if any English, it seems more than likely that among the Europeans, Menzies at least had mastered enough of the language to have convivial intercourse.

By 12 February the party was at the base of the main massif, where the Kilauea volcano was erupting, causing irritation to the party's eyes with dust, smoke and ash. Mark Twain, estimating the diameter of the crater at three miles, gives a vivid description of such an eruption on Kilauea as seen from the crater lip at night in 1866:

> The greater part of the desert floor under us was as black as ink … but over a wide square of it was ringed and streaked and striped with a thousand branching streams of liquid and gorgeously brilliant fire! … here and there were gleaming holes twenty feet in diameter, broken in the dark crust, and in them melted lava – the colour of dazzling white just tinged with yellow – was boiling and surging furiously … many years have elapsed since any visitor has seen such a display.[42]

At the higher altitudes, the natives in Menzies' party complained bitterly about the cold, with the snowline not far above their encampment. Nevertheless, the whole journey to this point at the upper edge of the forest was accompanied by not far short of a hundred local people, many of them there out of sheer curiosity. Heavy frost reduced the morning temperature to 28 degrees at a mere 6500 feet altitude, which astonished the British party. By this time, the barefoot porters were shivering continuously with the cold, and the old chief Luhea entreated them not to go further. Menzies arranged for most of the porters to go back into the forest while he and the other officers, helped by a few of the hardier locals, kept climbing over the most barren terrain and eventually reached the snowline after an exhausting journey.

They would have encountered both the jagged *A-a* lava whose pinnacles tore cruelly into the feet, and the pillow-like *pahoehoe* forming wrinkled folds and hummocks. Midshipman Heddington pressed on further but became very ill, no doubt with altitude sickness, exacerbated by strenuous effort, and had to be sent down to lower altitudes. (Modern tourist guides warn of this hazard and the need for proper footwear and high altitude clothing, none of which Menzies' party had.) They had, in a relatively short time, moved from the warm tropics at sea level to a semi-arctic environment, and were now surviving on a small quantity of chocolate, some ship's biscuits, and a quart of rum. Their shelter at these frigid altitudes was a modest parapet of lava boulders, while they huddled together under some thin local cloth:

> Our minds were variously occupied, sometimes on meditating on the dreadful consequences of a snowstorm coming on whilst we were thus situated; at other times in contemplating the awful and extended scene around us, where the most profound stillness subsisted the whole night, not even interrupted by the least chirp of a bird or an insect. The moon rose out of the sea at an immense distance, and her orb appeared uncommonly large and brilliant …[43]

The next day, Howell, whose shoes had been cut to pieces on the lava, was forced to retreat down the mountain, while Menzies, Baker and McKenzie pushed on with virtually no food. By noon on 14 February, after a most arduous trek around the rim of an immense crater not less than three miles in circumference, they reached the summit. With his portable barometer, Menzies calculated this at 13,634 feet, a mere 45 feet below the modern official altitude. Their return down the mountain, desperately hungry, thirsty and exhausted, was not helped by the discovery that Howell had gone on with the liquor which they had hoped might revive them for the rest of the long journey down through the forest to their main encampment: only the three coconuts kept by the natives gave them sufficient strength to carry on. Menzies, no weakling, accurately defined the expedition as 'the most persevering and hazardous struggle that can possibly be conceived'.[44] However, Vancouver was clearly annoyed by Menzies' late return, which had delayed the vessel's departure.

It was the first known ascent of the mountain by a European, and almost certainly by anyone, until it was climbed some 40 years later by Menzies' colleague and fellow-countryman David Douglas. (The first woman to make the ascent was the intrepid Victorian traveller Isabella Bird in 1873 when she was fortunate to see the 'fountains of fire' with the mountain in eruption, and who gave a very vivid account of her hair-raising experience riding to the summit on the back of a mule.) This established Menzies as a true explorer in his own right, with a determination that overcame considerable odds – the party was singularly ill-equipped for such a venture – and the single-mindedness to take the first barometric and temperature readings throughout the arduous climb. He was still remembered by the islanders when Douglas arrived as 'the red-faced man who cut off the limbs of men and gathered grass'.[45,46]

NOTES

1. Menzies Journal, 20 February 1793
2. Ibid., 13 March 1792
3. Wilson (1920), 76, 80
4. Lamb (1984), 1145
5. Menzies Journal, 14 January 1794
6. Ibid., 25 February 1793
7. Ibid., 25 March 1793
8. Lamb (1984), 124
9. Ibid., 60
10. Menzies Journal, 21 February 1793
11. Ibid., 22 February 1793
12. Ibid., 22 February 1793
13. Wilson (1920), 67–90
14. Menzies Journal, 26 February 1793
15. Ibid., 22 February 1793
16. Ibid., 2 March 1793

17. Naish (1996), 211
18. Menzies Journal, 4 March 1793
19. Lamb (1984), 1158–60
20. Menzies Journal, 29 February 1793
21. Ibid., 26 February 1793
22. Lamb (1984), 121–2
23. Menzies Journal, 11 March 1792
24. Ibid., 14 March 1793
25. Ibid., 13 March 1793
26. Lamb (1984), 473
27. Naish (1996), 129
28. Lamb (1984), 462
29. The ethnic Polynesian Hawaiians have in recent years rediscovered their traditional boat building and navigational skills. In 1993 a boat was built called the Haiwai'iloa which subsequently has made a number of trips across the Pacific to other Polynesian islands such as Tahiti. Originally the boat was to be built using indigenous koa (a type of acacia tree) but as there was not enough timber of the right size to complete the task, two great Sitka Spruce logs were subsequently gifted, in a show of solidarity between native peoples of the Pacific, by native Alaskans. Each log was more than 400 years old and each weighed more than 25 tons. The reference above by Menzies to the native peoples using pine logs which drifted from the Pacific Northwest of the North American continent to build their large craft accords with this re-enactment. These were considered 'gifts from the gods'. (Source: Personal observation by Syd House and story of the Outrigger, Waikaloa Hotel on Big Island, Hawaii, July 2000)
30. Manby 13–14 March. Thomas Manby – letters Coe Collection of Western Americana, Yale University, in Lamb (1984), 469 note 2
31. Menzies Journal, 15 February 1793
32. Wilson (1920), 54
33. Menzies Journal, 15 February 1793
34. Ibid., 17 January 1794
35. Ibid., 26 February 1793
36. Ibid., 17 January 1794
37. Ibid., 19 January 1794
38. The Hawaiian flora has been very much threatened over a number of years by intensive agriculture, invasive alien plants, pests, and urban development. Some 38% of all plants on the list of endangered species in the USA are native to these islands, which are home to some of the rarest plants on earth. Menzies was fortunate in being in Hawaii before this degradation.
39. Menzies Journal, 23 January 1794
40. Ibid., 24 January 1794

41. Ibid., 11 February 1794
42. Twain (1938), 209–11
43. Menzies Journal, 13 February 1794
44. Ibid., 16 February 1794
45. David Douglas, Botanist, at Hawaii, quoted in Wilson (1920), 199
46. Plants which were found by Menzies in Hawaii and named after him include *Abutilon menziesii, Astelia menziesiana, Bidens menziesii* and *Bonamia menziesii* (as recorded in Wilson (1920), with corrections by C. L. Justice and D. E. Justice in Justice (2000)).

11

'A Spot more Delightfull could hardly be met with in the Whole Globe'

The expedition paid three visits to California between 14 November 1792 and 9 December 1793, totalling over three months. They visited Santa Cruz, Bodega, San Francisco Bay, Santa Clara, and San Diego. The *Discovery* passed through the Golden Gate where Menzies was delighted to see herds of black cattle grazing in the foothills and, after their first season surveying on the northern coasts, he confessed to '… a pleasing glow of hope that there we should be able to obtain the comforts and refreshments which the vitiated state of our constitutions … required'.[1] The country was under a loose form of administration as a colonial province of the Spanish empire between 1769 and 1821, when it became part of independent Mexico. At the time of the *Discovery* voyage, the Spanish were at an early stage in establishing three forms of settlement: forts or praesidios, missions, and townships or pueblos; several of each of these were visited by Menzies.

On arrival at San Francisco in mid-November, the British party were made immediately welcome by the Spaniards, who provided generously of their stock of vegetables and meat, displaying great skill in lassoing a bullock from a herd to be slaughtered for their use; the Franciscan friars were especially kind in attending to the crews' needs. Together with the other ship's officers Menzies met the commandant of the settlement and the principal father of the mission. Referring to the elderly commandant, he states:

> He no sooner came on board than he told Capt. Vancouver with the honest frankness of an old Castilian, that we should be supplied with every kind of refreshment which the country afforded, & that during our stay he would further have a particular satisfaction in contributing to our amusements by furnishing us with Horses & Guides whenever we wishd to ride or traverse the Country. These offers were certainly gratifying to us, & still more so from the gratifying manner in which they were offered by a man whose heart seemed to glow at such a favourable opportunity of exercising his hospitality and kindness, for with that candour inseparable from real merit he further added, that these were the orders of his Sovereign, which he believed were general all over the country respecting us.[2]

These orders would have certainly come from Juan Francisco de la Bodega (1744–94), the distinguished 52-year-old naval commander and Governor of the Spanish settlement at Nootka.

Later, the officers were invited to ride to the *praesidio* or garrison headquarters. Menzies gave a detailed description, possibly the first in English, of these key settlements on this Spanish frontier.[3]

> The Soldiers constantly rode on Horseback fully accoutred with Target Lance Musket & sword secured to the Saddle before them ... generally stout Men capable of bearing great fatigue & without any exaggeration the most dextrous and nimble Horsemen we ever saw; They are allowed a relief of five or six horses each by Government, & when mounted they carry a target with which they parry off the missile weapons of the Indians; Their Body is defended by a quilted buff coat of several folds of leather without sleeves, which is impenetrable to Arrows; They have a kind of Apron of thick leather fastened to the pummel of the saddle & falling back on each side covers the Legs and Thighs & affords considerable defence either in passing through thorny bush woods with which the Country abounds, or from such weapons as the Indians generally make use of.
>
> Their offensive weapons are a Musket, a broad sword & a pair of large pistols all of which are generally carried in leather cases secur'd to the Saddle; they also carry a Lance in their hand which they manage with great dexterity. Thus equipped and with a large Cloak thrown over his shoulders to keep himself and his accoutrements dry, a Californian soldier makes a formidable and curious appearance. His Spurs are very large and clumsy, weighing I dare say upwards of a pound weight, and his Stirrups are form'd of heavy pieces of wood, with a cavity dug out of each to admit the Toes, and seem a good contrivance to defend them in riding through the Bush Wood, etc.[4]

The detail of this description could suggest that Menzies might have been assessing the military attributes of a potential foe, but he was also very accurately describing the original cowboy of future western legend.

The *Discovery* had on board two young women from Hawaii who had been illegally taken from there by Captain Baker commanding the British schooner the *Jenny* and who now wished to see them returned to their home. They were lively and likeable girls and one day were invited to ride out with the officers:

> Hitherto these Women had only been distant Spectators of the Country and its produce, black Cattle they had some idea of from having seen a few of them at Nootka, but horses and their fleetness with which they saw them carry people about on their backs produced much admiration & afforded a fertile theme for conversation between them since they came into this port; the proposal of a ride therefore much excited their curiosity & was readily accepted, & we no sooner

landed than they mounted on Horseback & kept their seats throughout the journey without shewing the least sign of fear or timidity, in short with as much ease & apparent satisfaction as if they had been brought up or accustomed to such mode of Conveyance from their infancy. The party was accompanied to the nearest mission by the commandant and an escort of soldiers, being received most warmly by the fathers who provided an elegant and plentifull dinner for the whole party, which at their particular request was Cooked in the English Stile by our own servants ...[5]

Because of his indisposition, Menzies did not accompany a party that was got up to visit the Mission of Santa Clara, which perhaps is just as well as the distance was seriously misjudged and several officers were too exhausted even to dine at the mission on arrival. Fortunately *en route* the accompanying military escort drove a posse of fresh horses which substituted at intervals for those which had been ridden, expertly lassoing them. What they did discover was a beautiful and fertile country, 'a spot more delightfull they all agreed could hardly be met with on the whole globe'. Again, they were received most cordially at the mission by the two venerable fathers, 'who took the greatest pains in contributing every means in their power to comfort & entertain them, & could the pain and fatigue be brought on by the journey be at once relievd, no strangers ever had greater reason to be satisfied with their situation ...'.[6] The party also noted the fine crops of grain and a wide variety of good quality fruit which was raised by the fathers. Menzies' friend Lieutenant Johnstone gives a good description of a cattle roundup:

[The soldiers] surrounded a large herd of black Cattle & began to catch them. This was done by riding in amongst the herd & singling out the one they wished to take, which was instantly pursued by two Soldiers on Horseback at full speed, till each threw a Noose made on the end of a long leathern thong over its neck or horns, & which they generally effected in a short chace with great dexterity & then were able to manage the wildest of them and keep a due distance between the two Horses, without suffering to hurt either. In this manner they caught about twenty & led them to the Mission where they were slaughtered & seventeen of them were divided amongst the Indians to make it a day of festivity in compliment of the visit of the English Officers to the Mission.

The visitors were told that a nucleus of 15 head of cattle had been introduced some 20 years previously, and as a result of natural increase, the plains now swarmed with them. Menzies declares that there could not be less than 30,000 head of cattle belonging to the two settlements of Monterey and San Francisco, besides huge numbers of horses, sheep and goats, despite the slaughtering of 3000 cattle annually for these stations.

For all of this generous hospitality, neither the missions nor the military would accept any payment on the orders of Señor Quadra, but the fathers were grateful for gifts of those utensils and tools which they were short of from the stock carried by the ships, together with trinkets for the natives and spirits. However, they were punctilious in observing the formalities, and at Monterey, south of San Francisco, on 27 November they exchanged 13-gun salutes, and met up again with Señor Quadra, renewing a warm friendship which had begun at Nootka. Menzies delights in the attractive countryside around Monterey with its 'beautiful Lawns & rising eminences of clear pasturage diversified with Clumps of Trees & scattered Pines, & enlivened with Horses and Cattle grazing in numerous Herds'.[7]

Again, with Señor Quadra, the Spanish Governor and his wife, and a number of soldiers, the British officers rode out in a substantial cavalcade to the nearest mission at Carmillo, where they were as usual received with bountiful hospitality and warmth, and shown the church, granaries and the impressive agriculture. In the evening, the party was invited to a dance at the Governor's house in the *praesidio* of Monterey:

> ... it was to begin at seven, but the ladies had such unusual preparations to make that they could not be got together till near ten, & as they entered they seated themselves on Cushions placed on a carpet spread out at one end of the room: They were variously dressed, but most of them had their Hair in long queues reaching down to their waist, with a tassel of ribbons appendant to its extremity: They danced some Country dances, but even in this remote region they seemed most attached to the Spanish exhilarating dance the Fandango, a performance that requires no little elasticity of limbs as well as nimbleness of capers and gestures. It is performed by two persons of different sex who dance either to the Guittar alone or accompanied with the voice; they traverse the room with such nimble evolutions, wheeling about, changing sides & smacking with their fingers at every motion; sometimes they dance close to each other, then retire, then approach again, with such wanton attitudes and motions, such leering looks, sparkling eyes & trembling limbs, as would decompose the gravity of a Stoic.

Apart from being a vivid and accurate description of the dance by Menzies, there is just a suggestion that perhaps he should not, from a Calvinistic upbringing, fully approve of the overt sexuality of the performance, while being impressed by it. However, a performance by the two Hawaiian women was not well received:

> The two Sandwich Island Women, at the request of Captain Vancouver exhibited their manner of singing and dancing, which did not appear to afford much entertainment to the Spanish Ladies, indeed I believe they thought this crude performance was introduced by way of ridiculing their favourite dance the Fandango, as they soon after departed.[8]

By way of returning hospitality, Vancouver arranged for an entertainment for the Spaniards and their womenfolk and a considerable number of British officers from both vessels in a large tent pitched on the shore, accommodating 40 to dinner:

> After dark, a selection of Fireworks were exhibited with which the whole Company particularly the Spaniards were highly delighted, for many of them we believd had never seen anything of the kind before, and on that account their admiration was more excessive. Most of the sky rockets went off well & were much admired, but the Water rockets being exceedingly good, never faild of exciting most wonder & applause from the gazing multitude. The evening was spent with hilarity mirth & mutual good humour between us and the Spaniards, with whom we parted at a late hour; but some little altercations took place amongst ourselves which was not so pleasant, & certainly shewd the Spaniards the characteristic of English Sailors, who on these occasions are apt to quarrel with their best friends.[9]

It is not difficult to imagine that while the ships' crews revelled in California's abundance of food and hospitality after the rigours of northern survey work, equally the Spaniards would welcome this diversion of exotic company amidst the monotony of serving on the frontier of their empire and that the British habits and behaviour would be the subject of endless comment in the missions and *praesidios* which they visited.

Throughout their stay, the British officers dined almost daily with Señor Quadra, were provided with horses and guides for explorations of the local countryside for shooting and hunting, and generally were given a very good time at the hands of their Spanish hosts. Menzies comments: 'Whenever we went out in this manner Sr. Quadra's Plate and Cooking Equipage etc travelld along with us, so that we had always the luxury of dining in those retreats off Silver, & on the best of everything he could afford.'[10] Menzies made good use of this freedom to collect plants and observe wildlife, but also drew on the journeys of his colleagues, 'who were in general extremely liberal in presenting me with everything rare or curious they met with'.[11]

Despite the season, his collections of plants from Monterey were his most successful in California, totalling 42 species (see Appendix 5). This included the conifer *Pinus radiata* which he found on the headland known as Punta de Pinos and which was subsequently to become such an important commercial plantation tree in the sub-tropics, not to mention the most impressive tree of the coast, the huge *Sequoia sempervirens* or Coast Redwood, which was first found at Santa Cruz across Monterey Bay in 1794. He is also credited with becoming the first bird collector in California:

> The Thickets every where were inhabited by great variety of the feathered tribe, many of which were also new, among these was a species of Quail of a dark lead colour beautifully speckled with black white & ferrugineous colours with a Crest of reverted black feathers on the crown of its head …[12]

What he had seen was the California Quail, providing its type locality.[13] Later:

> We returned through the Wood by a different path and shot a number of small birds, a new species of Hawk & several Quails, but the Country was so exceedingly dry and parch'd that we found but few plants in Flower in our whole excursion.[14]

The so-called 'hawk' was later confirmed as the type specimen of the Californian Condor.[15] These two bird species were the first birds to be named scientifically from California and according to Grinnel 'remain today [1932] as perhaps the two most conspicuously peculiar birds of this State'. Thus Menzies has been properly accredited with being the first collector of Californian birds. Subsequently, he observed a 'large variegated Squirrel which burrowed in dry sandy grounds ...', later identified as the California Ground Squirrel, but not formally described until 30 years later.[16,17]

Menzies did in fact make an extensive herbarium collection of plants from Monterey, more than from any other part of California, and was the first botanist to make a thorough examination of the interesting coastal pine forest.[18] While at Monterey he encountered two Spanish botanists who had been with Quadra during the summer at Nootka:

> ... they tell me they are part of a Society which has been employed of late years at the expense of his Catholic majesty in examining Mexico and New Spain, and collecting materials for a Flora Mexicana which they say will be published before our return to England; and as they have promised me a copy of it, I have requested them to address it to you [Banks] with seeds or any other things they may be inclined to send from Mexico. I cannot help envying them the assistance they have in being accompanied by an excellent draughtsman.[19]

Californian Condor, photographed by Michael Quinn.
(Courtesy of the US National Park Service.)

Menzies must have been very envious of the resources available to the Spanish scientists, and not a little piqued at the prospect of their early publication in the area in which he himself was collecting.

He records at this time the loading of 12 cows, six bulls and the same number of breeding sheep on board the supply ship for transport to the penal colony of Port Jackson in New South Wales, but that the shortage of hay in the parched country resulted in most of the animals dying on the passage, half of them expiring even before they reached Hawaii. He also reports the suicide of the carpenter's mate, Joseph Margetdroit, who appears to have somehow squeezed through a porthole in the gunroom, an event which was incomprehensible to the crew. However, Menzies notes that he had been 'severely punished' for theft some months before and 'his guilt might have preyed on his mind, especially as he was always observed to be of a gloomy religious cast'.[20] Again it is interesting to note that Menzies refers to 'severe punishment' rather than more directly to flogging, which the miscreant would certainly have received.

The opportunity was taken to send Mr Broughton, master of the *Chatham*, with Señor Quadra, who was proceeding on 14 January to San Blas in Mexico so that a copy of the dispatches from Nootka could be taken home via that territory, a challenging overland journey which Señor Quadra promised to facilitate in any way possible and in which he was as good as his word. With Broughton went a box of seeds for Kew Gardens and a letter from Menzies to Sir Joseph Banks, both of which arrived safely and in record time. Quadra refused all payment for all the valuable services and provisions he had rendered to the British, accepting only a receipt for the latter. The parting with Vancouver and his men would have been an emotional one after their very close association and deepening friendship.

In his letter to Banks, Menzies complained at some length that Vancouver had not chosen his long-standing friend Johnstone as the new commander of the *Chatham*, selecting the younger and less experienced Peter Puget instead, prefacing his letter with the phrase '... like many other strange things, in this Voyage ...'. He also complained and apologised for the fact that the plant frame, if opened, was penetrated by the many forms of livestock on the ship, or his plants were poisoned from drips of tar from the rigging.[21] This was not the only hazard to these plants, as the changes from tropical to sub-arctic climates killed off many others. During heavy seas, the frame inevitably became penetrated by salt water.

In the same letter, Menzies takes another dig at Vancouver when he says:

> I forgot to tell you that our Commander has already perpetuated his name on this coast, for the great island we circumnavigated last summer of which Nootka is a part, is modestly named Quadra & Vancouver island tho' it should I think, with more propriety be named after his Majesty, as the name of King George's Sound is now extinct which Capt. Cook first intended for him.

Since Menzies himself had several features named after him, he is presumably making a distinction between these and the largest single island encountered by the expedition.

After a season in Hawaii, the expedition was back in California, anchoring at Port Trinidad on 2 May, where after provisioning and repairs to the vessels, they sailed for San Francisco. Here they had a completely different reception from the previous year, even by the same commandant who had received them so hospitably. Letters were sent to Vancouver demanding why he had entered the port and restricting landing to Vancouver, attended only by an officer midshipman. Other wooding and watering parties would be supervised by a Spanish guard, with no tents or places of shelter to be erected. Nor were they allowed to go to the nearby mission. (His subsequent easing of these restrictions suggests that the official letters were to 'cover his back'.) However the commandant, Señor Sal, was in person just as friendly as before, offering to provide whatever the ships required in the way of provisions. The British were confused, to say the least, but noted that the defences of the garrison had been improved. In Señor Quadra's absence, it was clear that different orders had been received from above.

> As Capt. Vancouver had already obtaind leave for some of the officers to go on shore on pleasure & even exceed the limits of the restrictions, I was in hopes he would be equally inclind to favour my pursuits, & therefore ask'd his leave to go on shore on the morning of the 22nd. if I should only have the scope of the parties who were daily landed & employed on the ship's duty, which he refused, consequently I had no opportunity while we remained here of collecting either plants or seeds for his majesty's Gardens, which I the more regretted as my state of health when here last year precluded me in great measure from extending my excursions or examining the shores of this Harbour with that minuteness I could wish.[22]

No reason is given for Vancouver's refusal on this occasion – it may be that he was unwilling to risk further restrictions, or simply that he was out of sorts and wanted to exercise his authority. However, it became clear that relations between Vancouver and Menzies had seriously deteriorated over the contentious plant frame. Vancouver's intemperate outbursts had got to such a pitch that Menzies could not speak to him directly on the subject, and on 18 November 1793 was obliged to write a formal letter of complaint:

> Sir, It has really become so unpleasant to me to represent to you verbally anything relative to the plant-frame on the Quarter-Deck that I have now adopted this method to mention to you all the alterations or rather additions which I wish to make to its original plan for the security of the plants within it, together with the occasional aid that may be required to look after it in my absence; that my solicitations for its success may not be subject to me hereafter to such treatment.
>
> I beg leave to inform you that the Fowls have been in again last night, and have done irreparable damages. It is therefore absolutely necessary to have the upper

> part of the frame as well as the sides covered over with netting of sufficient strength and sized-meshes and to be constantly kept in repair to prevent Poultry, Pigeons and other animals from destroying the Plants, while they are receiving the necessary advantages of light and air.
>
> It will likewise in the future be necessary that you appoint a Man who will be suffered from his other duty to look after it, and execute my orders concerning it, while I am out of the Ship or pursuing my Duty on Shore.
>
> These Sir are all the requisitions I at present make concerning it, and trust that they will meet with your approbation as you can fully satisfy yourself with the necessity that requires them.
>
> I am, Sir, your Obedient Humble Servant. A. Menzies

A copy of this was made available to Banks with a telling postscript, almost certainly written at the end of the voyage:

> The first of the above requisitions was complied with two months after but the other I have been frequently obliged to request one of the Gentlemen to look after it when I could not leave my servant on board.
>
> You will see by the above that Captain Vancouver's disinclination for the success of the Garden has been pretty evident for some time back, and it was no unusual thing with him to be passionate and illiberal in his abuse whenever anything was represented to him relative to its safety, which made me always cautious in giving him as little trouble as possible and I believe I have not had a boat from the Ship on the particular duty of my department above four or five times during the Voyage and that only for a few hours at a time.

Naish considers that the above postscript was intended for Banks' eyes after the termination of the voyage and might even have been part of the evidence required by him in his attempts – which were well known – to blacken Vancouver's name at the instigation of Lady Camelford. It is difficult not to feel some sympathy for Menzies after all the trouble he had taken to collect his plants, often in difficult circumstances, but his letter, which is quite peremptory in tone, would have been like a red rag to a bull, with Vancouver on such a short fuse. But Menzies would not have written it had he not felt at the end of his tether too, or had he not thought that he would have the influential Banks behind him. One can hardly imagine the atmosphere between the two men, especially since the surgeon had to attend the captain in his medical capacity. This issue of the plant frame was to culminate in the most serious breakdown between them, with the potential to affect both their careers.

When the two principal mission fathers from Santa Clara and San Francisco paid a courtesy call on the ships, it became quite clear that they thoroughly disapproved of the reception suffered by the British, but could give no reason for this. In contrast to his experience the previous year, Vancouver had to pay for any provisions received, but to the hospitable Franciscans, he gave 'about a Ton of iron besides an assortment of such Tools & Utensils of our manufactury as they had made choice of from the Trading articles we had found'.

Their reception at Monterey was no better, where it was clearly intimated that Vancouver's proposed call at San Diego would not be welcomed by either the Court of Spain or the Viceroy of Mexico. Vancouver received similar official letters such as those from the commandant at San Francisco and soon after, all communications were broken off. All this appears to have resulted from the assumption of command by a new Governor, which had not been confirmed by the Spanish court. The British were understandably aggrieved and humiliated.

The whole situation was reversed yet again when they reached Santa Barbara where they were warmly received by the commandant Don Felip Goyoshea and by the fathers at the nearby mission. Menzies went botanising 'but the season of the year & the arid state of the Country was much against it … I was able to receive but little pleasure or advantage from my excursion', although he comments on encountering beautiful groves of evergreen oak, and he shot a variety of birds. The usual hospitality and entertainment was exchanged between the British and the Spaniards. One of the fathers who had arrived had travelled from a mission about 20 miles away.

> This worthy father was much afraid what we would pass his Mission without his having the satisfaction of seeing us or contributing to our comforts, & he therefore brought with him nine Mules loaded with various articles for us, such as sweet and common Potatos, Onions, Maize, Wheat, some Baskets of Figs & what are called prickly pears, etc.[23]

Before the ship left, Menzies remarks on the almost embarrassing quantity of provisions of very good quality received from the Spanish, but for which they would not take any payment. However, items were traded with the soldiers: an ox could be obtained for three axes and a sheep for small culinary utensils. The three vessels between them killed and carried away 18 head of cattle and about two dozen sheep. One of the most interesting descriptions by Menzies is of the native equivalent of a sauna:

> At each Village we observed a sweating place made by digging a deep pit or cavity of from ten to 15 feet square in a bank near the water side and covering it all over with Spars & earth so as to be scarcely distinguishable from other parts of the bank, excepting by a small hole left at the top for an entrance through which only one person could descend at a time by means of a post notched with steps; … one evening near the landing place we observed them make a large fire with dried faggots in the middle of this subterraneous oven & when it was sufficiently heated & the smoke subsided a number of the Natives went down in order to be sweated,

> by the time they were in a state of profuse perspiration they came up again one by one & instantly plunged themselves over head into the sea ...[24]

Menzies saw them repeat this procedure many times but could not work out whether it was simply a custom or whether it was to assist with ailments.

> They arrived at San Buenaventura, where the small boats were enabled to land our much esteemed Father Vincenti in safety to the no small satisfaction of his faithful adherents and a numerous tribe of Converts who flockd round him kissd his robes & expressed their joy on his arrival with every mark of veneration & grateful affection, nor was the venerable father less wanting in testifying his regard & received the caresses of his flock with tears in his eyes ...[25]

Here Menzies received plants and branches gathered by the ships' crews 'that greatly excited my curiosity'. However, on an excursion on the following day he 'saw a vast variety of Plants that were entirely new to me but to my no small mortification I met with only two plants in flower & very few in Seed ...'.[26] Menzies also received from one of the fathers a branch in bloom of *Parkinsonia aculeata* (Mexican Palo Verde) but he was equally pleased to receive a quantity of kernels and growing plants of the medicinal plant *Simmondsia californica* (Jojoba) which were successfully brought back to Kew Gardens.

Menzies also notes: '... as there were many other Plants growing on the shore near the landing which appeared new & ornamental, I employed two men this and the following day in digging them up and planting them in the same frame ...'.[27,28]

Some indication of Vancouver's pleasure at their hospitable reception was his gift to the *Padre Presidente*, the most senior of the fathers, of 'a small organ he had in the cabin, set to a miscellaneous collection of about thirty different tunes to the music of which he seemed very partial in his different visits aboard last year. This present he said he would carry with him to the seat of government at Monterey & there deposit in the Church where it would be carefully preserved as a memento of our visit to this Country'.[29]

What is clear from all this is that despite official coolness towards the British company at the higher levels of distant Spanish bureaucracy, relations at the personal level in California were warm and companionable.

Before they left San Diego, a cow and two young bulls were taken aboard for transhipment to Hawaii:

> As we were so unsuccessfull in carrying Bulls last year that none of them hardly survived the Voyage to the Islands, these two were chosen very young & by the care and attention of the Sailors who made pets of them, they soon became very fine animals, and we conceive that taking them on board in a young state, by which they soon became inurd to the Vessel is the most likely way to succeed in transporting these Animals to distant regions.[30]

NOTES

1. Menzies Journal, 14 November 1792
2. Ibid., 15 November 1792
3. At the *praesidio* in San Francisco, the original commandant's house of 1791–92 can still be seen.
4. Menzies Journal, 5 January 1793
5. Ibid., 18 November 1792
6. Ibid., 22 November 1792
7. Ibid., 27 November 1792
8. Ibid., 2 December 1792
9. Ibid., 10 December 1792
10. Ibid., 19 December 1792
11. Ibid., 7 January 1793
12. Ibid., 6 January 1793
13. Grinnel (1932), 246
14. Menzies Journal, 6 January 1793
15. Grinnel (1932), 251
16. Ibid., 247
17. The California Quail (*Lophartyx lophartyx*) became the official state bird in 1931 and is widespread. The Californian Condor (*Gymnogyps californianus*) is one of the largest flying birds, with a wingspan of over three metres, and lives up to 60 years. By the mid-1980s its wild population had been reduced to eight individuals. As a result of an intensive captive breeding programme, there are now 273 birds, 127 of these living in the wild. It is surprising that Menzies did not provide a fuller description of this dramatic vulture. The California Ground Squirrel (*Spermophilus beecheyei*) is widespread and by its burrowing habits is now regarded as a major pest on agricultural land and canal banks.
18. Galloway and Groves (1987), 20
19. Menzies to Banks, Monterey, 21 January 1793
20. Ibid., 21 January 1793
21. Ibid., 14 January 1793
22. Menzies Journal, 22 October 1793
23. Ibid., 16 November 1793
24. Ibid., 17 November 1793
25. Ibid., 20 November 1793
26. Ibid., 29 November 1793
27. Ibid., 6 December 1793
28. All of the plants collected were subsequently identified from Menzies' descriptions and specimens by Alice Eastwood: see her introduction in *California Historical Society Quarterly* of January 1924.
29. Menzies Journal, 7 December 1793
30. Ibid., 7 December 1793

12

'An Awful Silence Pervaded the Gloomy Forests'

After the expedition's first stay in Hawaii, Vancouver's survey of the Northwest coast could be said to have commenced when he entered the Strait of Juan de Fuca (in present day Jefferson County in the state of Washington) at the end of April 1792. Menzies' plant collecting commenced just east of Port Angeles, ending that season at Menzies Point on the mainland immediately north of the northern tip of Vancouver Island.[1] On 28 April, they had passed the mouth of the great Columbia River without Vancouver recognising this – one of his few navigational mistakes. He became aware of this on meeting the American Captain Robert Gray, an experienced fur trader, of the Boston Brig *Columbia Rediviva.*

Lieutenant Puget and Menzies had been sent to the ship to make first contact, presumably because of Menzies' previous knowledge of the Northwest coast and his ability therefore to ask informed questions. By this time, Menzies would have been recognised by Vancouver as one of the most valuable members of his team, with his tact and good judgement. (Because of these characteristics, together with his age, experience and scientific training, he was almost certainly given a larger role than would be expected of a supernumerary officer, and accompanied Vancouver on all important meetings, such as the difficult negotiations with Señor Quadra.)[2] Gray was able to give them valuable information, not only on the geography of the coast, but also on the temperament of the various Indian tribes: he himself had suffered the loss of his chief mate and two seamen to the warlike Haida.

Their next anchorage for several weeks was off Protection Island in Discovery Bay, as it was named by Vancouver. (Subsequently Menzies was to take a dig at Vancouver's naming of Port Discovery: '... we afterwards found that the Spaniards had named it Port Quadra the year before, and having then anchored in it, surely gives their name a prior right of continuing, to prevent the confusion of names which are but too common in new discovered countries'.)[3] Here the first of the fixed astronomical observation points was established in a tent on shore. Here too the men were delighted to stretch their limbs after the confines of a long and tedious voyage, while Menzies was dazzled by the thick pink patches of wild valerian or sea blush.[4] Both Vancouver and Menzies were enchanted by the landscape: the captain viewed it as 'a rich lawn beautiful with nature's luxuriant bounties', and Menzies was equally effusive. The 'lawns' so frequently mentioned and admired among a matrix of scattered trees were miniature prairies maintained by fires set deliberately by the Indians to encourage food plants and game – at least 80 of the plants were used by the Indian people for food.[5]

Despite all this mellow contemplation, following the unfortunate loss of a stream anchor by the commander of the *Chatham*, Lt. Broughton, the latter was refused the varnish required for the repainting of his vessel by an angry Vancouver. Given that the very able Broughton was second-in-command of the expedition, and a person on whom Vancouver would depend for assistance in case of trouble, this was short-sighted to say the least.[6]

Here at the head of the bay they also found the remains of a deserted village of a few houses:

> On a Tree close to it we found the skeleton of a child which was carefully wrapped up in some of the Cloth of the Country made from the Bark of a tree and some Matts, but at this time it afforded tenement to a brood of young Mice which ran out of it as soon as we touched it.[7]

At another canoe burial, Peter Puget, another young officer, observed:

> This … argues Strongly that the Indians believe in a future State, or else why bury with them Eatables with their Weapons for procuring more & place the Body in a canoe suspended in the Air, which we may reasonably suppose is to prevent it being damaged by Insects or Animals, that it may be of Service to the deceased herafter.[8]

However, the Indian's attitude to children horrified the ships' crews when they were offered two children aged about six or seven, in exchange for copper sheeting or muskets.

Subsequently, two human heads were found impaled on the top of 15-foot poles; the party assumed they were the heads of enemies killed in battle. Other tall poles were for a quite different purpose: the Indians used nets strung between them for catching wildfowl.[9] Later they were to encounter small parties of Indians who were willing to trade fresh fish and venison for trinkets and who were entirely peaceable. Menzies recognised their dialect as being of the Nootkan language and comments on the likely extent of this, indicating his own familiarity with Indian speech.

In the course of a small boat expedition – the first of many which Vancouver was to authorise for coastal survey – Menzies considered much of the land suitable for cultivation and settlement:

> … a pleasant and desirable tract of both pasture and arable land where the Plough might enter at once without the least obstruction, and where the Soil though light and gravely appeard capable of yielding in this temperate climate luxuriant crops of the European grains or of rearing herds of Cattle who might here wander at their ease over extensive field of fine pasture.[10]

From this point at Whidbey Island they were able to view the snow-covered peak of Mount Rainier beyond, which provided for Menzies an idyllic setting.

Among the several tree species which Menzies recorded, perhaps the most memorable was a madrone which, as *Arbutus menziesii*, now commemorates the botanist. It is notable for its striking smooth reddish-brown bark, which peels off in long curled strips. (The species is characteristic of the rainshadow area of the northeastern Olympic Peninsula which Menzies was exploring and which is now part of a national park. One of the finest, and possibly oldest, specimens of this striking tree is appropriately to be found at Castle Menzies, near Menzies' birthplace and where he worked as a young gardener.) On an excursion into the woods Menzies was entranced by a 'vast abundance' of that rare plant *Calypso bulbosa*, the Venus or Fairy Slipper Orchid, with its beautiful nodding single flowers.[11] He also found the now widespread but localised *Rhododendron macrophyllum*, or Pacific Rhododendron, now adopted as the state flower of Washington. Here he also found the Hairy or Columbia Manzanita

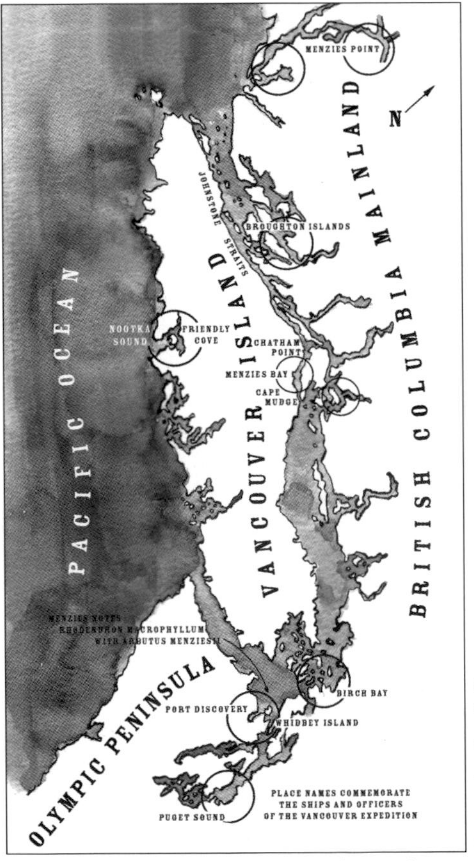

Drawn by Sarah Batey

A map showing the locations botanised by Menzies during his time on the coast of British Columbia. Based upon a map in Clive L. Justice's work *Mr Menzies' Garden Legacy: Plant Collecting on the Northwest Coast.* (Redrawn with kind permission of Clive L. Justice.)

(*Arctostaphylos columbiana*) growing with the *Arbutus* and the rhododendron, all three ericaceous plants inhabiting the forest edge.[12]

Despite his plant discoveries Menzies was unhappy, with the boat expeditions which he accompanied being 'not very favourable for my pursuits as it afforded me so little time on shore at different places we landed'.[13] Normally, the cutters and pinnaces would keep a cable length's distance from the shore, providing little opportunity for plant identification, and even when they landed, Menzies had to take opportunities for botanising only while other activities, such as meal preparation, were going on. It would have been frustrating for Menzies to have to carry out his plant collecting usually in a hurry, even if he understood that the main purpose of the expedition was coastal survey, and not natural history. In the next 150 years, this botanical treasure house and its unique habitats, supporting almost 1500 plant species, was to be decimated by timber cutting and settlement, so that only a tiny fraction of the original forest now remains.

Drawn by Sarah Batey

The lowering of the long boats from *Discovery* for a day of botanising. Based upon an original drawing by Greg Foster in Clive L. Justice's work *Mr Menzies' Garden Legacy: Plant Collecting on the Northwest Coast.* (Redrawn with kind permission of Clive L. Justice.)

These boat expeditions from the main vessels were crucial to all of the survey work, since the smaller boats, suitably provisioned for up to three weeks, could penetrate the long inlets for a considerable distance, using their shallow drafts. Eight yawls, launches, cutters and jolly boats were carried by *Discovery* and *Chatham* and were used constantly. Both sail and oars were used as necessary, and the men, under the charge of an officer, might be required to row for many hours, while they were not infrequently short of food.[14]

Most of the small boat expeditions were led by the very experienced James Johnstone and Joseph Whidbey who were responsible for making the initial calculations and also the sketches of the areas surveyed – sketches which were of a high quality and which were passed to Joseph Baker for conversion onto a fair sheet held on the *Discovery*. Vancouver had a very high opinion of Baker's work and it was he who prepared the charts for engravings which accompanied the final report of the expedition. The method was known as a running survey, with a portable observatory, usually in the form of a pavilion-like marquee, being established at suitable points several hundred miles apart to establish a fixed frame of reference for the detailed work of the small boats.[15]

The process of survey was standardised by what was known as 'taking angles'. A compass bearing was taken on any suitable landmark, and its bearing was then taken again after sailing a measured mile. The latter was measured by monitoring the speed of the boat every few minutes by trailing a chip-log and counting the knots on the line as the log drifted astern. Each new bearing was carefully entered into a survey journal, and from this a chart would be drawn later, indicating all the features passed. Likewise from depth-soundings by the 'lead', the sea depths would be recorded wherever bottom was reached, which in the deeper fjords was rare enough.

Initially, the lack of shelter on these boats was a serious limitation if circumstances prevented them from landing and erecting a tent. (Parties of armed marines accompanied these expeditions.) Menzies took advantage of these excursions for botanising although being usually on his own, he had to keep within hailing distance of the boats or within sound of a musket shot if he climbed a hill. The drying of the plants between sheets of paper in this frequently damp climate would have been a real difficulty. His dried specimens were mounted on small herbarium sheets on the reverse of which he wrote the locality and date of collection, with those he collected himself marked 'A.M.'. Given that the localities in his journal and on these sheets are often imprecise and lacking in habitat descriptions, it is almost certain that he also kept a field notebook which most unfortunately has been lost.

The days were often long and arduous, as Menzies records towards the end of the expedition:

> … next morning we were again in motion at day break as we had the comfort of fair weather, but we did not long enjoy it when it came on to rain again very hard

> with fluctuating gusts of wind that greatly retarded our progress. As we had this day but a single meal, every exertion was used to reach the vessel both by rowing and sailing, and after persisting in our endeavours with fatiguing toil till ten at night we were obliged to stop about five leagues from the ships and spend the night in the boats very uncomfortable as it rained incessantly and all the shelter we could make from the boats, sails, etc was very inadequate to defend us from its inclemency. In this situation we anxiously looked forward for daylight, when we again set out, cold, stiff, wet and hungry.[16]

Menzies also made very skilful drawings and paintings of plants collected, a considerable number of which have still survived. A young Indian chief came aboard the *Discovery* while Menzies was painting a plant further up the coast and 'took pleasure in observing the manner I proceeded ... painting is an art [to] which the Indians appear particularly partial'.[17] He goes on to express his admiration for the Indians' own regular but intricate designs and was later (at Bella Bella) to consider their painted carvings as evidence of high civilisation. At one point Menzies gives a very succinct description of the sort of activities which engaged the ships' crews whenever conditions were suitable: 'The carpenters were now employed in Caulking & on the various necessary repairs – the Blacksmiths had their Forge going on shore – a party were cutting down fire wood – another brewing Beer from a species of Spruce – in short the weather being so favourable & vivifying every spring was set in motion to forward our refitment.'[18]

On 3 June, Menzies writes:

> The latter being the King's Birth Day, Capt Vancouver landed about noon with some of the Officers on the south point of the small bay [Tulalip Bay in Washington State] where he took possession of the Country with the usual forms in his Majesty's name & namd it New Georgia & on hoisting the English Colours on the spot each Vessel proclaimed it aloud with a Royal Salute in honor of the Day.

By the end of May, the survey of Puget Sound had been completed, an epic surveying and mapping expedition, accurately charting some 210 miles in six days. It was also one of the most attractive coastlines they were to encounter and Menzies was moved to comment in somewhat purple prose on this fine country:

> To the Southeast seen through a beautiful inlet, Mt. Rainier augmented by its great elevation [5000 m] and bulky appearance begins the background panorama of rugged and peeked summits covered here and there with patches of snow ... Between us and the above ridge and between the two mountains a fine level country intervened, chiefly covered with pine forest abounding here and there with clear spots of considerable extent. These clear spots, or lawns, are clothed with a rich carpet of verdure and adorned with clumps of trees and a surrounding verge of scattered pines which, with their advantageous situation on the banks of these inland arms of the sea, gave them a beauty and prospect equal to the most admired parks of England.

> A traveller wandering over the unfrequented Plains is regaled with a salubrious and revivifying air impregnated with the balsamic fragrance of the surrounding Pinery, while his mind is eagerly occupied every moment on new objects & his senses riveted on the enchanting variety of the surrounding scenery where the softer beauties of landscape are harmoniously blended in majestic grandeur with the wild and romantic to form an interesting & picturesque prospect on every side.[19]

Here also he writes of finding many species of trees in the coastal woods, including spruces, yew, oak, maple, poplar, ash, hazel, alder and many new species of other plants, with various vacciniums and many berried bushes, speculating on the reasons for so few inhabitants, concluding that the land is particularly suited to the hunter-gatherer mode of life, of which he gives an accurate description. In the middle of the month, a boat expedition under Lt. Whidbey had an unexpected meeting with two Spanish vessels, the *Sutil* under Don Dionisio Alcala Galeano and the *Mexicana* under Don Cayetaqno Valdes. They were surveying the Straits of Juan de Fuca, where they anchored at Port Discovery, naming it Port Quadra after their Governor at Nootka, and where there were a number of other Spanish vessels. Later in the month Vancouver refused the Spanish offer to join survey forces: he was deeply disappointed that the Spaniards had got there before him.

From his own experience in a small vessel Raban provides an imaginative reconstruction of the passage of the ships on 25 June 1792 in the vicinity of Malaspina Strait:

> … picking their way through the rocks and islets, the ships sailed so slowly that it was 9.30 p.m., nearly dark, and sixteen miles on when the flotilla arrived at a gap in the mountains … . … the water was now fathomless. A thin persistent drizzle had fallen since mid afternoon, thickening the visibility and dampening the spirits of the explorers. *Discovery* was first to ghost through the entrance, which opened on a strange, watery crossroads of black precipices and inky canals, leading off in every direction like the arms of a starfish … I could see, as they could not, that they were floating over a sheer-sided submarine valley 1,500 feet deep.[20]

'The night was dark and rainy,' commented Vancouver, 'and the winds so light and variable that by the influence of the tides we were driven about as it were blindfolded in this labyrinth'.[21] On the following morning, the maze was revealed with vertical cliffs covered with black pines rising to nearly 6000 feet, while the water, in the dull morning light, reflected the darkness of the trees in this canyon, interrupted only by cataracts pouring from rock overhangs. Something of the sublime nature of their surroundings with their gaunt cliffs and snow-capped mountains wreathed in mist – which Vancouver did not appreciate – was conveyed in the drawings of the midshipmen John Sykes, Thomas Heddington and Henry Humphrys. The small boat expeditions could be extremely arduous, such as the 11-day investigation of the Burrard Inlet (which leads to the present day city of Vancouver) where at one point Lt. Puget's crew rowed till 11 at night i.e. about 14 hours on their oars and 4 hours before breakfast, having 18 hours of 'constant and hard rowing' in one day covering over 300 miles. At another point Lt. Johnstone narrates of going for two days 'on a single scanty meal & without rest or out of the boats in 24 hours'.[22]

Lieutenant Manby's expedition almost starved over three days, and he was deeply offended when Vancouver very intemperately accused him of getting lost. Likewise, the very competent Lt. Brougham was publicly humiliated by Vancouver for losing an anchor – both of these flare-ups may have been exacerbated by a combination of Vancouver's vexation at the earlier Spanish arrival and his own increasingly choleric disposition.

Throughout this period, Menzies was collecting and naming plants and on 15 June he found the Mock Orange *Philadelphus lewisii* var. *gordonianus.* On an expedition to one of the Gulf Islands with Lt. Johnstone he discovered several new species, including Coast Juniper, and watched Indians weaving with the shredded bark of Western Red Cedar, *Thuja plicata.* He is always interested in the habits of the local people:

> ... the Women were employed in making Mats and large Baskets for holding their provisions stores and Luggage. In one place we saw them at work on a kind of coarse Blanket made of double twisted woollen Yarn & curiously wove by their fingers with great patience & ingenuity into various figures thick Cloth that would baffle the powers of more civilizd Artists with all the implements to imitate, but from what Animal they procure the wool for making these Blankets I am at present uncertain.[23]

In Discovery Passage, Menzies landed at Cape Mudge, where he gave what is now accepted as the first accurate description of the Kwakiutl Indians, including their tools, canoes, burial customs, etc., in considerable detail. (The nearby perfectly formed small bay was named in his honour.)

Here Menzies got the Indians to count numerals which seemed to him to be much the same as those of the east side of the Gulf of New Georgia. He found the natives of this large village under Chief Cathlagees obviously used to trading but 'tho they were free and unreserved in their manners & conversation, yet none of them would suffer any of our people to offer them any indecent familiarities, which is a modesty in some measure characteristic of their Tribe'. This suggests at least some of the crew had offered 'indecent familiarities'. At this village, which was about 60 miles north of Nootka, Menzies records that 'upwards of 200 Sea Otter skins were procured ... at more than double the value I ever saw given for them ... consequently many of our Articles of Commerce begin now to lose their intrinsic value amongst them ... iron is scarcely valued'.[24]

On a boat journey, Menzies notes the presence of seals, porpoises and whales. As a naturalist, Menzies would have been filled with awe at the sight of a surfacing killer whale and even more, if in close proximity, by the shock wave of its 10 tons smashing back into the water, showing the unique black and white patterns of its polished body. It is hardly surprising that the Indians stood in awe of such creatures, and which were so fearsomely represented in their art.

But Menzies has an encounter with a form of wildlife at the other end of the size scale in a village on a high rocky promontory. The deserted huts gave out an appalling stench, but also:

> … myriads of fleas which fixed themselves on our shoes Stockings and cloths in such incredible number that the whole party was obliged to quit the rock in great precipitation, leaving the remains of the Assailants in full possession of their Garrison without the least desire of facing again such troublesome enemy. We no sooner got to the Water side than some immediately stripped themselves quite naked & immersed their Cloth others plunged themselves wholly in the Sea in expectation of drowning their adherents, but to little or no purpose, for after being submersed for some time they leaped about as frisky as ever; in short we towd some of the Cloths astern of the Boats, but nothing would clear them of this Vermin till in the evening we steepd them in boiling water.

It was appropriately named 'Flea Village' and Menzies reckons this scourge was probably the reason the Indians had quit the village and might have been the reason for the number of deserted villages they encountered.[25] Interestingly, Vancouver, in his published account of the voyage, includes this story among a number related by Menzies, which apparently gave him the reputation of a congenial raconteur.[26]

Early in July, Menzies climbed Nipple Hill and measured its height accurately by portable barometer. In the surrounding area of the rugged Desolation Reach he discovered four new species of *Pyrola* and two of *Penstemon*, as well as the tree species *Pinus contorta* and *Pinus strobus*. Around a lake he found *Drosera rotundifolia*, *Myrica gale*, *Menyanthes trifoliata* and others typical of Scottish bogs. Later he was to find *Empetrum nigrum*, *Cornus suecica* and *Rhodiola rosea*, all characteristic of a cool wet oceanic climate.

Near the village of Chief Cathlagees, he also found *Menziesia ferruginea*, which he had previously collected in Alaska when he was with Colnett. It is one of seven species in the genus which bears his name, in the *Ericaceae* family, and is commonly called False Azalea. It has tiny urn-shaped copper-coloured flowers.[27] Menzies' portrait by Eden Upton Eddis, painted in 1836 by subscription and now in the Linnean Society lecture room in London, displays a vase with a sprig of this plant by his side. (A great-niece of Menzies records that in 1893 the species was to be seen in the rock garden of the Royal Botanic Garden Edinburgh.)

However, he could not find the spruce which was normally used for making beer and resorted to using what he called *Pinus canadensis* which was later identified as *Tsuga heterophylla* (Western Hemlock) which happily made an entirely palatable substitute. On several occasions, Menzies was required to advise the brewing parties on which species to select, although it is likely that a number of conifer species would have served the purpose.[28]

Much of the country north of Puget Sound appeared to the crews as barren and forbidding; Vancouver named it Desolation Sound and thought of it as '... truly forlorn; an awful silence pervaded the gloomy forests'.[29] This remark has to be seen in the light not only of the circumstances of such a voyage, where physical comforts were few and far between, but also that, as a result, any semblance of civilisation and human cultural activity would have been welcomed. However, Menzies and Vancouver differed in their appreciation of these overwhelming landscapes, with Menzies using words such as 'beautifull' [sic] and 'romantic', while his captain felt that 'gloomy' and 'dreary' were entirely appropriate epithets.

Between 13 July, when the expedition quitted Desolation Sound, and 6 August, when they reached Queen Charlotte Sound, the sailing up Discovery Passage and Johnstone Strait was uneventful, the weather remained fine, food from the Kwakiutl villagers was plentiful, and the crews were able to collect many sea otter pelts, as well as numerous Indian artefacts – masks, conical cedar hats and weapons. In return, some of the tools traded with the Indians subsequently resulted in a huge enhancement of local art, especially by carving with the new iron chisels replacing the previous bone and shell implements. With the addition of copper, beads and mirrors, the local people were able to produce highly decorated artefacts of every description, which are now often considered 'original' but which date from the time of such European penetration.

I Name This Place Desolation Sound, a painting by John M Horton, Marine Artist. (Courtesy of John M Horton, CMSA, FCA, Marine Artist, www.johnhorton.ca)

On 6 August 1792, the expedition almost ended in the notoriously dangerous Queen Charlotte Sound (an area known for its thousands of islands, both large and small, making it exceedingly dangerous for navigation), when the *Discovery* stuck fast on some submerged rocks, with her stern deep in the water.

A very critical situation developed, and it was only by a combination of calm conditions and the jettisoning of water, wood and ballast that the ship refloated in the early hours of the following morning. In the evening of the same day, the *Chatham* also came to grief, but was fortunately floated off by a high tide. Here the crews suffered very bad weather for several days, although in the vicinity of the Burke Channel, Menzies was impressed by 'ridges of high snowy mountains adorned with foaming Torrents tumbling headlong down their steep sides over rocks and precipices ...'.[30] It was at the junction of this channel and Bentinck Arm that Menzies Point was so named, although Menzies himself, on a boat expedition in the middle of the month, was not enamoured of their situation:

> ... we pitched our Tents on a small Isthmus for the night which continued to rain very hard throughout so that we were all wet & uncomfortable particularly the Men who had no other shelter but what they formed by the Boat Sails which were found very inadequate to screen them from the inclemency of such boisterous weather & such deluge of rain.[31]

HMS *Discovery on the Rocks, Queen Charlotte Sound.*
A contemporary watercolour by *Discovery* crewman Zachary Mudge.
(Courtesy of the Edward E. Ayer Collection, The Newberry Library, Chicago.)

Two days later, running out of food, they had to spend another very uncomfortable night in the open boats, with a wind and swell against them. With the weather now becoming continuously very cold and wet at this latitude, and the men exhausted:

> The men were no longer able to endure the fatiguing hardships of distant excursions in open Boats exposed to the cold rigorous blasts of a high northern situation with high dreary snowy mountains on every side, performing toilsome labor on their Oars in the day, & alternately watching for their own safety at night, with no other Couch to repose upon than the Cold Stony Beach or the wet mossy Turf in damp woody situations, without shelter sufficient to screen them from the inclemency of boisterous weather, & enduring at times the tormenting pangs of both hunger and thirst, yet on every occasion struggling who should be most forward in executing the orders of their superiors to accomplish the general interest of the Voyage.[32]

It was at the end of this arduous small boat journey that the crews of the *Discovery* and *Chatham* learnt of the fate of Lt. Hergest, Mr Gooch and the murdered seaman on the *Daedalus*: Menzies expends considerable space detailing the circumstances of their deaths. To add to their woes, Vancouver's health was deteriorating, with a deep disturbing cough and shortness of breath, while his appearance was not improved by his increasingly bloated figure.[33]

Menzies goes on to say that they could not have achieved what they did in a relatively short time except by the exertions of all concerned. Vancouver had had enough and decided then to retreat south to Nootka. Menzies had completed four months of botanising in very poor weather and made collections of more than 250 terrestrial plant species, including mosses, with an additional 20 or 30 lichens and an equal number of marine algae.[34]

An engraving from the published edition of Vancouver's journal, *Voyage Of Discovery To The North Pacific Ocean, And Round The World In The Years 1790–95.* The Spanish fort is to the left of the image at the area marked with a cross.

The Spanish settlement at Nootka on Friendly Cove was situated on the west coast of what is now Vancouver Island. It had been established to verify Spain's claim to sovereignty over the whole of the Northwest coast and to resist encroachment by the Russians from the north and other nations from the south. However, the most serious challenge came from the British, who used the confiscation of the very modest property of the trader John Meares as a pretext for threatening war against the Spanish. It was agreed that Spain should 'relinquish' Nootka and Vancouver had been given instructions to accept the settlement on behalf of the British Crown, but without very particular conditions.

On entry into the cove, Vancouver was punctilious in observing the formalities, firing off a 13-gun salute, which was returned by the brig of Don Juan Francisco de la Bodega y Quadra. Quadra was an aristocrat who did not believe in 'roughing it' and the expedition was impressed by his relatively luxurious house on two storeys, where he laid on quite lavish hospitality, not only for Vancouver and his officers, but also for the officers of other vessels which used this anchorage freely. Menzies identifies no fewer than 10 vessels of different nationalities at one point.

In fact, Nootka had become something of an *entrepôt* for ships of many nations, with the local Chief Maquinna orchestrating contacts and trading arrangements. The fort was well stocked with goats, sheep and cattle, while a variety of vegetables and crops were grown, which were made available to the visiting crews.

In early September they were visited by Maquinna, the most important of the Indian chiefs in this area who took a close interest in the relationships between the Spanish and the British. Quadra cleverly arranged for a combined Spanish–English party to make a preliminary visit to Maquinna at his village to show their mutual friendship, while the British arranged *en route* to have fifes and drums played which 'gave a martial solemnity to our Visit'. With Quadra's example, the Spanish and the British got along splendidly and Menzies declares that 'the party spent the evening with our new friends in social hilarity and mirth'.

Next morning the navymen provided a musical parade, were received very hospitably by Maquinna and his brothers, and introduced to Maquinna's successor, the teenage girl Apinnas, with the young princess suitably seated on a throne with her father. At this point, Menzies reports on a moving reunion:

> On turning to those seated on the other side of the house I instantly recognised in the Wife of Maquinna's Brother an old acquaintance the daughter of an elderly Chief who had a numerous family … and to whose friendship and kindness [I was indebted] when I was here about five years ago. She & her Sisters were then very young, yet they frequently shewed so much solicitude for my safety, that they often warned me in the most earnest manner of the dangers to which my Botanical rambles in the Woods exposed me & when they found me inattentive to their entreaties, they would then watch the avenue of the Forest where I enterd, to prevent my receiving any insult or ill usage from their Countrymen. But it was not

A Spanish portrait of the time of Chief Maquinna.

> until after I left them that I became sensible how much I owed to their disinterested zeal for my welfare by knowing more of the treacheries & stratagems of the Natives on other parts of the Coast – I emptied my pockets of all the little Trinkets they containd in her lap and begged her to come on board the Vessel with her Father who she told me was still alive, that I might have an opportunity of renewing our friendship by some gratifying present.[35]

Ample gifts were exchanged and the Spaniards indicated that the English were friends. The chief put on a dance, representing the different nations (Spanish, Chinese, Hawaiians) whom they had known and portrayed a mock hunt and battle, dressed for the occasion, with Maquinna himself later joining in. Instructed by Vancouver, some of the sailors did a dance. Then the party all sat down to a generous meal of porpoise and tunny served on Quadra's silver plate and with all his fine utensils, which apparently set the requisite tone of dignity. Vancouver was sufficiently impressed by this astute chief to lay on a fireworks display several days later in his honour. Vancouver apparently went out of his way to establish friendly relations with natives, and his own high respect for authority gave him a sensitivity as to what was required in the way of paying respect to important chiefs.[36]

A different sort of honour was bestowed on Menzies when, on 8 September, with the formal invaliding of the expedition's surgeon Cranstoun and his retirement to

England, he was asked to become surgeon. Initially Menzies was reluctant to accept, surmising that the duties might well interfere with his natural history activities and that this would place him much more directly under Vancouver's authority.[37]

However, Vancouver was insistent, and gave assurances on this point. He went as far as to demand that if Menzies refused, he would require to have this stated in writing for the Admiralty, which would not have been helpful to Menzies. In any case, it is clear that Menzies had been acting virtually in the capacity of ship's surgeon (including treating Vancouver) since they left South Africa, with the increasing illness of Cranstoun.

> Captain Vancouver's earnest solicitations has induced me to accept of his place, with the proviso that he will be careful it will interfere as little as possible with my other pursuits. Indeed I have in some measure attended the surgeon's duty since we left the Cape of Good Hope ... I have by this means got an additional cabin which will be serviceable in preserving my collections.[38]

Menzies also treated Quadra at his request: 'On my arrival at Nootka he put himself under my care for a severe headache, of which he said he complained of upwards of two years, and I was extremely happy that my endeavours was in some measure serviceable toward his recovery before his departure.'

While Vancouver and Quadra remained on the friendliest terms, they made little headway on the handover of Nootka. They clearly had different views on what was involved, with Quadra politely being prepared to concede the small area previously occupied by Meares, while Vancouver was preparing to take possession of the whole settlement and the raising of the British flag there. Both used the undoubted lack of precise instructions from their superiors to suspend negotiations, though apparently entirely amicably. In the meantime, Menzies was able to send a package of seeds via Lt. Mudge who was taking dispatches back to England, reporting that subsequently a number of these were successfully germinated and grown by William Aiton at Kew. It was at Nootka that he had first met the Spanish botanists Don Jose Mozino and Atanasio Echevarria – the latter he considered an excellent artist and draughtsman. Before Quadra's departure for California, where he was to take up post at San Blas, there was a round of entertainments and dinners with much reciprocal hospitality. On board the *Discovery* on its departure for California on 12 October were two young Hawaiian women whom Captain Baker of the *Jenny* now wished to return to their homeland, after he had quite illegally taken them from the islands.

On the route south, the expedition was able to view the snow-covered Mount Olympus. Vancouver decided to explore the Columbia River and sent the *Chatham* as the smaller vessel on ahead, under Lt. Johnstone. Due to very unfavourable weather, by 22 October the *Discovery* was forced to retreat from the Columbia. The incident exposes how vulnerable these vessels were to sudden storms while they were in narrow passages of unknown depths, which could spell disaster at any moment.

NOTES

1. Justice (1991a), 127–30
2. Turnbull (1954), 282–3
3. Menzies Journal, 16 May 1792
4. Ibid., 1 May 1792
5. Gorsline (1992), 21
6. Lindsay (2005), 130
7. Menzies Journal, 2 May 1792
8. Puget, quoted in Raban (1999), 63–4
9. Menzies Journal, 8 May 1792
10. Ibid., 7 May 1792
11. Justice variously calls this Fairy Slipper and Pink Lady Slipper, but the Lady's Slipper Orchid is a separate if related genus, *Cypripedium.*
12. Menzies Journal, 4 May 1792
13. Ibid., 20 May 1792
14. Groves (1998), 97
15. Turnbull (1954), 280
16. Menzies Journal, 24 July 1794
17. Ibid., 1 June 1792
18. Ibid., 5 May 1792
19. Ibid., 6 June 1792
20. Raban (1999), 176
21. Ibid., 176
22. Menzies Journal, 12 July 1792
23. Ibid., 19 June 1792
24. Ibid., 20 July 1792
25. Ibid., 27 June 1792
26. Turnbull (1954), 283
27. Justice (2000), 85
28. In Eastern Canada, the equivalent is *Tsuga canadensis*, i.e. Canada Hemlock. Western Hemlock is found as an amenity tree on many British estates.
29. Lamb (1984), 601
30. Menzies Journal, 13 August 1792
31. Ibid., 15 August 1792
32. Ibid., 18 August 1792
33. Apart from Menzies Point in the Burke Channel, there were two other locations named after the botanist: Menzies Bay in Discovery Passage opposite Quadra Island on Vancouver Island, and Menzies Island in the Columbia River, which has subsequently been renamed Hayden Island. Mount Menzies (1239 m) situated just north of the Campbell River was also named in his honour. All the other senior officers

had locations named after them, which remain on today's maps.

34. Justice (2000), 77
35. Menzies Journal, 5 September 1792
36. Turnbull (1954), 280
37. Keevil (1948), 800
38. Menzies to Banks, Monterey, 14 January 1793

13

'Such Diabolical Treachery'

After a very tedious and frustrating journey of seven weeks from Hawaii due to contrary weather, the expedition arrived at Nootka on the British Columbia coast on 20 May 1793 for their second season of surveying. (By contrast the *Chatham* had taken a mere two weeks and was anxiously awaiting the main vessel.) They had learned a hard lesson from their previous work in the Northwest and Menzies details the considerable improvements which had been made to shelter both men and officers on the small survey boats, and covering provisions and dry clothes, and to provide greater security for their arms. Both of these were to prove very necessary in the coming months of demoralising weather, while they investigated probably the most convoluted and intricate coastline in the whole world.[1]

In a letter to Banks, Menzies asked to be considered for the post of medical officer to any settlement which Britain might establish on this coast. This says a great deal about Menzies' commitment to his studies and also his attachment to this country which has some similarities to the West Highlands of his native Scotland. 'I continue daily, with much delight, augmenting my knowledge and collections of the Natural History of this country which keeps my mind in a continual scene of amusement.'

In the same month Menzies witnessed the historic meeting between the powerful Chief Wackanish and Chief Maquinna, for the betrothal of Wackanish's teenage son to Maquinna's daughter, Apinnas, at a highly ceremonial occasion. Wackanish and his tribespeople arrived with about 40 canoes, some with 10–15 paddlers and holding up to 40 people, which Menzies reckoned must have totalled 1000 people. There was a great choreographed arrival with the canoes lined up abreast, the paddlers beating time with their paddles on the sides of the canoes, while the people sang, creating a great echo in the bowl of the surrounding hills. All of the chiefs were impressively robed in furs, while others were dressed as animals such as deer, fox and bear. Tribespeople on the beach had painted their faces and hair, to produce what Menzies called the 'most grotesque figures'. The British party were very fortunate to be in time to observe such an unusual and colourful sight, while Menzies was very impressed by the fine physiques of the chiefs and their brothers, and the display of robes and dresses.

There were impassioned and lengthy speeches by both Wackanish and Maquinna, lasting over four hours, with exchanges of expensive gifts, although the onus was clearly on the groom's father to ensure that his presents were sufficient to secure the hand of Maquinna's daughter. In the event, and despite the number of skins, furs and sheets of copper, he had to send back for more to satisfy him. In all of this, Menzies was apparently received in the most friendly fashion and was able to question the young groom, a youth of about 14 years, who revealed that he had not seen his future bride, which was the accepted custom.[2]

It is clear from this that while Vancouver had little time for what he considered outlandish native dances and ceremonial, Menzies, by contrast, took such Indian traditions seriously. Likewise, Vancouver was very slow to recognise that along this lengthy coastline, different tribes had very different customs and cultures and their reactions to white visitors depended very much on the extent of previous contact with them. Menzies for example noted that at Nootka, the going rate for otter skins had multiplied by some 200% since his previous visit with Colnett.

On 23 May, the *Discovery* sailed out of Nootka to rendezvous near Queen Charlotte Sound with the *Chatham* whose officers were very much relieved to see Vancouver's ship, thinking that after such a delay, some misfortune must have befallen her. Here they set up the observatory marquee (where because of weather conditions they encountered great difficulty in obtaining accurate astronomical fixes) and brewed spruce beer 'from *Pinus canadensis*' (*Tsuga heterophylla*). Johnstone set off in one of the small boats to recommence the survey carried out in the previous year. On 3 June, Menzies records the astonishment of one young chief that by Vancouver's embargo, the crews were unable to barter for his plentiful otter skins, but also adds the interesting comment: 'They [the Indians] had no women with them this time more than formerly tho' they had been solicited to bring them.'

Elsewhere, in the vicinity of Fisher's Channel, Menzies records his surprise at the size of Indian houses, supported by huge beams, and the engineering skills that had gone into their construction. Of the monumental house posts ('totem poles') he stated: 'These monstrous figures were fantastically ornamented with carvings of smaller human faces in different parts, particularly in the eyes of each figure.'[3] One of the regular characteristics of Indian ornamentation was symmetry in the form of doubles of each image – the mirror image which the Indians would have seen so frequently in reflections from water, and which Raban ascribes to the maritime environment which dominated every aspect of their culture.[4]

On one of his solitary shore excursions in this area, Menzies captures very well the unnerving atmosphere of a very silent coastal valley:

> ... I found a good deal of low meadow land, but no traces of human beings were to be seen, nor no Animals whatever to enjoy the pasture; an awfull stillness pervaded the whole valley. The sheet of water before me presented a smooth glassy surface reflecting from its bosom the dark verdurous forest that covered the steep ascent on each side, the shrill notes of a few gulls, the wild croaks of some passing Ravens & the tedious hissing noise of distant Cataracts could hardly be said to interrupt the general silence which prevailed in this solitary gloom,

> circumscribed on all sides by a barrier of high mountains whose summits were whitened over with the stormy produce of many winters.

Menzies had a difficult journey back to the beach without a compass through thick forest and with many dead trees across his path.[5]

Something of this forbidding atmosphere of the grey-green waters and endless forest affected Vancouver himself:

> ... as desolate inhospitable a country as the most melancholy creature could be desirous of inhabiting. The eagle, crow, and raven, that occasionally had borne us company in our lonely researches, visited not these dreary shores ... and the ruins of one miserable hut was the only indication we saw that human beings ever resorted to the country before us.[6]

What Vancouver considered 'dreary' landscapes and their wildlife is now the basis of a very flourishing tourist industry paradoxically exploiting this sense of wild remoteness as the great cruise ships negotiate the famous 'Inside Passage' to Alaska.

The boat expeditions often encountered more practical problems, with weather so bad that even the protective awnings had to be taken in while the men attempted to sleep aboard, huddled together in considerable discomfort. On these rocky and precipitous shores they found it difficult to locate a suitable camping place, and on more than one occasion their tent was flooded by the incoming tide, forcing them to seek shelter in the dripping woods higher up. Several of these expedition boats would be away from the mother ships simultaneously, and considerable skill had to be exercised in maintaining communications and making arrangements for a rendezvous, complicated by fog and ferocious gales.

On the shores of the Kitimat Arm Menzies found *Linnaea borealis* (Twinflower) in great abundance and at his insistence, the boat's crew gathered and boiled the leaves of '*Ligusticum scoticum*' (Beach Lovage) and the whole plant of *Salicornia virginica* (American Pickleweed) in order to supplement their diet with green vegetables. '*Ledum groenlandicum*' (now *Rhododendron groenlandicum* or Labrador Tea) was gathered in quantity to make substitute tea, which Menzies said 'made a drink that was very palatable and salubrious beverage not inferior in those qualities to the manufactured teas of China'.[7] On 10 July 1793 he found a number of alpine plants on some islands in the Douglas Channel which were new to him, including two new species of *Gentiana*, a dwarf *Vaccinium*, and a new species of *Sanguisorba* (Burnet), among an assemblage of species which would not have been out of place in the upland bogs of Scotland.

One medical emergency which Menzies had not anticipated was a lethal case of food poisoning. On a boat journey headed by Lt. Johnstone, food became short and the crew devoured mussels which they found on shore. The results were immediate, with virtually everyone prostrated. Despite their best efforts, one seaman, John Carter, died, while the remainder were out of action for a week after their return to the main ship. Menzies described their symptoms as numbness in the limbs and extremities, giddiness, with men unable to stand, and nausea. Lieutenant Manby says:

> In a few minutes, the whole were seized with convulsive pains, unusual swellings, and every other symptom produced by poison … the Rocky inhospitable shore not affording sufficient Earth to receive the remains of our departed Countryman, the Body was consigned to a watery grave, and to commemorate the name of the deceased, this inland Navigation was called after him Carter's Passage.[8]

Concentrations of sea otters were scattered but on 10 July Menzies observed several hundreds of the animals. The young who were unable to dive were left on the surface when the females dived at the approach of the boats, but the females immediately resurfaced to carry off their young. Menzies records that they succeeded in getting one young otter into their boat, but the noise of a gun 'brought the Dam after us & she made frequent attempts to rescue it by approaching near the boat at the hazard of its own life, which shews the great affection of these Animals for their young'. At this time he was very anxious to capture a sea otter as he had not seen a whole animal out of the water; he subsequently wrote one of his few scientific papers on this species' morphology.[9] The scarcity of otter skins is hardly remarkable considering Menzies notes that the English ship the *Butterworth* had collected more than 3000 skins and had only been prevented from gathering more by lack of trade goods.[10]

There would have been no lack of food for the otters, according to his description of a run of salmon in July:

> … this being about the beginning of the spawning season for the Salmon on this coast, a stream of fresh water that emptied into the bay swarm'd with them, though there was scarcely water sufficient to cover them, so that they could be caught with the hand in any quantity we chose; in shooting the Seine across the entrance to this Stream it surrounded such a prodigious quantity of the Salmon that it was impossible to haul them all on shore without endangering the Seine …

(One account says that in a single set of the seine they captured 2000 salmon.)

There were many encounters with native people of different tribes and Menzies used his usual technique of getting them to count up to 10 to identify similarities and differences in their languages, which seems to have been quite successful. He gives detailed descriptions of their customs including the lip ornament, or labret, noting the link between this and the status of women. Earlier the men who had not been on this coast before were appalled to see that a number of them wore these wooden mouthpieces, some as long as three inches. According to Menzies:

> … it gives these women a most unnatural and disgusting appearance, as they have the power of depressing it over their chin or elevating it over their nose at pleasure. … This horrid custom of piercing the underlip prevails among the women from Queen Charlotte Sound all along the Coast to Admiralty (Yakutat) Bay near

> Mount St Elias; what was the origin of such strange deformity we could not learn, but it is now so general among them, particularly with women of rank, that they vie with one another in putting their lips upon the utmost stretch round these pieces, at least we observed in our former visit to this Coast that the Chiefs Wives always had the largest pieces, which are sometimes carved or neatly inlaid with pearly shells or bits of Copper.[11]

Not all of their meetings with the Indians were harmonious and on 12 August Menzies provides a minute-by-minute account of a potentially lethal encounter:

> ... four of these canoes containing about 36 natives approached the launch, carolling and holding up Sea Otter Skins with all the alluring signs of friendship; as soon as they joined us they threw two of these skins into the boat & took the first things that were offered in return with apparent satisfaction without driving a bargain for them as the Natives we had hitherto met with generally did; after some more were offerd, in doing which, they crouded close in at different times to take hold of the Boat, but as they were at first easily kept off by gentle admonition, we thought only that their eagerness for Trafic might induce them to be thus forward.

One of the larger canoes was apparently commanded by an old woman, directing the Indians to harass the surveyors, who were obliged to surreptitiously get out their arms from the chests. Then, as Menzies recalls, things turned nasty:

> The Pinnace was about quitting the Point after Captain Vancouver had taken the angles, when we approached her & were alarmed to see her closely surrounded by the Natives brandishing their Spears, though we were uncertain what they were about till Lieutenant Puget called upon us to fire upon the natives, that they were attacking the Pinnace; we were then within pistol shot of them with all our Arms at hand & already loaded; on seeing our promptitude they dropped their Spears & kept waving their hands at us calling Woagan, a word which implies friendship, notwithstanding which we instantly obeyed the order & discharged a Volley among them, on which the greater part of them plunged into the Water & and those that were able swam to the shore leaving their canoes adrift; others paddled to the shore expos'd to a heavy firing, among these we observed the old woman left alone in the large Canoe which she very coolly secured before she retreated to a place of safety for herself.
>
> As it was necessary to punish these natives with severity to deter them & others from such rash attempts in future we continued firing at them from the Launch with Muskets and Wall pieces till those that reached the shore escapd into the Wood and hid themselves behind Trees and Rocks. The pinnace having pulled immediately off from the scene of action made us apprehensive that some lives were lost or in imminent danger in her, which made us the more anxious to punish the authors of such cruel & savage barbarity by committing every depredation

> against them, and as their Canoes were in our power. Mr Swaine hail'd the pinnace to ask Captain Vancouver if he would destroy them, he answered to let them alone till he join'd us, on which we lay by, firing a Musket now & then whenever any of them were seen stirring in the wood, for when they saw us approach their canoes they began throwing stones from behind the Rocks & discharged a Musket or two at us, neither of which did us any injury.[12]

Two seamen were severely wounded and subsequently attended to by Menzies and it was a very dangerous situation before the launch came to their rescue. Another small boat crew from the *Columbia* had been murdered about two years previously near this location and Menzies considered that the success of the Indians on that occasion might have encouraged the attack on the *Discovery*'s boats. The Tlingit tribe here were known to be aggressive and treacherous. The wounded men, although kept comfortable, were not able to get treatment for their spear wounds until they reached the *Discovery* four days later, after an expedition of three weeks on only two weeks' provisions.

Menzies directs a diatribe against the Indians:

> ... when we considered their unprovok'd attack & the manner in which they were proceeding to butcher the Pinnace's Officers & crew in cold blood we can hardly think any punishment too severe for such diabolical treachery. Lenity on such occasions assumes the aspect of a crime, as Savages are apt to construe it into a Victory obtain'd over their opponents, & which afterwards stimulates them to the perpetration of cruelties with the most audacious temerity, but as a just resentment, a timely & severe chastisement would readily check their treacherous conduct & deter them from committing actions so disgracefull to humanity.[13]

What of course Menzies does not mention is that the British would have been regarded as intruders, notwithstanding the desirability of their trade goods. However, the seriousness of this incident served to put the crews very much on their guard in all future encounters with large groups of Indians. (Later that summer one of the boat expeditions was again seriously threatened by a large armed group of Tlingit Indians who initially professed to be peaceable but were clearly bent on plunder.)

Despite this, one of the Indians expressed a desire to journey to England with the ships, but at that time, according to Menzies: '... punishments were inflicted on board the *Discovery* of a very unpleasant nature, on seeing which all of the natives left the bay, & he that before was so solicitous to go with us now went away without taking leave of us & never afterwards returned to the Vessels'.[14] This was no doubt a flogging which the surgeon would have to attend and deal with the aftermath. In a subsequent visit to Alaska, it was deemed necessary to flog an Indian: an attempt by natives to steal the rudder chains of the *Discovery* resulted in the thieves, two women and a man, being put in chains for a night. The man was subsequently given four dozen lashes before being released – he was later very friendly and seemed to bear no ill will, while the women visited the ship for medical attention.

In late August and September the weather was very bad, with incessant storms and heavy rains, at one point forcing one of the small boats to remain in the same position for three days. Botanising was unsuccessful, as Menzies indicates on 11 September: '... took a stroll in the woods but found nothing new, nor indeed scarcely any Plant in flower, for the season was now so far spent that the cold boisterous weather set in & check'd the progress of vegetation, so that I made but a short excursion'.

NOTES

1. Menzies Journal, 29 May 1793
2. Ibid., 21 May 1793
3. Ibid., 12 June 1793
4. Raban (1999), 24
5. Menzies Journal, 6 June 1793
6. Vancouver, quoted in Raban (1999), 312
7. Groves (2001), 89
8. Manby, quoted in Raban (1999), 335
9. Menzies, A. (1796), 'Anatomy of the Sea Otter', *Transactions of the Royal Society*
10. Menzies Journal, 10 July 1793
11. Ibid., 16 June 1793
12. Ibid., 12 August 1793
13. Ibid., 12 August 1793
14. Ibid., 28 August 1793

14

'An End to a Laborious Exercise'

After wintering in Hawaii, the expedition was again back on the Northwest coast in 1794 for the third season of survey. Vancouver headed directly for the northernmost point for his survey at Cook Inlet, working his way southwards. Menzies was critical of Cook's assumption of a much larger inlet at the so-called Cook's Gulph which the navigator suggested might be the North West Passage. Thus there was a great deal of speculation that this was indeed the passage, but Menzies indicated that if his boats had proceeded a little way further, they would have found the termination of this inlet:

> ... we directed our course along the coast to Cook's River, which we pursued to its utmost extremity, and You will no doubt, Sir, be equally surprised as we were, when I inform You that it is only an Inlet of the Sea, similar to many other great Inlet[s] on this coast ... we were much entangled & perplexed with drift Ice, and about the latter end of April, experienced heavy falls of Snow, and intense frost, the Mercury in the Thermometer fell so low as the seventh degree of Fahrenheit's scale, and I am sorry to acquaint you, that this severe and quick transition of Climate, killed the greatest part of the live plants, I had in the frame on the QuarterDeck, & this is more to be regretted, as I am afraid it will not be in my power to replace many of them, particularly those from California & the upper regions of Owhyhee [Hawaii] ...
>
> ... we cannot well reconcile Capt. Cook's account of this part of the coast to his usual precision and accuracy.[1]

He tells of meeting with native people who from his description appear to be Inuit tribesmen or possibly Athabascans and who behaved quite differently from the Indians met with previously:

> They were well cloathd from head to foot with long frocks of Racoon skins; their hands were covered with fur mittens, and their legs with leather boots, so that they were well equipped to withstand the rigor of the climate. They had broad flat visages & wore their hair cropped short around the nape of the neck.

Later he was to develop his observations:

> The Natives of this great Inlet or Gulph [Cook Inlet] are of a low stature, but thick and stout made with fat broad visages black eyes and straight black hair, their

> mouth and nose are generally small. In their disposition they seemed to be good naturd friendly & peaceable & during our stay amongst them, they gave us very little reason even to suspect either their fidelity or honesty. Most of their implements exhibit a degree of neatness in the execution, that far surpassed all other rude nations we met with, for if we examined their clothing & see with what care they form & sow them, so as not to admit the least drop of rain; and their canoes are equally neat having their Seams sowd so tight as not to admit any water. Their harpoon darts cordage & little leather belts shew a degree of art that would do credit even to the most civilised nations.

This is a typical example of Menzies' acute observation and ability to convey characteristics succinctly. Later he observes the natives in not fewer than 150 canoes accompanying the ship to try to sell their handiwork.

Menzies continues:

> In our dealings with this Tribe we could not but be struck with their candour and implicit confidence for as few of them were admitted on board & the canoes were too numerous to get all close alongside, they would frequently hand on board their little bags containing the articles to be disposed of from the furthest off canoe & suffered as many of us as pleased to overhauls them, & to fix upon what we likd, whilst the Owner sat composedly in their canoes without shewing the least uneasiness or apparent suspicion.

By 19 March, when they had reached the Knik Arm in Cook Inlet, a little further than where Cook himself had turned back, the crews were suffering from the change in climate: '... the frost was now so very intense, that a little before we got under way this morning the thermometer was so low as 7 degrees, at eight it was 13 degrees & at noon it was no higher than 18 degrees the effect of which was that several of our people were frost bit in performing their duty on this and the preceeding day'. In Glacier Bay and vicinity, they found large icebergs, and masses of drift ice which impeded their progress, while off Prince William Sound, Johnstone endured the most serious storm of his long life at sea.

At the end of April, the expedition had its first meeting with the Russians, a party of about 10 in a large whaleboat, rowed by 14 natives: '... they were very desirous of spirituous liquor & tobacco, of both which they had a small supply ...'. The Russians under Bering had explored this area as early as 1741 and shortly afterwards established settlements for fur trading on a considerable scale, using local people as hunters. The extent of this trade is indicated by a report by Johnstone at Comptrollers Bay where he met a party of nine or ten Russians, with a fleet of about 450 skin canoes containing more than 900 Indians from Cook's Gulf and the island of Kodiak, all hunters and warriors, headed by the Russian Egor Purtov. He reported that they had left Cook's Gulf five or six weeks previously with a fleet of 700 canoes, dropping off groups of these along the coast to hunt for sea otters.

On 10 May Vancouver visited the Russians:

> On entering [the settlement] we observed several men drawn up under arms, which they immediately laid down on our approach, & we were then conducted into a large log house by a narrow passage guarded by a sentinel, after passing which, we entered a long area in the middle of the house, and were desired to walk to the further end of it, where we were seated on a bench by a small table.

After describing the primitive beds of bare boards covered only by a deer or bear skin, Menzies reports:

> ... they set upon the table before us, some cold dryd halibut & narrow stripes of dried raw salmon as a substitute for bread, but we could not make use of it, for the stench which assailed our Nostrils on entring the settlement made us loathe everything, it was really suffocating & such as we could not long endure – it rose from the putrid filth & garbage of animals that had been strewd about the place during the winter time, which being now thawd, and the effluvia set in motion by the suns eschalation, produced such a penetrative and putrid stench round the place that we were much astonished how any human beings could exist in such a tainted & pestiferous atmosphere, & yet these people had all a very healthy appearance, though they have neither bread nor flour nor liquor but live entirely on the Produce of the country like the natives.

Menzies records sickness and vomiting among some of the British sailors, apparently caused by a quantity of tobacco accidentally falling into their soup – the only men affected were those who did not use tobacco, hence the severity of their symptoms. More seriously, he describes a quarrel between shipmates which resulted in a quite accidental but serious wound from a spear used by one of the officers to separate the men. Although the wound was successfully treated by him, the other man involved was given four dozen lashes for quarrelsome behaviour. More happily, on 4 June, the ship's crews celebrated the King's birthday with a double ration of grog to drink His Majesty's health, which according to Menzies 'we were sure was done with as much fervency and loyalty in this remote corner of the globe as in the capitals of his dominions. The evening was afterwards spent in jollity and mirth'.[2]

Meeting up with the Russians at their substantial settlement at Port Etches, Menzies writes how they were apparently received very well:

> ... the commandant spread out his little table with such fare as he had before them, which consisted of a piece of boild seal with part of the hairy skin still adhering to it, some fish oil & a few boiled eggs; these articles not being very inviting to people accustomed to a different diet, & as their politeness could not on this occasion overcome the delicacy of their appetite, Mr Johnstone beggd leave to add some chocolate beef and bread to the repast on the table, which was readily granted & to which their host & the next to him in command did ample justice.[3]

Later Johnstone, by way of return for the commandant's hospitality, presented him with a gallon and a half of rum, with predictable results:

> Mr Colomnee [the commandant] joyfully expressed that he had not had such a quantity of spirituous liquor in his possession in a long time, & indeed the intemperate use he soon made of it provd it to be a fortunate circumstance for him that it had been so, for Mr Johnstone observes that most of the Russians hitherto met with in this country were immoderately fond of spirituous liquors & whenever it was in their power, used them to the greatest excess … it was distressing now to behold a man far advanced in years & whose venerable deportment & superior station had justly entitled him to their respect suddenly become the object of their pity by indulging in that obnoxious vice.[4]

By mid-June the weather was balmy, and Menzies was entranced by the beautiful mountain scenery in Prince William Sound near Stockdale's Harbour where in the woodland clearings he collected many plants including a new species of whortleberry and two new species of *Vaccinium*: he was obviously in his element with the late thaw. Later he reports Johnstone's observation of a large avalanche plunging into the sea and how the ice floes had worn the copper bottoms of the ships, which had to be repaired.

The crews were greatly impeded by wind and rain on a boat expedition in the vicinity of Point Whidbey, coupled with a strong current which according to Menzies:

> … put almost everyone in bad humour at the extent & direction it was likely to carry us, but for my own part the little acquisitions I was able to make here and there to Botany, more than compensated for whatever I felt on the score of repining. Amongst them was a beautiful new species of *Caltha* which I named *Caltha celiarius.* I also met with *Caltha palustris* for the first time on this coast. After a fatiguing row we advanced this day about 24 miles …

(Menzies' descriptions of these boat expeditions suggest that he took his share on the oars.) At Port Armstrong he collected quantities of Marsh Samphire (*Salicornia*) as greens for the men and whortleberries for pies and made daily excursions on shore to fill his plant frame 'to be added to His Majesties' valuable collection of Exotics at Kew'. By this time, Menzies had become seriously concerned about the state of health of many of the men.[5]

At Point Brightman the crew of one of the small boats found they were on the last day of their provisions, barely sufficient to reach the ships which were at least 120 miles distant – a journey of at least four days, largely by rowing. They eventually arrived via Cross Sound having travelled some 600 miles in the open boats in about 16 days – a remarkable feat of seamanship and endurance. By 15 August at Port Armstrong, Vancouver and his crew were anxiously awaiting the return of the last survey party now long overdue – double the time expected. Menzies wrote: 'Nothing but a tedious state of suspense occupied our minds.' Vancouver, who had become acutely melancholy and depressed during this anxious time, was hugely elated and relieved at the sight of the four boats after three days of waiting, and uncharacteristically gave way to his emotions in writing:

> ... exciting in the bosoms of our little community sensations of a nature so pleasing and satisfactory that few are likely to experience in the same degree ... for as they returned altogether, it was to our minds a presumptive proof that they had finished the laborious & intricate examination of this coast ... thus put an end so successfully to a tedious & laborious enterprise for the completion of which an uncommon zeal had activated every individual to the most unwearied and persevering exertions, under all the circumstances of hardships & laborious toils of dangers & difficulties to which the nature of the service unavoidably exposed them they on all occasions performd their duty with alacrity, & cheerfulness, & with a manly perseverance that contributed to the highest degree to attain the great object in view. Every one was elated with the most pleasing sensations & the fondest hopes of returning home to enjoy repose in the bosom of their country & amongst their dearest connections. All work was suspended & the rest of the day was devoted to festivity & convivial mirth, enlivened by an additional allowance of grog, whilst the social pleasure of recounting past dangers & future expectations alternately beguiled the happy hour over the flowing cup.[6]

If some of this appears 'over the top' it is worth remembering that at this point the expedition had been away from home for three years and four months and only that summer, via an English ship, the crews had learnt of the death of Louis XVI some 18 months earlier. Many of them were comparatively young: the midshipman George McKenzie of Edinburgh was only 16 when he joined the expedition, and only two of the ships' complements were over 40. The exaltation at having completed the work was marred by one of the very few casualties of the voyage, when one of the seamen, Isaac Wooden, accidentally fell, hitting his head on the gunwale of one of the boats and disappearing over the side, despite the efforts made to retrieve him. According to Menzies he was '... a quite peaceable man much respected by all his shipmates'. (In fact he had been given 72 lashes in August 1792 for being party to 'the embezzlement of the King's canvas' when he received some of this material from the sailmaker who stole it.)

Menzies also makes the point, in comparing the surveys of the different cutters, that these had revealed a number of omissions from the previous season which if they had known about would have considerably reduced their work. He says:

> These & other instances ought to teach us to speak with the utmost diffidence of our having all along traced the continental shore, notwithstanding that every degree of precaution was in general made use of yet such was the expeditious nature of the service, performed often in obscure & inclement weather & such the difficulty

> of tracing al the windings of such an intricate labyrinth through a region so dreary and broken that it is impossible to pronounce such a laborious task as infallible.[7]

For his part Vancouver was quite clear on what had to be done next:

> Mr Whidbey had my directions to take possession of the said continent from New Georgia north-westward to Cape Spencer, as also of the adjacent islands we had discovered within those limits; in the name of, and for, His Britannic Majesty, his heirs and successors ... the colours were displayed, the boats' crews drawn up under arms, and possession taken under the discharge of three vollies of musketry, with all the other formalities usual on such occasions ...[8]

Lieutenant Whidbey had taken charge of most of the boat surveys from mid-summer onwards, since Vancouver's own health had deteriorated rapidly and he was confined to his cabin for days at a time, becoming increasingly morbid and morose while he was out of touch with the survey parties.

They entered Nootka Sound on 2 September 1794, having delineated the North American coast from Baja California to Cook Inlet in Alaska, including an estimated 10,000 miles of survey in small boats. By any standards it was a remarkable achievement. Vancouver had completed one of the longest journeys in the history of exploration with only accidental (if a presumed suicide is discounted) loss of life. This had been achieved despite often atrocious weather conditions on a coast renowned for its topographical complexity, while their encounters with local native peoples had on the whole been peaceable.[9] Apart from the charting of this difficult coast, Vancouver had once and for all disproved the existence of a so-called North West Passage which some had thought might lead from the Cook River at latitude 60 degrees North.

It was said that they had concluded one of the greatest and most strenuous voyages of discovery.[10] The expedition had undoubtedly had its dangers and adventure, but also no doubt its periods of boredom for many of the crew, which Menzies largely overcame by his passion for plant collecting and identification, not to mention his interest in native languages and customs. However, referring to an enforced delay at Nootka while Vancouver awaited further orders from home apropos the Nootka affair, Menzies was to write to Banks on 1 October 1794: '... we do not know how long we may still remain in this dreary country, of which we are all heartily tired & look for the moment of our return with a considerable degree of anxiety'. One wonders if he still wished to be appointed to a future British settlement as he had previously requested.

From Monterey, the expedition had a very tedious journey south, with unfavourable winds which slowed their progress to only 40 miles a day for over a month. They suffered 'the most parching and oppressive heat we ever experienced at sea', with water supplies running low.[11] However, by 23 January they reached Cocos Island where they found plentiful wood, water and coconuts and where they also found, by a curious coincidence, a message in a bottle left by Colnett on his voyage in the

Rattler two years previously. But here Menzies was saddened by the loss of the seeds and seedlings from the island when the surf washed them out of his boat.

However, their next stop at the north end of the Galapagos chain was said by Menzies to be '... the most dreary, barren and desolate country I ever beheld ... whose sides here and there covered with tufts of dry shrivelled grass, with a few low scattering bushes, but all the lower ground was strewed over with black rugged lava and scoria, without the least appearance of either soil, vegetation or fresh water'. But when he and Whidbey landed, they found it teeming with life, an extraordinary conjunction of polar and tropical life forms with 'Seals and Penguins in abundance, while the surface of the adjacent sea ... swarmed with large Lizards'.[12]

Although in this part of the Galapagos Islands there were none of the famous tortoises and turtles on land, there were many porpoises and whales offshore, and he discovered a new dove which he named '*Columba leucoptera*'.[13] When they eventually arrived at the Spanish port, Menzies was not impressed by Valparaiso: '... like the other Spanish settlements to the northward, falls far short of our expectation, it is at best but a shabby appearance, scattered round the bottom of the bay, though it seems to be a place of considerable traffic ...'.[14]

However, they were well received, and Menzies writes:

> ... the distant inland mountains are seen covered with perpetual Snow. Peaches, Apples, Grapes and vegetables in general are here in great abundance, and other refreshments are very reasonable which is very fortunate for the Scurvy a little before our arrival had made its appearance among our people in our long ill-chosen passage from Monterey, but they are now perfectly recovered again; and I have the pleasure to tell you that in both vessels we have only lost one man by disease since we left England and he died of the Flux [dysentery] soon after we left the Cape of Good Hope.
>
> Our tedious and sultry passage from Monterey proved fatal to many of my little favourites, the live plants from the Northwest coast of California notwith-standing my utmost attention and endeavour to save them, but I have now again filled up most of the vacancies, and as it is supposed we shall touch somewhere to the southward between this and Cape Horn, I hope I shall be able further to augment my Collection – here I have been able to make but a very small addition to my Hortus siccus, owing to the particular season of the year, and the dry scorched state of the country.[15]

This is interesting on a number of counts, not the least being the implied criticism of Vancouver for his 'ill-chosen passage' but also for the remarkable survival of the crew over a very extended voyage covering a wide range of climatic regimes. Menzies is also making it clear to Banks that despite the vicissitudes of the voyage, he is attending to his duty regarding His Majesty's plants.

As anticipated, the voyage round Cape Horn was difficult, with violent storms and ships which were badly in need of serious repairs and refurbishment, the ropes and cables worn, sails patched, and barely enough anchors to secure the ships. However, they reached St. Helena in sufficiently good order to seize as a prize the Dutch ship *Macassar*, since Vancouver had learned that Britain was now at war with Holland. (This seizure resulted in an extended wrangle for prize money, with both the Governor Colonel Robert Brooke and the Vice-Admiral of the Fleet Elphinstone claiming a part for their actions.) Lieutenant Johnstone was put in charge of this slow and leaky ship to sail her back to England with a reduced crew of 17, which also inevitably depleted the manpower on board the other two expedition ships after their departure on the last leg home on 15 July. This may have contributed to a serious altercation between Menzies and Vancouver on the issue of securing the plant frame.

NOTES

1. Menzies to Banks, Nootka Sound, 8 September 1794
2. Menzies, 4 June 1794, in Olson (1993), 118
3. Menzies, 8 June 1794, in Olson (1993), 128
4. Ibid., 131
5. Ibid., 168
6. Lamb (1984), 1371
7. Menzies Journal, 19 August 1794
8. Lamb (1984), 1382
9. Naish (1996), 351
10. Turnbull (1954), 280
11. Menzies Journal, 15 January 1795
12. Menzies to Banks, 7 February 1795
13. Coleman (1988), 119. (The dove referred to is probably the Galapagos Dove *Zenaida galapogoensis* – R. Mitchell, pers. comm.)
14. Menzies to Banks, Valparaiso, 28 April 1795. Banks Correspondence 2: 121, Royal Botanic Gardens, Kew
15. Menzies to Banks, 28 April 1795. Banks Correspondence 2: 121, Royal Botanic Gardens, Kew

15

'This Fatal Neglect'

Following a period of torrential rain after leaving St. Helena, it was found that the covers of the plant frame had not been replaced and virtually all of Menzies' treasured plant collection, garnered with such effort and difficulty, was ruined. Unfortunately the *Discovery* had no scuppers, so that when rain fell heavily, or the sea washed in, the plant hutch acted like a bathtub with no drain, if the wooden gratings and protective tarpaulins were not replaced.[1] (In a letter to Banks Menzies refers to previous losses and those of 'the live plants from the Northwest coast of California notwithstanding my utmost attention and endeavour to save them'.)[2]

He discovered that the man delegated to look after the frame had been put on watch without informing him, and a furious Menzies remonstrated angrily with Vancouver over what he considered dereliction of duty, demanding that the man be punished. He realised that this was a real disaster for him, with the result of the loss of many plants which would otherwise have been introduced to cultivation in Britain earlier than they were.[3] Probably to his quiet satisfaction, and notwithstanding his own frequent recourse to punishment, Vancouver was able to show that the man had been given legitimate orders by his superior officers. The fact of the matter was that throughout the expedition the plant frame had never been a success, with Menzies advising Banks on more than one occasion of how, apart from the depredations of the ship's livestock, many plants had suffered severely from drastic changes in climate.

Vancouver also reminded Menzies at this point that he was still waiting for him to surrender his journal, which in itself was a controversial issue. All officers were required to keep journals, which were the property of the Admiralty, and which were required to be given, together with any other sketches or collections, to the captain of the vessel for security and onward transmission. This requirement was much resented, since these documents could have value for potential publishers. Menzies was quite clear that his instructions were to hand over his materials to Banks, and with the exception of the surgeon's sickbook, refused Vancouver's request point-blank, considering his work to be that of a botanist with responsibility strictly to his patron:

> I have received your order of this day's date, Addressed to me as surgeon of His Majesty's Sloop *Discovery*: demanding my Journals, Charts, drawings etc of the voyage, but I can assure that, in that capacity, I kept no other Journals than the Sickbook which is ready to be delivered if you think this is necessary ... I there-

> fore beg leave to acquaint you that I do not conceive myself authorised to deliver these Journals, etc. to anyone till they are demanded of me, by the secretary of State for the home department, agreeable to the tenor of my instructions.[4]

Here Menzies is quite cleverly using his position as official surgeon to avoid handing over anything other than the required sickbook, knowing full well that he had kept his naturalist's journal as instructed by Banks.

Menzies wrote to Banks: 'I mentioned in my last two letters that when the journal of the Voyage etc are demanded by Captain Vancouver I mean to seal up mine and address them to you, so that you will receive them I hope through the same channel as the most part of my correspondence during the voyage'.[5] This was written on 28 April 1795 at Valparaiso, indicating that Menzies was by then already becoming anxious about their fate. Banks' original instructions to Menzies were unequivocal: 'You are to keep a regular Journal of all occurrences that happen in the execution of the several Duties you are to perform … which Journal … you are on your return to deliver to His Majesty's Secretary of State for the Home department, or to such person as he shall appoint to receive them from you'.[6] According to Lamb, the over-riding consideration on the Vancouver expedition was Banks' conviction that Menzies should keep a journal for his own protection. In the same letter in which he expressed doubt about Vancouver's treatment of Menzies, he stressed this point. As it could be 'highly imprudent' of Vancouver 'to throw any obstacles in the way of your duty I trust he will have too much good sense to destruct it if he does the instances whatever they are will of course appear as they happened in your Journal which as it will be a justification of you will afford ground for impeaching the propriety of his conduct which for your sake I shall not Fail to make use of'.[7]

Clearly, given what transpired between Vancouver and Menzies, Banks was not only prescient, but shrewd in his warnings. What Menzies might not have appreciated immediately was that his formal assumption of duties as surgeon to the expedition, after Cranstoun's repatriation, changed not only his professional status, but also his relationship to Vancouver in matters of discipline and authority. Up to that point, he might well have been considered a civilian, but from then on, he was a naval officer subject to the normal rules of service.

This was the last straw as far as Vancouver was concerned, especially as the quarrel seems to have taken place publicly on the quarter-deck. Deeming Menzies to have been insubordinate, he became quite abusive and ordered him to be placed under arrest and confined to his cabin for the remainder of the voyage – a quite extraordinary situation which reflected badly on both men. (Nor would it have been comfortable for Menzies, given that his cabin would have been tiny.) Vancouver would have been well aware that, under the often strained relations between the two men, Menzies might have been critical of his captain in the pages of his journal. In fact, the relatively few criticisms, more often than not veiled, are to be found in the correspondence between Menzies and his patron, Banks.

Menzies was not the only member of the ship's personnel who had difficult relations with Vancouver. The journals of other officers reveal that after the incident of the flogging of the 16-year-old Thomas Pitt at Matavi Bay in Tahiti, although they might respect their captain's seamanship and his rank, his intemperate outbursts and sometimes vengeful behaviour induced a cool and correct attitude towards him rather than any warmth. The atmosphere created was well described by Thomas Manby in a letter to a Captain Barlow from Monterey on 9 January 1793:

> We are my good fellow spinning about the Globe like a Whorligig, seldom in a place, and as seldom like true Seamen contented with our situation. Good health continues in our little squadron, but I am sorry to say not that good fellowship which ought to subsist with adventurers traversing these distant Seas, owing to the conduct of our Commander-in-Chief who is grown Haughty, Proud, Mean and Insolent which has kept himself and Officers in a continued state of wrangling during the whole Voyage … . Capt Van has got quite fat though has not got clear of his Cough. His language to his officers is too bad, and I am sorry to [say] what with his pursuing business, and a Trade he has carried on, are unbecoming the Character of an Officer in his Honourable exalted station.

Given that Vancouver was Manby's superior officer, the use of the word insolent, certainly in its modern meaning, sounds odd, but perhaps the reference to 'trade' and 'character of an officer' provides an explanation. Like many before him – including Cook – Vancouver had certainly purchased otter skins for his own profit, but this was not usually regarded as abnormal. What it helped to confirm in Manby's mind however was that since only lesser mortals engaged in 'trade', Vancouver was not a 'gentleman' by the definition of the times and therefore his inferior. However, there is good evidence that Manby did some trading on his own account.[8]

It was Manby who in the same letter accused Vancouver of dubious trade practice in the course of survey:

> A great many skins were bought by the rich Merchants on board and from a party of fishermen we purchased Two hundred Salmon, at the price of two buttons each … a vast quantity of all kinds of skins were purchased, those people who were intrusted with the various Articles sent out by Government, made to their disgrace an amazing harvest – Bales of Cloath and blankets were sold with lavish hand for Skins, at a time when many … of our own Crew were shivering with cold from want of woollen cloathing.

As purser for the expedition, Vancouver was responsible for this situation and there is no doubt about who Manby was pointing to when he referred to 'those people'.

Although Manby is one of that cadre of 'gentlemen' who had a snobbish and patronising attitude towards Vancouver, and which coloured their relationships with him, the letters of other officers tend to confirm their estimation of their captain, and give the lie to Coleman's inference that it was Menzies who was the *provocateur* fomenting trouble alongside his accomplice, Hewett. He 'behaved like a Madman raged and swore', according to the latter. 'His salutation I can never forget, and his language I will never forgive', said Manby after another of Vancouver's outbursts. Even the moderate Menzies commented: '... it was no unusual thing with him to be passionate and illiberal in his abuse'.[9]

It is curious that Menzies' journal apparently ends abruptly on 16 February 1794, as did those of other officers prior to the formal ending of the voyage.[10] This date coincides with the ships' departure from Hawaii, where, astonishingly, Pitt, the presumptive Lord Camelford, who had been recruited as an able seaman, was left behind to make his way home on the store ship, the *Daedalus*; this was a considerable humiliation, since it precluded his arrival in England with the triumphant *Discovery*. Some infringement of discipline by the young man had been the last straw for Vancouver, and given Thomas Pitt's connections and influence within the Establishment, Vancouver's action was injudicious to say the least.

It was a fatal error on Vancouver's part, given that the young man was closely related to the Prime Minister, William Pitt, and to John Pitt, Earl of Chatham and First Lord of the Admiralty, while Pitt's sister had married Lord Grenville, the Foreign Secretary – a formidable line-up of potential enemies. Vancouver, after his arrival in England, was relegated from being the commander of an important expedition to being a mere naval captain on leave.[11] There is considerable suspicion that the final entries of the officers' journals, including that of Menzies, were deliberately destroyed to remove any evidence of this incident by persons unknown. Likewise, the pages from the punishment book for 27 May to 10 June and 16 August to 6 September appear to have been torn out, so that all references to the disciplining of Pitt mysteriously vanished.

This has meant the loss of Menzies' journals relating to the journey south via San Francisco and Valparaiso, his collecting round Monterey and Santa Cruz, including the type specimen of *Sequoia sempervirens* (Coast Redwood), his journey with Vancouver to the Pinnacles of San Benito Country, his landing at Cocos Island, Costa Rica and the Galapagos, and the journey to visit Santiago with other officers.[12] Given that Menzies did not hand over his journal to Vancouver, this excision is likely to have been done by others higher in the chain of command, with the inference that, not surprisingly, the Establishment of the time did not wish the humiliation of a scion of the aristocracy to become generally known. Nor is there any mention in Vancouver's journal of his dispute with Menzies over the plant frame. It was Vancouver's misfortune to return to England when both government and the people were absorbed by the war in Europe and were hardly in a mood to celebrate his very real achievements, so that he was received almost with indifference, no doubt exacerbated by his transgression of the mores of a very hierarchical society.[13]

The affront to the young aristocrat culminated in him beating Vancouver in a London street encounter, resulting in a notorious newspaper cartoon by James Gillray, entitled 'The Caneing in Conduit Street' which lampooned the captain as a vulgar and bloated plebian.[14]

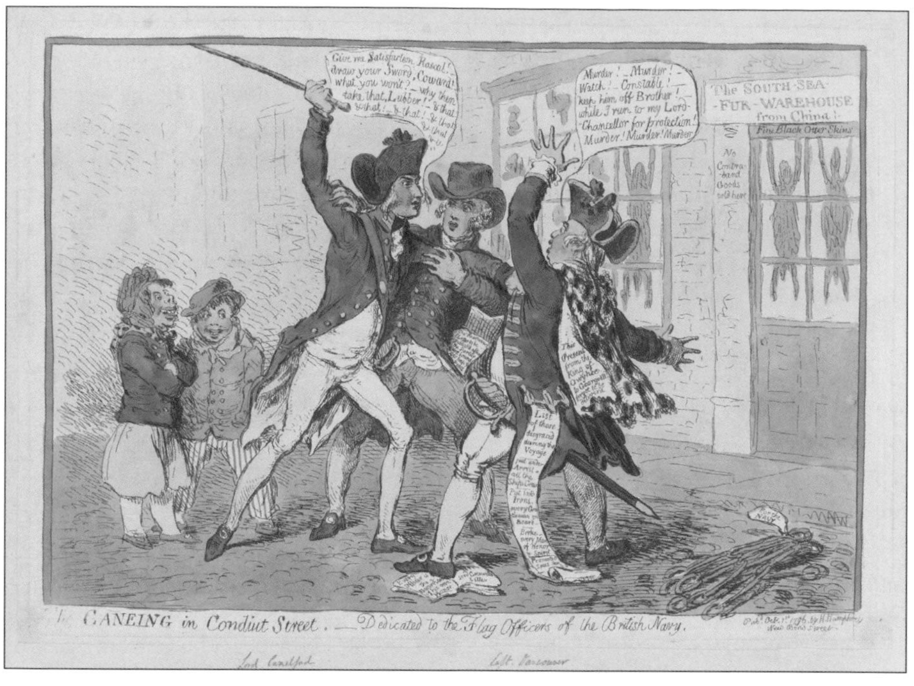

The cartoon *The Caning in Conduit Street* by James Gillray, published in October 1796. (Courtesy of the National Portrait Gallery, London.)

This is referred to in a letter from Menzies to Banks, enclosing a very revealing quote from Joseph Whidbey:

> Lady Camelford has been anxiously collecting information relative to the treatment her son met with in the late voyage from Capt. Vancouver, and after informing her of all I knew of it, I was anxious that she should have the opinion of others and wrote to Mr Whidbey, late master of the *Discovery* now of the *Sans Pareil* who favoured me with the following particulars which afforded her Ladyship much satisfaction, especially as they came from one who was the chief confidant of C. Vancouver most part of the voyage. He says … The first time he was punished was at a very early part of the Voyage, at a Gun in the Cabin, before all the officers for cutting up an Iron Hoop, which C. Vancouver brought under the head of purloining, but I am convinced had C. Vancouver not been the Purser of the Ship, no such construction would have been annexed to the Crime, if an act of that kind may be called a crime. If such a construction as Purloining is applicable to the cutting up of an Iron Hoop I am afraid there are few officers in the Navy that are not guilty of Purloining … The time Lord Camelford was put in Irons, I was on deck and as far as I can recollect his Lordship had the forecastle watch and did not answer the call from the Quarter deck the first time. Capt. Vancouver accused

him of being asleep and ordered him in irons amongst the ship's company where I believe he stayed ten days or a fortnight. After that time, excepting bad language, I don't recollect Lord Camelford receiving any other punishment during his stay in the ship ... Lady Camelford and his Lordship's Guardian, you say they wish to know from me what crimes Lord Camelford was guilty of during his stay with us; to that request I can easily answer – I know of none – excepting what is incidental to Boys in general. I ever conceived Lord Camelford to be a well disposed young man, and I have not the least doubt but he will prove an Ornament to his profession – that was always my opinion.

Signed J. Whidbey[15]

However, Whidbey was to make a much more damning and comprehensive indictment of his commander in a letter to Captain Barlow, apparently in Menzies' handwriting who must therefore have copied it. He tells how the armourer had some copper chippings left over from a job which he apparently sold to Lord Camelford for a pair of pistols, and Camelford then traded the copper to the Indians. Seen by Vancouver, Camelford was forced to disclose the source of the copper and the armourer was severely punished, while the pistols were thrown overboard. Whidbey commented:

... ill natured constructions on any trivial act was always most pleasing to Capt. Vancouver and I declare I never knew him put a favourable construction on any part of the follies of youth, but where his own pecuniary interest was concerned – I never knew him make the least allowances either for youth or situation, but where he has some point to gain. I am sorry to say that he lost all respect to the Navy and thought of nothing but himself ... the Capt'n has introduced into the two ships such a spirit of Trade that little else was thought of, and was the cause of every little altercation that happened afterwards. I strove with all my power to stop it, but without effect, and contented myself with not following so disgraceful an example.[16]

This evidence comes from a man who was an experienced master, of whom Samuel Smiles said: '... he was greatly beloved and respected by all who knew him',[17] and who was to be elected as a fellow of the Royal Society for his engineering accomplishments.

In notes by Banks, he actually refers to a 'mutiny' when he states:

Lord C [Camelford] was on all occasions the spokesman of the Midshipmen, hence the charge of mutiny in among them ... a Mr. Robinson, educated at Christ's Hospital, and recommended by Mr Vales, had been received on board, but was put among the people [i.e. the seamen] and treated by V and by his Boatswains' mates as a servant lad, in course of time the Midshipman who had the charge of the timekeepers, owing to some treatment he did not approve, relinquished the charge, on this Robinson, who was very capable and was called to it, and V ordered him upon the quarter-deck, and directed that he should mess with the

> Midshipmen – which both the mates refused, and gave their reasons openly, as ordered by V upon the quarter-deck – on their refusal, V ordered the Midshipmen's berth to be pulled down, by which they were exposed to the men and had no harbour between decks to separate them.

Banks then goes on to describe the incident in which Lord Camelford was accused of sleeping on deck and put in irons and where apparently his lordship had broken the glass of the compass in the binnacle. At one point, things got to such a pitch after Camelford had been flogged that another scion of the aristocracy, Mr Stuart (the future Marquess of Bute) drew out a razor in front of Vancouver at dinner, promising to cut his throat if Vancouver ever threatened to flog him as 'he would not survive the disgrace'. After that, not surprisingly, Stuart was often sent to the masthead as a punishment 'for trifling offences' according to Banks, who was anxious to build up his case against Vancouver, even if at second hand.[18]

On 13 September 1795, after bidding his officers and men farewell, Vancouver left the *Discovery* in the Shannon for London, when he 'took leave of my officers and crew, not however without emotions … natural on parting with a society with whom I had lived so long, shared so many dangers …'. Menzies lost no time in informing Banks of the circumstances of his arrest. The following day, 14 September 1795, anchored at Limerick, he wrote to Banks giving his version of events, under threat of court martial. Because of its significance, a substantial portion of this letter is reproduced here in full:

> … I beg leave to inform you that I am now under arrest since the 28th July last for insolence and contempt as it is termed and as Captain Vancouver will no doubt report me as such on his arrival at the Admiralty. I trust you will have the goodness to make it known to their Lordships, in my vindication, that the alleged complaint for which I have been put under arrest by Captain Vancouver has wholly arisen from his own proceedings in depriving me of that servant which I was particularly allowed by Government, to aid and assist me in the different pursuits I was instructed to fulfil in the voyage, particularly for taking care and for looking after those live plants I was directed to bring home for his Majesty's Royal gardens … and when I flattered myself with the most pleasing expectations of being able to make considerable and valuable additions to his Majesty's extensive collection, had Captain Vancouver's adverse conduct not proved so inimical to my endeavour in executing this part of my instructions by putting my servant in a watch in common with the ship's company on leaving St. Helen; however while he executes my order respecting the garden I could have no objections to his giving every assistance in working the ship, nor had I any during the whole voyage, when his particular duty did not require his attendance; and I believe it will be allowed by the officers that he did more ship's duty before he was watched than any other idler on board.[19]

> But on the 28th July last I found him guilty of a very notorious neglect in disobedience of my particular orders by not covering the garden before a very heavy and sudden deluge of rain crushed down the tender shoots of many of the plants that never afterwards recovered it. As this fatal neglect merited some chastisement to prevent a repetition of it; I made a complaint of him to Captain Vancouver for that purpose; and I found that he discharged him, still to his duty in a watch without inflicting any punishment or disgrace or giving the least satisfactory redress to my grievance; merely because he had obeyed some other person's orders at the time, in preference to mine ... I however coolly and without either insolence or contempt complained to Captain Vancouver of being unjustly used in this proceeding; He immediately flew into a rage and his passionate behaviour and abusive language on the occasion prevented any further explanation – and I was put under arrest because I would not retreat my expression while my grievance remained unadressed ...
>
> ... However while I am confident in my own mind that I have done nothing to forfeit your friendship and good offices; but on the contrary on this as on every other occasion exerted my utmost endeavours to fulfil the object of my mission, to the best of my abilities; I rest satisfied and will cheerfully submit to whatever mode their lordships and you may think proper to settle this business.
>
> Though Captain Vancouver made a formal demand of my journals, etc. before he left the ship; I did not think myself authorised to deliver them; in my present situation particularly till I should hear from you or the secretary of State for the Home Department; when I shall be ready to deliver up everything I have written, drawn or collected during the whole voyage, agreeable to the tenor of my instructions.

While he was on board after the ship's arrival in London on 20 October 1795, Menzies was still under arrest and could not go ashore, nor land his papers or those plants which had survived.

This lengthy justification of his actions is revealing. It certainly confirms Vancouver's violent disposition, at least verbally, and possibly even the vindictiveness which others attributed to him. It is most probably true that Menzies did not reply in the same coin, given reports of his style. Certainly, for the senior ship's surgeon to be put under arrest for such a complaint, whether justified or not, seems quite disproportionate. On the other hand, in writing to Banks as he did, Menzies appears to swing between blaming his servant on the one hand and Vancouver on the other, but there is little doubt about who is being aimed at. It has to be said also that notwithstanding his treatment, a degree of self-righteousness is evident, and he cannot forbear from emphasising how he has done his duty in the interests of His Majesty's garden. Perhaps more importantly, in one telling phrase above he is actually accusing Vancouver of deliberately putting Menzies' servant in a situation where his jealously guarded plants would be jeopardised, although there is no evidence that Vancouver himself actually gave the order to put the man on watch, though he may have been aware of it.

In the event, Menzies was persuaded, no doubt by Banks, to submit an apology to Vancouver, who in turn was pressed, through Banks' intervention, by Evean Nepean, the new Secretary of the Admiralty, to drop any proceedings for a court martial. As a result, Vancouver withdrew his request for a court martial in a letter to Nepean on 24 October 1795, when Menzies was allowed to go ashore. (His commission as the *Discovery*'s surgeon ended on 3 November 1795.) Neither of the men referred to it again in writing, nor did anyone else.[20] Thus the issue was effectively hushed up yet again by the Establishment in the usual influential way.

The whole question of Vancouver's character and his relationship with Menzies and other officers is a fascinating one. On the positive side, he seems to have been greatly respected for his seamanship and to have been concerned for the health and welfare of his crews, even if he was something of a martinet. By the standards of the time, he was also humane in his attitude to native peoples and was able to establish good relationships with native chiefs such as Kamehameha and others, certainly to be respected by them. He modelled himself on his hero, Cook, but did not appear to have the latter's natural authority or charisma, with the result that he was constantly obsessed by discipline and not letting things get out of hand to the point that some of his punishments seem arbitrary and excessive. Although some have claimed that these were about average when it came to ordering floggings, others indicate that he was excessive in this regard, averaging 30 a year and involving around 50% of all crewmen. In his account Vancouver tends to gloss over this.

There is no doubt that he was feared by his officers for his violent temper and irrational outbursts which seemed to go beyond reason: it is doubtful if any of them, not excluding his very experienced second-in-command Broughton, escaped a tongue-lashing.[21] Lieutenant Manby never forgave his own humiliation at his captain's hand. It is also clear that he was concerned about his status, with a particular sensitivity towards those young 'gentlemen' who overtly or otherwise seemed to challenge his authority, and he may have suffered from what was once called an 'inferiority complex' in that regard.

Certainly he was self-righteous and unpopular, and displayed a rigidity almost certainly derived from a basic lack of confidence. One officer reported that 'some trivial inattention to duty on the part of one or two of the midshipmen' prompted Vancouver not only to forbid midshipmen to go on shore except on duty, but to prohibit visiting between the ships as well, 'an order so strange and unaccountable created no little surprise and astonishment ... and was at once conceived as harsh and unhandsome', going on to say that Vancouver had 'rendered himself universally obnoxious to all'.

This question of authority must have played a considerable part in his relations with Menzies who, on the face of it, with his gentle manners and obsession with botany, seems to have been an unlikely challenger. (In later years he appears to have been noted for his amiability and kindness and these are likely to have been characteristic of his earlier life.) For much of the voyage, the two men appear to have got on tolerably well and to have respected each other's strengths and interests – on occasions they went on shore expeditions together, and Vancouver's final report on Menzies indicates his admiration for the way in which he had carried out his duties, not only as a naturalist, but as a surgeon, stating in the preface to his journal of the voyage that not one man died of ill-health under his care. Vancouver said Menzies was 'always a gentleman', which in this era counted for a great deal and was an epithet not usually accorded a 'mere surgeon'.[22] Banks said that 'they agreed perfectly well, and M always had leave to go on shore – as he had stipulated when he accepted the surgeoncy' – which is not quite how Menzies himself recorded it.[23] Menzies was four years older than his superior (and considerably older than many of the other officers) and had a long experience at sea, even if he was not by the conventions of the time, or by his modest status as a surgeon without independent means, a 'gentleman'. But the issue of personal authority and control must always have been at the back of the commander's mind, with the knowledge that Menzies was the only officer who was not directly under his supervision, but had received his instructions personally from Banks. The latter in turn had the ear of the mightiest in the land, including the King himself.

Menzies had the privilege, at least in theory, of having access to boats for plant collecting expeditions and to resources for maintaining his plants, including fresh water (which might be in short supply) and a servant specifically designated as 'botanist's assistant'. He was therefore effectively outside the range of Vancouver's command, which Vancouver guarded jealously. The plant frame and all that it symbolised on the captain's beloved quarter-deck was not unnaturally the focus of his lack of authority over the naturalist and his displaced ire directed towards Menzies: it is questionable whether relations between the two men would have broken down if this 'excrescence' had not existed.

One writer, Coleman, contrary to all others, tends to play down Vancouver's faults and to criticise Menzies, claiming that 'there can be no doubt that Menzies frequently tested Vancouver's patience to the limit. ... When at great risk of encountering an overwhelming enemy [Spanish] the petulant surgeon's continued complaining about this plant frame would have tested the patience of the mildest of men'.[24] More understandably he suggests that Menzies frequently wrote with an eye to the approval of Sir Joseph Banks, but he reserves his greatest condemnation for the surgeon's assistant, George Hewett, whom he accuses of resorting to 'writing notes that verged almost on a hatred of his captain'. Referring to the Indian attack led by the old woman described previously, Coleman says: 'The surgeon's mate, George Hewett, following his leader Menzies, in his hostility towards Vancouver, took a different view of the attack and its outcome.' (Hewett claimed Vancouver was at fault in ignoring another officer's warning of impending attack, so that arms were not available.)[25] Hewett was subsequently to make copious annotations to his copy of Vancouver's journal of the voyage.

This writer continually excuses Vancouver's behaviour, suggesting that the several officers who criticised their captain were in the wrong. However, Coleman's judgement in this respect has to be questioned when he says:

> … Menzies, at the time of his reluctant acceptance of the Surgeon's appointment … had noted that he had constantly prescribed for Captain Vancouver himself since leaving England. Assuming that his illness had remained the same over the 27 months, it is also reasonable to assume that Menzies' prescriptions were not having much effect. Furthermore, it would have been easy for the hostile Menzies – supported by the equally antagonistic surgeon's mate, George Hewett – to have been somewhat less than benevolent in the medication he was supplying to Vancouver.[26]

This last comment is an extraordinary imputation on the actions of a medical man known for the care of his patients.

What has to be recognised is the cumulative strain on the leader of such a voyage over an extended period of time, with the peculiar isolation of high command. With the evidence of previous voyages, he was constantly concerned about the health of his men and the dangers they were exposed to in open boats, either from weather or from hostile natives, which must have been heightened with the news of the murder of Hergest, Gooch and a seaman on Hawaii. Maintaining stores of wood, water and food and the need to find suitable anchorages for essential repairs to his weather-beaten ships were other worries, not to mention keeping contact with his escort, the *Chatham*. Vancouver was deprived of precise instructions from the British Government over Nootka, and he was seriously discountenanced by the attitude of the Spanish authorities on his second visit to California.

Nor was he immune, with the example of Captain Bligh only a few years previously, to worries over possible disaffection amongst his crew and their immorality in the presence of native people. One writer has suggested that maintaining discipline was difficult where the crews were 'separated from the steadying influence of the fleet, with no unifying military duties to perform, and the ship's companies constantly broken up into boat parties'.[27] Neither would he have been unaware of the possible personal consequences of punishing and discharging the Honourable Thomas Pitt, with all his highly influential friends.

The survey of the Northwest coast was often plagued by bad weather and the hazard of shipwreck, while the overcrowded base ships provided little privacy for either officers or men. They were cooped up with a poor diet and under unhygienic conditions for long stretches at a time. To cap it all, Vancouver was seriously ill for much of the voyage, with severe attacks of vomiting and pain.[28] His symptoms, which have been ascribed to a form of hyperthyroid condition known as 'Grave's disease', no doubt contributed to his ill-temper.[29] The most authoritative modern diagnosis is that he probably suffered from myxoedema or thyroid deficiency, possibly with Addison's disease.[30]

NOTES

1. Justice (2000), 17
2. Menzies to Banks, 28 April 1795. Banks Correspondence 2: 121, Royal Botanic Gardens, Kew
3. Groves (2001), 764
4. Lamb (1993), 14
5. Menzies to Banks, 28 April 1795. Banks Correspondence 2: 121, Royal Botanic Gardens, Kew
6. Instructions from Banks to Menzies, in Lamb (1993), 232
7. Brabourne ix: 95. Banks to Menzies, 10 August 1791, in Lamb (1993), 233
8. Lamb (1984), 217
9. Manby, quoted in Raban (1999), 138–9
10. The word 'apparently' has been used here, because although the British Library manuscript of the Menzies journal and the Linnean Society transcript end in February 1794, Menzies' narrative of the final survey season in Alaska has been located in the National Library of Australia by Olson – see Introduction.
11. Lindsay (2005), 140
12. Anderson (1960), 24
13. Naish (1996), 351
14. Ibid., 23–4
15. Menzies to Banks, 21 October 1796. Banks Correspondence 2: 150, Royal Botanic Gardens, Kew
16. Banks Correspondence, Dawson Turner Collection 10(1): 87–8 (n.d.), British Museum (Natural History), London
17. Smiles (1861), 275–6
18. Notes by Sir Joseph Banks: Dawson Turner Collection 10(1): 83–6, British Museum (Natural History), London
19. Lamb makes the valid point that Vancouver may have felt that the *Discovery* was short-handed, as he had transferred 17 men to the prize ship *Macassar* at St. Helena. (Lamb 1984, 1630).
20. Naish (1996), 437
21. Lindsay (2005), 130
22. Justice (2000), 22
23. Notes by Sir Joseph Banks: Dawson Turner Collection 10(1): 83–6, British Museum (Natural History), London
24. Coleman (1988), 149
25. Ibid., 85
26. Ibid., 84
27. Keevil (1948), 802
28. Naish (1996), 263
29. Anderson (1960), 67
30. Lamb (1984), 211–12

16

'A Slow Hand at the Pen'

On 14 September 1795, Menzies wrote to Banks:

> I am at present hard at work, in bringing the clean copy of my Journal of the Voyage, & I am much afraid, I shall require the indulgence of a few months after I get back home to have it completed; as I am but a very slow hand at the pen, and our constant & frequent movements during the Voyage, took up much of my time on Shore, in examining the different countries we visited.[1]

Banks wrote to William Henry Cavendish Bentinck, Third Duke of Portland, to ask that Menzies' salary of £150 be continued to allow him to complete his journal, enclosing a catalogue of the articles he had collected on the Vancouver voyage. This material had been sent direct to Kew as instructed and was now with Banks to be sent to wherever the Duke wished.

> In consequence of this double duty as naturalist and surgeon on board *Discovery* he found it impossible properly to arrange and digest the journal he was ordered to keep, tho' he lost no opportunities of making and writing down necessary observations respecting the produce of the soil, the manners of the natives, and such other matters as he was instructed to remark upon. My petition in his favour was therefore that his salary, being 150 a year, might for the present be continued in order to enable him to complete his journals which when finished are to be delivered to your grace.[2]

The Duke replied that apart from the live plants and seed which were to be retained at Kew, the other items should be sent to the British Museum, but the continuation of salary was rejected.[3]

In late November 1795 Menzies became involved in an Admiralty experiment in controlling disease considered as 'contagious infection' but which is most likely to have been typhus, which is carried by lice. There was a frightening spread of this infection among the sailors of several Russian ships anchored off Sheerness, lying at anchor in the Medway, commanded by Admiral Hannikow. The authorities were much concerned that this might spread to the nearby British hospital ship, the *Union*, which was receiving the Russian casualties. Even the medical attendants and others were by now going down with the fever and there was considerable alarm over its spread.

Menzies was put in charge of the experiment and immediately ordered the ports and scuttles to be closed while the wards were fumigated with gaseous nitric oxide created by pouring sulphuric acid and potassium nitrate onto pots of hot sand. This was a drastic and potentially harmful 'remedy' which must have caused distress to both attendants and the sick in their beds from the choking fumes. But he also decreed that all dirty clothes and bedlinen be steeped in cold water and hung out on deck for fumigation prior to being washed. This fumigation was carried out twice daily and was accompanied by a complete ventilation of the ship. The appalling lavatories were cleaned and covered to reduce the stench. The rate of deaths and infection dropped, and by early February the epidemic had ceased. Although his success was attributed largely to the nitric fumes, based on the initial work of Dr James Carmichael Smyth, there can be little doubt that this was due to the improvement in hygienic measures which are more likely to have reduced lice infestation.[4]

In the spring of 1796, Vancouver heard that the Admiralty favoured a combined publication of his journal with that of Menzies (almost certainly at Banks' instigation, based on his own experience with the Cook journal). Vancouver's response to the Earl of Chatham was robust:

> As I find it the intention of the Admiralty, that the observations made by Mr Menzies, of the various objects of the Natural History of the different Country [sic] we visited, should in some way be connected with my account of the Voyage; and that under such conditions Mr Menzies is to be benefited by a proportion of the profits that may result from the sale of the work, and that on that subject in a letter to the Board [of the Admiralty] I have pointed out the disadvantages that I labour under ... the pay of Mr Menzies during the Voyage was much more than double mine which together with his expenses, has been paid him since his return; and hence it is natural to conclude; since he has been so amply paid by government that the results of his employment are the intire property of government and totally at their disposal.[5]

Vancouver was not only successful in his protest, but the latter may have persuaded the Admiralty subsequently to refuse Banks' request for Menzies to be paid to complete his own journal. What the whole episode and others reveal is how parsimonious the government was in its recompense to personnel who carried considerable responsibility: in these circumstances, it is hardly surprising that they sought other sources of remuneration, including trading on their own account in the course of expeditions, or indeed the capture of 'prize' enemy vessels. In the event, Vancouver's journal (completed by his brother John Vancouver) did not appear before his death and that of Menzies was never published, largely due to his own tardiness to provide a finished copy. Menzies' failure in this respect frustrated Banks in his attempt to steal a march on the Vancouver publication, and could have been the cause of a cooling of the relationship between himself and Menzies.

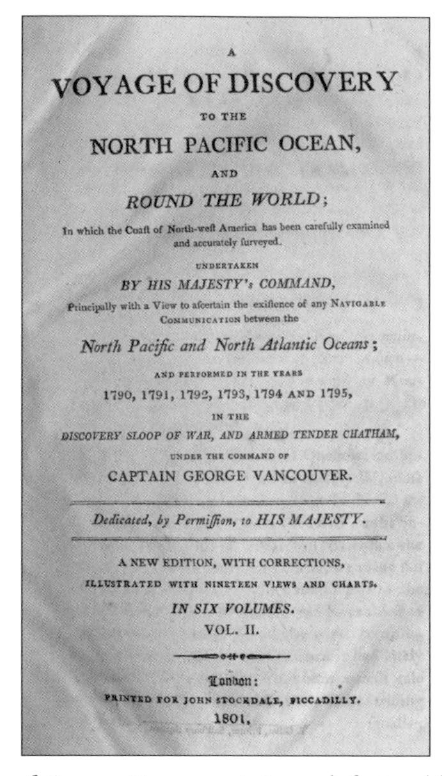

A

VOYAGE OF DISCOVERY

TO THE

NORTH PACIFIC OCEAN,

AND

ROUND THE WORLD;

In which the Coaſt of North-weſt America has been carefully examined and accurately ſurveyed.

UNDERTAKEN

BY HIS MAJESTY'S COMMAND,

Principally with a View to aſcertain the exiſtence of any NAVIGABLE COMMUNICATION between the

North Pacific and North Atlantic Oceans;

AND PERFORMED IN THE YEARS

1790, 1791, 1792, 1793, 1794 AND 1795,

IN THE

DISCOVERY SLOOP OF WAR, AND ARMED TENDER CHATHAM,

UNDER THE COMMAND OF

CAPTAIN GEORGE VANCOUVER.

Dedicated, by Permiſſion, to HIS MAJESTY.

A NEW EDITION, WITH CORRECTIONS,

ILLUSTRATED WITH NINETEEN VIEWS AND CHARTS.

IN SIX VOLUMES.

VOL. II.

London:

PRINTED FOR JOHN STOCKDALE, PICCADILLY.

1801.

The title page of George Vancouver's journal, first published in 1798.

Menzies resumed naval service on 30 November 1796 – he had received no pay for over a year up to this point – as surgeon on the royal yacht *Princess Augusta* which, although something of a sinecure, slowed down the completion of his journal. (It is something of a coincidence that Princess Augusta herself had been instrumental, through her interest in botany, in helping to found the Royal Gardens at Kew with which Menzies was so closely associated.) That commission lasted until May 1799, by which time he was 45 years old. However, by 1798 he had still not completed his journal and wrote to Banks on 3 January of that year:

> I received your letter this morning and return my sincere thanks for your friendly admonitions & solicitations respecting the finalising of my Journal before Captain Vancouver's is published – It is what I most ardently wish, for more reasons than one, and have therefore applied to it very close – I generally get up at five in the morning and continue at it, with as little interruption as possible till six or seven in the evening daily ...[6]

Menzies goes on to say how much he will apply himself to this task – but the interesting phrase above highlights Banks' and possibly Menzies' desire to pre-empt Vancouver's publication.

Menzies was nothing if not meticulous in his identification and description of his plant material, while at the same time he was much engaged in cataloguing the many 'curiosities' he had gathered *en voyage*. In the event Vancouver died in the same year, but due to his brother's efforts, his journal was published before that of Menzies, and Banks by this time seems to have lost interest.[7] Menzies' collection lay unavailable for study in Banks' herbarium for some years after the return of Vancouver's expedition in 1795, although Menzies had access to it, under the guidance of Jonas Dryander and others. He would not however have been able to use it later when he was still on naval service, nor would he have had access to the herbarium and his own plant collections, other than intermittently.

Menzies prepared his plant material over three years and distributed duplicates of his collection to colleagues in Britain and Europe, establishing a reputation as a very knowledgeable plant collector, perhaps to the detriment of his own publication. He seems to have been more at ease in allowing others access to his collections than publishing on them himself.[8] Despite his undoubted achievements, Menzies appears to have been peculiarly modest about his scientific credentials and it has been suggested that as he did not publish many of his important discoveries; this indicates someone who regarded himself as an agent of other men more eminent in the scientific world and greater in fundamental knowledge than himself.[9] However, he kept up an irregular correspondence with Dawson Turner (1775–1858), an expert on seaweeds, and with Olof Swartz in Stockholm, among a number of botanists who appreciated his invaluable collections and knowledge of plants from around the globe, not least his expertise in the cryptogams, or non-flowering plants.

Menzies was particularly generous in giving many plants from his voyages to expand Turner's extensive collection of cryptogams. In a letter to him on 3 November 1798, he shows that despite his normal geniality, he is not above criticism of sloppy work. Referring to the work of another *Fucus* expert, E. J. C. Esper of Nuremberg: 'The text is a mere farrago of Synonyma without the least selection, along with Gmelin's description copied verbatim ... as a specimen of accuracy the *Fucus sinosus* is given as a variety of *F. palmetta*, ie. *F. membranifolius*'.

Despite his age, Menzies could not afford to retire from the Navy, and in the last year of the 18th century he was given appointments to the vessels *Prince of Wales*, *Sans Pareil* and *Tamer*, spending several years on the last two ships, stationed in the West Indies.[10] On 24 July 1799 he was able to take leave to travel to Aberdeen to receive the degree of MD (*Honoris Causa*) which would certainly have gratified him. But his later years in the Navy in a tropical climate took their toll, and he began to suffer quite seriously from asthma, exacerbated by living and working in the distinctly unhealthy environment of the cockpit, with its overcrowding and unventilated conditions. (In Jamaica, he was often obliged to sleep ashore or on deck.)

It seems that the Vice-Admiral of the West Indian fleet, Lord Hugh Seymour, had a sufficiently high opinion of Menzies to appoint him as acting Physician to the Squadron, although this was very abruptly terminated by Evan Nepean who felt that the Admiral had exceeded his authority. Menzies must have been disgruntled that, despite having worked in this capacity for several months, he received no extra pay, confirming the Admiralty's habitual penny-pinching attitudes. It was also unfortunate for Menzies that his supporter Seymour died in post in the West Indies. Menzies returned with the *Sans Pareil* to England in September 1802 and retired from the Navy, having been too unwell to carry out any botanical work while preoccupied with his medical duties in the Caribbean. Given his state of health and his treatment by the Navy establishment, he would not have been sorry to leave both the West Indies and the naval service.

Over a period of four years between 1801 and 1805, Menzies applied to the Admiralty for half-pay for his service of more than 20 years, emphasising his health problems as a result of his West Indian service: he was at this time only on the half-pay of an assistant surgeon. In his memorial to the Admiralty, Menzies reviewed his service with the Navy, mentioning in passing that Carmichael Smyth had received a recompense of £5000 for his part in the discovery of the effect of the 'Nitrous Acid Gas' on the suffering Russian sailors at Sheerness. Referring to his last period in the West Indies, he goes on:

> And that from the crowded and sickly state of the *Sans Pareil* and the excessive fatigue in performing his duties in that sultry climate, Your Memorialist's health became greatly impaired by frequent and severe attacks of asthma, which induced him on his return to England, to change his mode of Life, by settling for a time on shore; as the most likely means of alleviating his sufferings, & thereby Shun the repeated attacks of a Disorder which constantly assailed him with the greater violence in the Cock-pit. In doing this he little expected that he should be deprived of his half-pay by the Commissioners of the Medical Board; such however was the Case; but on producing a certificate from Doctor Blair Physician of the Fleet, of the Actual State of his Health, the Sick and Hurt Board reconsidered his case, & allowed him to remain on his Old Half-pay which he now finds is only equal to that of an Assistant Surgeon for two Years services.
>
> That Your Memorialist therefore humbly implores Your Lordships to take into consideration his long and active Services, and the misfortune of losing his health in the performance of his Duties; And he ardently hopes that Your Lordships will be pleased to allow him to be put upon the New Half-pay according to his servitude & rank on the list of Navy Surgeons especially as he knows that others enjoy it, who have not served in the late War and are in other respects similarly situated with himself.[11]

The Fleet's official physician, a Dr Primrose Blair, supported his case, claiming that in Jamaica, Menzies had been obliged to sleep on shore because of the foetid atmosphere of the ship's cockpit:

> I am ready to take Oath to the fact, that for nearly twelve months, he laboured under such severe fits of Asthma as to oblige him frequently to come up to the Ward Room in the middle of the night, and at last the returns of the Disease became so certain on his breathing the air of the Cock-pit, that he was obliged to sleep on shore at Port Royal. And I feel convinced from his even now breathing rather laboriously in a pure air, that he could not sleep in the Cock-pit of a Man of War without the fits of Asthma again recurring.[12]

The Sick and Wounded Office of the Admiralty eventually relented, almost certainly due to Dr Blair's submission, and restored the former half-pay to Menzies.[13]

In the spring of 1802 Dawson Turner wrote to Olof Swartz, saying that neither he nor anyone else seemed to have heard from Menzies for a long time.[14] Swartz replied by saying he had heard nothing from Menzies for the last five years.[15] Later Swartz, referring to Menzies, was to say: 'He has communicated not a few things of his beautiful discoveries in his voyage with me, and I am much indebted to him.'[16]

In fact, in the same month (January 1803) Menzies took up correspondence with Turner, thanking him for his gift of specimens and giving him permission to include in any publication the new species of *Fucus* which Menzies had collected. He offered to help in any way he could with this publication which was nothing less than a compendium of all the species of this genus known at the time. What this correspondence with eminent botanists confirms is that, perhaps not surprisingly, Menzies did little active botanising in his last years with the Navy in the West Indies and elsewhere, but was typically generous with both plant specimens and assistance wherever he could offer it.

By 1807, both Turner and Swartz were expressing concern that Menzies did not seem to have progressed any publication of his own, despite his intention of completing a work based on his collection of mosses and liverworts. It was left to William J. Hooker (1785–1865), the subsequent Director of Kew Gardens, another appointee of Banks and whose son Joseph was to succeed him, to bring his work together many years later. (No fewer than eight distinguished taxonomists had attempted previously to correct mistakes in the classification of many plants in the Menzies collection.)[17] Although this procrastination seems to have been a personal characteristic of Menzies, partly due to his meticulous approach, and reflected in his erratic correspondence, it may also have been due in some degree to the demands of medical work following naval service.[18]

After his retirement from the Navy in 1802, Menzies established a medical practice, setting up as both a doctor and a surgeon, practising at 6 Chapel Place, between Cavendish Square and Oxford Street in London. The practice prospered for the next 23 years. In the same year he married a Scotswoman, Janet Brown, the sister of Adam Brown, who had sailed with Menzies while the latter was temporarily on board the

Chatham. She was 32 years old, some 16 years younger than Menzies, and although there were no children, it appears to have been a happy marriage, which lasted until her death 34 years later in 1836. In 1826 he retired from medical practice and set up house at 2 Ladbroke Terrace, Notting Hill. During these years, Menzies frequently attended meetings of the Linnean Society (of which he had been a member since 1790)[19] and kept contact with many botanical friends at home and overseas, while much of his spare time was spent at Kew Gardens. He was highly regarded in the botanical world, and in 1822 received a diploma from the University of Leipzig.

Through his generous hospitality, Menzies' home at Ladbroke Terrace became a regular meeting place for many of the great botanists of the time: there are records of lunches with John Smith, the chief gardener at Kew, discussions with Sir William J. Hooker, Professor at the University of Glasgow, and talks with George Don junior who had recently returned from a botanical expedition to West Africa and the West Indies. Dr Ward no doubt took Menzies' advice on his invention of the 'Wardian case' – the glazed box used for transporting plants around the globe – while the Scottish botanist Thomas Drummond sent Menzies samples of mosses, as did many others.[20]

Groves describes a happy home where 'Menzies and his wife kept open house to visiting botanists, often having them to dine after which Archibald delighted in discussing plants or exchanging travel experiences … Menzies, in his mid-seventies, was still alert and never more happy than when recounting his tales of travel, particularly those on the northwest coast of America'.[21] The younger botanists and collectors, starting out on their own travels, came to him to seek his advice, notably the Scottish plant hunter David Douglas. Writing to W. J. Hooker in 1828, Douglas said: '… I was all day with Mr. Menzies … and just on the evening who came in but Scouler in search of me … the three North Americans under one roof'.[22]

He might have said 'three Scots' since John Scouler (1804–71) had studied at Glasgow University, had been a surgeon and naturalist to the Hudson Bay Company and travelled extensively in North America, while Douglas was a fellow-countryman. For his part, the generous and affable Menzies would have been delighted to welcome these young botanists and to give them the benefit of his experience. Scouler was unequivocal in his appreciation: '… the knowledge acquired from Mr. Menzies was particularly interesting as he had already explored the very coast I had to visit … and directed my attention to those [plants] which were most likely to be useful when cultivated in this country'.[23]

When Douglas was preparing to go to North America on his first expedition in 1823 he obtained much advice from the now elderly Menzies, and between his first and second expeditions in 1827 and 1829 he again met Menzies, and wrote of his appreciation for the advice received from him.[24] In fact, many others came to his door to seek his counsel, and it might be said that in a number of ways Menzies was a pathfinder for others in this part of the world. All the indications are that Menzies took great pleasure in his meetings with other plantsmen, not least in encouraging

A miniature of Janet Menzies thought to be painted at the time of her marriage in 1802. Artist unknown. (Courtesy of the Royal British Columbia Museum, British Columbia Archives.)

and inspiring younger men to explore the wider botanical world, retaining an almost boyish enthusiasm for his subject right up to the end of his life.[25]

From the late 1820s onwards, Menzies entertained a wide range of scientific colleagues, including Dawson Turner's son-in-law William Jackson Hooker, who was to have Menzies' wholehearted support in his successful application for the post of Professor of Botany at Glasgow University, and whom Menzies subsequently encouraged to apply for the chair of botany at Oxford University, as he 'knew of none in the whole Empire more able and fit to fill that chair than yourself'.[26] As usual, they exchanged plant specimens, but it is clear from their correspondence that the two men had established a warm friendship, despite almost 30 years' difference in their ages:

> ... Both Mrs Menzies and myself were very sorry to be informed of poor Mrs. Hooker's indisposition and sufferings, and we sincerely hope that long 'ere this

A miniature of Archibald Menzies *c*.1785 by an unknown artist.
(Courtesy of the Royal British Columbia Museum, British Columbia Archives.)

> She is recovered from her critical situation to a permanent state of good health … you will receive this from your friend Mr. Scouler who is just returned from Columbia River, NW Coast of America and as I understand with a rich collection of plants seeds etc. for you. If on looking them over, you find that you can spare any of the Cryptogamic Plants – *Gramineae, Junci, Carices* etc, do not forget an old friend.[27]

Five years later, Scouler's friend, David Douglas, wrote to Hooker from Monterey: 'The first plant I took in my hand in full flower was *Ribes stamineum* (Smith) remarkable for the length and crimson splendour of its staminea, a plant not surpassed in beauty by the finest *Fuschia*! For the discovery of which we are indebted to the Good Sir Arch'd Menzies in '79 …'.[28] Of course the 'Sir' here is a mark of Douglas's own respect for his one-time mentor. Later, he was to remind Hooker that the older natives of Hawaii still remembered Menzies:

> ... I made a journey to the summit of *Mowna Roa* [Mauna Loa] or the Big or Long mountain which afforded me inexpressible delight. This mountain of 13,517 feet elevation is one of the most interesting in the whole world – I am not sure whether the venerable Menzies ascended or not, I think he did and the natives say he did, (*for the Red faced Man who cut the limb of men off and gathered Grass*) is still much known here did go to *Mowna Roa* ...[29]

Another of Menzies' firm friends in later life was the gardener John Smith (1798–1888). Smith followed his father as a gardener and worked for two years (1818–20) at the Royal Botanic Garden Edinburgh before going to work under W. T. Aiton. He was first offered a post in the Royal Gardens, Kensington then in 1822 he moved to Kew where he was finally promoted to curator, a post he held from 1841 to 1864.[30] They had many convivial dinners together, and the still-enthusiastic Menzies was always enquiring about new acquisitions to Kew, particularly from North America, and whether they had flowered or seeded.

W. H. Harvey, Keeper of the Herbarium at Trinity College, Dublin met Menzies towards the end of his life and commented that he was 'One of the finest specimens of green old age that it has been my lot to meet ...', and who was able to 'recall with vividness the scenes he had witnessed and loved to speak of the plants he had discovered. His plants, the companions of his early hardships, seemed to stir recollections of every circumstance that had altered their recollection at a distance of more than half a century'.[31] The American botanist Asa Gray described Menzies, at his first meeting with him, as 'that Nestor of botanists, Mr. Menzies, whom I found a most pleasant and kind-hearted old man; he invited me most earnestly to come down and see him ...'.[32]

The impression given is of an honoured elder statesman of botanical exploration who modestly enjoyed both his reputation and being a mentor to the younger generation of botanists, and who very properly indulged himself in his memories.

The German botanist J. A. Schultes noted when Menzies was 75 years old that

> ... no less venerable and highly amiable sage is the good old man of the mountains (e monte Grampio) Sir [sic] Archibald Menzies ... Flora has presented this valuable old man with a truly viridem senectutem, in reward for the homage which he offered to her in his twice repeated voyage rounded the world. 'And were another expedition going, I would immediately set off again', said Sir Archibald to us ... a neater herbarium than that of Sir A Menzies I never saw ...[33]

That amiability came through in his 80th year, when a mellow Menzies, notwithstanding the vicissitudes of his relationship with Vancouver, accorded him a final epitaph:

> What days these were – a fine group of officers – all gone now – a credit to the Captain – he chose them all except me – they became Captains too – Mudge and Puget – Admirals both of them. These books that Vancouver wrote – strange that he could put so much of himself into the printed page. He was a great Captain.[34]

Menzies maintained his interest in botany to the last and was still checking records in his final years – a letter to John Smith three months before his death refers to the identification of fern species. He died peacefully at his home on 15 February 1842, the day after making his will. In that will dated as proven on 4 March 1842 he left 1000 francs in the form of French Government stock to his surviving sister, Mrs Betty Crearer, and 100 pounds to each of his nephews and nieces, the children of his three deceased sisters, among other similar sums to other relations. His nephew Charles Geddes received the house at 6 Chapel Place and all the furniture, etc. in the residence at Ladbroke Terrace, including all his books and manuscripts. His considerable herbarium was donated to the Royal Botanic Garden Edinburgh, while the Linnean Society received 100 pounds.[35,36]

He was buried the day after his death in All Souls Cemetery, Kensal Green, next to his wife Janet. His headstone states:

> … many years a surgeon in the Royal Navy in which station he served in the fleet commanded by Admiral Rodney on the 12th of April 1782. He afterwards twice circumnavigated the globe first with Captain Colnett, and again in the voyage of *Discovery* under the orders of Captain Vancouver as the naturalist to that expedition.
>
> He added greatly to the knowledge then possessed of the natural productions, especially the plants, of the various countries visited. After practising his profession for many years in London, he retired to Notting Hill where he died on the 15th February 1842, aged 88 years. Sincerely respected and deeply regretted by his numerous friends.[37]

NOTES

1. Menzies to Banks, 14 September 1795. Banks Correspondence 2: 127, Royal Botanic Gardens, Kew
2. Banks to William Henry Cavendish Bentinck, 3 February 1796. Banks Correspondence, Dawson Turner Transcripts 10: 15–16, British Museum (Natural History), London
3. Groves (2001), 71
4. Naish (1996), 441–3
5. National Archives 30/8/185, Vancouver to the Earl of Chatham, 8 April 1796, in Lamb (1993), 331
6. Menzies to Banks, 3 January 1798. Brabourne Papers ix: 185–6
7. Groves (2001), 77
8. Galloway and Groves (1987), 25
9. Naish (1996), 464
10. Groves (1998), 15
11. Menzies (n.d.), 'The Memorial of Archibald Menzies Surgeon in the Royal Navy. To the Rt Hon the Lords Commissioners for executing the office of the Lord High Admiral.' A. Menzies Papers, University of Washington Library
12. Dr Primrose Blair, 1805. A. Menzies Papers, University of Washington Library
13. Galloway and Groves (1987), 28
14. Dawson Turner to Swartz, 15 March 1802. Swartz Correspondence, Library, Royal Swedish Academy of Sciences, Stockholm
15. Swartz to Dawson Turner, 12 April 1802. Dawson Turner Correspondence, Trinity College Library, Cambridge
16. Swartz to Dawson Turner, 13 January 1803. Dawson Turner Correspondence, Trinity College Library, Cambridge
17. Justice (2000), 18
18. The *Dictionary of National Biography* entry claims that the delay in the publication of Menzies' journal of the Vancouver voyage was because he had given these to Banks, rather than publish the five volumes himself, but this is not confirmed by others. See Baigent (2004).
19. Forsyth, in Newcombe (1923), x
20. Lindsay (2005), 143
21. Groves (2001), 105
22. Douglas to W. J. Hooker, 17 January 1828. W. J. Hooker Correspondence 61: 112, Royal Botanic Gardens, Kew
23. Scouler (1826): 196fn
24. Aitken (1988), 6
25. Galloway and Groves (1987), 35
26. Hooker was appointed to this post in 1820, and in 1841 became the first full-time

Director at Kew. He shared Menzies' enthusiasm for bryophytes (ferns and mosses).
27. Menzies to W. J. Hooker, 20 April 1826. W. J. Hooker Correspondence, English Letters 1: 198, Royal Botanic Gardens, Kew
28. Douglas to W. J. Hooker, 23 November 1831. W. J. Hooker Correspondence 61: 104,Royal Botanic Gardens, Kew
29. Douglas to W. J. Hooker, 6 May 1834. W. J. Hooker Correspondence 61: 112, Royal Botanic Gardens, Kew
30. Groves (2001), 115 note 128
31. Harvey (1852–53), 42; Groves (2001), 106
32. Gray (1893), 308
33. Schultes (1829), in Galloway and Groves (1987), 4
34. Turnbull (1954), 11
35. Last Will and Testament of A. Menzies. Public Record Office, London – PROB11/1959, 322–3
36. Herbarium of grasses, sedges and cryptogams bequeathed to the Royal Botanic Garden Edinburgh. In 1886, other specimens acquired by the British Museum (*Oxford Dictionary of National Biography*, 826).
37. Galloway and Groves (1987), 34

17

'A Tree that God left on Earth for Us'

Of that legion of eminent Scots botanists of the 18th and 19th centuries there can be little doubt that Menzies was one of the foremost plant collectors. It has been said of him that few botanists had so many plants named after them, and perhaps even fewer have had a whole genus ascribed to them. Apart from the genus *Menziesia* created by Sir James E. Smith, nearly 100 flowering plant taxa, whether species, sub-species or varieties, have been given the epithet '*menziesii*'.[1] Justice, one of the foremost authorities on Menzies' botanical legacy, describes him as the first discoverer, describer and collector of most of the plants of the Pacific Northwest.[2] Many plants which are now commonplace in the gardens of Europe are the result of his assiduous plant collecting across the world, but primarily on the Northwest coast of America. In this huge region, his account of his finds and their circumstances represents one of the earliest collections of such observations made by a European.

Many of the plants discovered by Menzies in North America readily acclimatised to the similar conditions of Britain, and several tree species proved subsequently to be of considerable economic importance. Others, such as the Pacific Rhododendron (*Rhododendron macrophyllum*) and the Pacific Dogwood (*Cornus nuttallii*), became state or provincial emblems. The latter, discovered by Menzies in Admiralty Inlet in May 1792, was to become the first single species to be protected under British Columbian legislation. With its large creamy white bracts surrounding the dark clove-shaped seeds, it is considered one of the most spectacular of flowering trees in the Northern Hemisphere, but Menzies was not credited with its discovery. One of the first illustrations of this plant was by the great American ornithologist John James Audubon, who featured it as a background to his striking portrait of the Band-tailed Pigeon. He gave the plant species the epithet '*nuttallii*' some 40 years after Menzies discovered the species – yet another example of Menzies missing out in the naming of plants he first collected.[3]

Menzies did not confine himself to the collection of plant specimens as an academic exercise, but went to some length to find out their properties as possible sources of food or medicine, not least in search of new local plants for the treatment of scurvy. It was here that his facility for native languages and efforts to learn these were especially useful. The evidence also indicates a quiet and modest personality, allied to a natural curiosity: this encouraged native people – who more often than not had a considerable store of knowledge of the attributes of the plants around them – to open up to the unthreatening botanist. This was almost certainly helped by his willingness to treat them for common ailments or injuries. In his identification of the potential usefulness of previously unknown plants, he was undoubtedly one of the notable pioneers.

On the Northwest coast alone, Menzies collected over 300 plants; many more, such as the colourful *Ribes sanguineum* (Flowering Currant), were collected as seeds and sent back to Britain. However, it was said that from his most important voyage with Vancouver, he was able to bring back only two live plants, after the disaster with the flooding of the plant frame.[4] His own slowness in writing up the results of his endeavours, combined with the attention given to subsequent plant hunters such as David Douglas, and the epic trans-America explorations by Lewis and Clark, meant that he was not credited with a number of his original finds. (A good example is the Douglas Fir, *Pseudotsuga menziesii*, which Menzies first discovered.)

The eminent botanist Frederick Pursh (1774–1820) worked on the collections of the American explorers well before he turned his attention to those of Menzies, with the result that they got the credit for many plants originally introduced as seeds to Britain by the Scot. Much of his plant material did not become the basis of type descriptions as a result. It has been claimed with justification that had it not been for these circumstances and his failure to publish, Menzies would have been justifiably acclaimed as the pre-eminent plant collector of the period 1790–1810.

While much attention has been given to the plants Menzies collected on the Northwest coast of America during the Vancouver voyage, it was not until over a hundred years after his death that some of the specimens he collected while voyaging with Colnett came to light, as a result of investigations into the herbarium records of the Royal Botanic Garden Edinburgh by J. Macqueen Cowan. Of the 700 herbarium sheets from the Menzies collection deposited there, at least 11 sheets, from their geographical locations and dates, cannot be ascribed to the Vancouver journey.

These are mainly non-flowering cryptogams, notably seven sheets from South Sumatra, but with other specimens from Hawaii, New Zealand, Madagascar, the Cape of Good Hope and North America.[5] His herbarium record also includes some 40 bryophytes from Brazil, but the collector is unidentified: it is just possible that Menzies did land here in the course of the Colnett voyage. On that expedition there is however a clear record of collecting in China, including *Aster menziesii* and *Paeonia moutan* (= *suffruticosa*) var. *menziesii* (Chinese Tree Peony), and of finding *Drosera menziesii* in Tasmania.

Menzies may also have collected specimens of the Coast Redwood (*Sequoia sempervirens*), the tallest of all living things, on this voyage, since he called at Monterey, near the southern limit for the species. The largest surviving specimen of this, the world's tallest tree, is estimated at over 365 feet.[6] Due to cutting and development, the species, which is entirely confined to the coastal range, now occupies less than 40,000 hectares. During the 19th century, when much forest destruction occurred, it might take up to a week to fell one of these giants, weighing up to 300 tonnes each, with the tools of the time.[7] The most famous of the surviving groves of the species is on the slopes of Mount Tamalpias opposite the Golden Gate Bridge; this is now named Muir Woods after John Muir, yet another renowned naturalist hailing from Scotland.[8]

No complete list of plants collected by Menzies on his voyages either with Colnett or Vancouver is available: the surviving material has been dispersed, some to unknown locations. It may not be possible, despite the painstaking work of Groves and others, to determine the provenance of all his specimens.[9]

It was left to his great friend and collaborator William J. Hooker to put Menzies' name against many species, some 50 years after the Vancouver voyage, in his great work *Flora Boreali-Americana* (1829–40) in which he cited over 190 species attributed to Menzies.[10] One of the important tree species which Hooker listed was the Silver or Southern Beech (*Nothofagus*), of which there are more than 37 species (*N. menziesii* is named after the botanist). It is native only in the Southern Hemisphere, where it is widespread, and was collected by Menzies in Dusky Sound, New Zealand. (The distribution of this tree between the southern regions of South America and Australasia confirms the historical conjunction of these continents.)

While Menzies was undoubtedly an objective observer and scientifically trained collector by the standards of his time, he was by no means a detached technician, merely interested in the business of acquiring, identifying and listing his plants. His description of finding the great swathes of *Calypso bulbosa* (Fairy Slipper Orchid) near Discovery Bay in May 1792 indicates a perception of natural beauty, including wider aspects of landscape and the natural environment, which goes well beyond mere enumeration. He took a delight in the structure, colour and sheer attractiveness of his plants, not excluding those non-flowering mosses and lichens that others might ignore. There was a passion there which was quite emotionally expressed in his early letters from Nova Scotia to Professor Hope, indicating a real depth of feeling for his subject.

Published work on Menzies has naturally focussed on botany, while his ethnological collections, with the notable exception of King's research, have been largely overlooked. These collections, together with those of his assistant George Hewett, were 'the most extensive and best documented to the place of collection, of any before 1800'. (With his 500 artefacts, Hewett himself created the largest collection of ethnography to survive from before that date and was likely to have collaborated with Menzies in this field.)[11] Despite the importance of this collection, the all-important associated list was lost among the Banks papers and all knowledge of the collection disappeared in the following 200 years. Menzies' collection went to George III and eventually to the British Museum, where it forms an important early element in the collections from the Northwest coast of America, in addition to containing items from the South Pacific, including material gathered on the Colnett voyage. They range from clothing to weapons, from baskets to food bowls. However, they would have been of much less significance were it not for the existence of Menzies' journal with its detailed descriptions of the native peoples encountered during the Vancouver voyage in particular.

Apart from his plant collecting and observations on the geography and customs of the regions visited by him, one aspect of Menzies' scientific recording has only recently been examined in detail: his systematic weather recordings during the Vancouver voyage. These have come to light as a result of the finding of his tabulated daily observations (amounting to 39 pages of carefully listed records) in the archives of the Royal Meteorological Society.[12] In his journal entry for 1 April 1791, at the start of this voyage, Menzies wrote:

> I now began to register daily at noon the height of the mercury in the barometer which stood suspended in the great cabin together with that of the thermometer exposed in the open air in a shaded place ... I therefore ascertained it [ocean temperature] by immersing a thermometer in a bucket of water fresh drawn from the surface of the sea.

(This last was to ascertain whether in different climatic regimes, the sea temperature differed from the air temperature.) What is particularly interesting is that when recording wind strength, Menzies used descriptions very like those proposed by Francis Beaufort some 15 years later and which are still in use today.[13] Further, Menzies was able to predict gales and stormy weather by keeping watch on a falling barometer reading. This was more than a decade before Robert Fitzroy, the great exponent of this method of sea weather prediction, was born.[14] Taken together with Menzies' accurate determination of the heights of mountains in Hawaii using a portable barometer and his observations of differential cloud movements at different heights, for example, his recordings show him to have been a first class observational scientist. These recordings were the first systematic weather observations along the length of the North American coast and for this reason alone are important historically.[15]

There are a number of problems associated with the assessment of Menzies' contribution to botany. The first is obviously his tardiness in writing up and publishing his own work, much of which had to be left to others, notably W. J. Hooker. There is no doubt that the lack of any major published work to his name seriously affected his scientific standing. The second is that many of his papers and specimens were subsequently dispersed to various institutions and individuals: a number of memorabilia were lodged with the Provincial Archives of British Columbia, while his flowering plant specimens went to the British Museum, but his very considerable herbarium collection (valued at his death at a mere £60) was lodged with the Royal Botanic Garden Edinburgh. Here it was not kept as a discrete collection, but was dispersed within the classified system; Menzies had stipulated in his bequest that it should be placed in an appropriate locality for study. (See Hedge and Lamond (1970) for the index of collectors in the Edinburgh herbarium.)

A letter of 22 March 1920 from the Director at Kew, in response to a query from Sir David Menzies, categorically states: 'No catalogue of the plants collected and sent home by Dr. Menzies exists – his specimens are all dispersed ... there is no indisputable

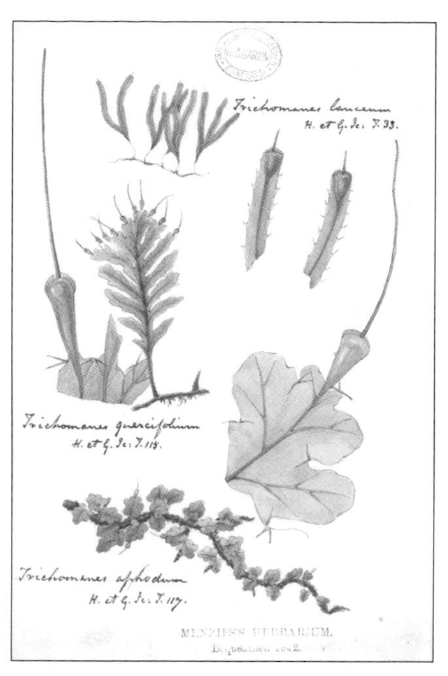

Menzies demonstrates his drawing skills in this fine sketch of non-flowering bryophytes, his special field of interest. (RBGE archive.)

evidence that he introduced any except the Monkey Puzzle.'[16] While this may be strictly correct, it does not take account of the very many seeds which were sent by Menzies from his various journeys, a number of which would have been successfully raised by others. (Part of the problem is that references in the literature to Menzies do not clearly distinguish between 'collected', 'noted', 'discovered' and 'identified'.) It has been remarked that, whereas other later botanists were in a position to bring home live plants, the conditions in which Menzies worked, often constrained by a shipboard existence, pre-empted this.[17]

One question which has vexed botanists in particular is why, especially during the Vancouver voyage in the years 1793 and 1794, there are so few specific botanical records in Menzies' journal. Jepson in 1929 commented:

> Menzies from time to time makes a few notes, in more or less general terms, of his botanical excursions ashore, but on account of the utter strangeness of the vegetation his comments are not, on the whole, of much significance ... on the other hand the journal is amply filled with other matters. Save for the reference to himself as a botanist just noted one might suppose from reading the manuscript that Menzies was the navigator or geographer of the expedition. The progress of the *Discovery* or its consort the *Chatham*, every storm that impeded, every wind that aided their movement, is faithfully set down.[18]

Lamb regards this as an extreme view, but suggests that apart from the very real possibility that Menzies' detailed botanical notes were kept in a separate notebook, now lost, it is just possible that the pressure from Banks to complete the journal obliged Menzies to omit such detail from the journal *per se*.[19] Lamb supports this by showing that there was a change in the latter part of the journal, suggesting that the copying from original notes by Menzies might have been abandoned after 1796 under the direction of Banks.[20]

Many of the species which Menzies collected have become favourite garden plants. Some of the most notable have been the broadleaf evergreen *Mahonia (Berberis) aquifolium*, the Oregon Grape, and the deciduous Flowering Currant, *Ribes sanguineum*. Others include *Nemophila menziesii* (Baby Blue Eyes), *Gaultheria shallon* (salal), *Chimaphila menziesii* (Menzies Pipsissewa) and many others.[21] However, perhaps the most obvious of the plants in the larger garden have been the tree-shrubs such as Lawson's Cypress, with its enormously varied forms and colours ranging from deep green to almost pure yellow, and widely used in parks and gardens.[22] Care must be taken however with the assumption that Menzies introduced into cultivation many of the plants which he collected (i.e. 'discovered'), as there is no evidence of this.

Monkey puzzle trees in their natural habitat in the Nasampulli Reserve, Chile. (RBGE archive.)

Although Menzies' collections of herbaceous and non-flowering plants are not unimportant, there is no doubt that it was the tree species he discovered which have been of most obvious economic significance, including such species as Western Red Cedar, Lawson's Cypress, Western Hemlock, Noble Fir, Douglas Fir, and Sitka Spruce. Some of these Menzies would have seen before the end of his life clothing the slopes of the hills of his native Perthshire, enhancing many of the large ancestral estates there, which would have undoubtedly given him much pleasure.[23]

He could not have imagined however that the planting of the last of these tree species, Sitka Spruce, with its rapid growth and toleration of the wet boggy conditions of western Britain, would have resulted in perhaps the greatest change in the landscape of Scotland in the last hundred years. Thriving in a climatic environment very similar to that of its homeland in British Columbia, huge swathes of this species have replaced many of the previous sheep runs and deer forests of the north and west, often to the distress of those who valued the open uplands for their distinctive wildlife and scenery.[24]

One species which has gained a certain notoriety is in part due to Menzies. This is the hybrid x *Cupressocyparis leylandii*, a dense conifer, which as a fast-growing hedge has been the cause of many neighbour disputes in the United Kingdom. Menzies first discovered it as *Chamaecyparis nootkatensis* or Nootka Cypress, before it was hybridised with *Cupressus macrocarpa* to produce the ornamental Leyland Cypress. Nootka Cypress was introduced into Britain as seed by Menzies' colleague David Douglas, whose friend, the nurseryman James Lawson, promoted another false cypress, Lawson's Cypress, brought back by Douglas, to become a favourite ornamental of many different forms and colours in British and North American gardens.

Menzies also discovered Western Red Cedar (*Thuja plicata*), not only a useful timber tree, but one which was used by the native Indians for a variety of purposes, including the making of house posts and longhouses.[25] It was Douglas also who gave his name to the Douglas Fir, although its discoverer is celebrated in its scientific name *Pseudotsuga menziesii*. The species is distinguished by providing the tallest tree so far recorded in the United Kingdom, a massive specimen of 64 metres growing in Reelig Glen in Inverness-shire, with its own local Gaelic name *Dughall Mhor* or 'big dark stranger'.[26]

Few other botanists have given their name to such a large number of plant species as Menzies. Close to one hundred flowering plants, and numerous non-flowering plants, have been named after him. Menzies' collection from western North America represents the most extensive, early gathering of dried plant material from that region and contains an unprecedented number of examples that have subsequently become the types [sources] of new species. It forms a most important source and baseline on which any historical study on western North American botany may be founded.

The above is the informed assessment of the foremost authority on Menzies as a botanist, E. W. Groves, and is perhaps Menzies' most fitting epitaph.[27] (See Appendix 4.) Groves selected several of the species collected by Menzies as exemplars of the many familiar to horticulturists and which bear his name, including *Arbutus menziesii* (Pacific Madrone), *Erysimum menziesii* (Menzies Wallflower), *Penstemon menziesii* (Menzies Penstemon), *Silene menziesii* (Menzies Catchfly), *Spiraea menziesii* (Menzies Spiraea) and *Tolmiea menziesii* (Youth-on-age, or Pick-a-back Plant).[28]

Of all the species which Menzies collected, one conifer stands out, partly due to its unique appearance, and partly because of the controversy surrounding its reputed 'collection' by Menzies. This is the Monkey Puzzle (*Araucaria araucana*). Within the genus there are 41 known taxa, with the largest collection (28) in the United Kingdom being in the Royal Botanic Garden Edinburgh and its associated gardens such as Benmore, which is appropriate given that Menzies is generally accepted as being responsible for its introduction to Northern Europe. *Araucaria araucana* remains the most widespread in cultivation. As a native species, it grows in large natural stands in Chile and Argentina. In its native haunts, the tallest specimens have been measured at over 165 feet (50 m).

It is a very ancient tree, having existed during Jurassic times. In its natural environment it can live up to 2000 years, but is unfortunately threatened at the present time by timber cutting and forest fires, sometimes caused by volcanic eruptions. It has both male and female trees (i.e. dioecious) but very rarely, trees with both male and female branches have occurred. Usually the sex cannot be confirmed until the specimen is mature, after about 40 years. It produces spectacularly large (up to 1 kg) green ball-like female cones with up to 200 large edible seeds; these provide a staple food of the Pehuenche Indians, and are sold in local markets in Chile. The name Pehuenche means people of the Pehune or Monkey Puzzle, who traditionally based their diet on the tree, with a single family collecting up to 4000 kg at harvest time.[29]

> In Chile and Argentina, the spirit of the Pehue'n tree (*Araucaria araucana*) known as the monkey-puzzle tree, provides food during periods of scarcity and is also believed to have a positive influence on the harvest. The spirit is especially kind to women and children. This tree is also connected to the god who lives in volcanoes and is the creator of storms and thunder.[30]

A Pehuenche Indian spokesman, Alfredo Melenir, has said: 'The monkey puzzle is our tree. It's a symbol for us. It's a tree that God left on earth, for us, the Pehuenche. We cannot cut it down, because it gives us our daily bread. In the end, we would rather die than give up defending this tree.'[31]

There is now an international effort to preserve the natural araucaria forests of southern Chile, a leading role being played by the Royal Botanic Garden Edinburgh as part of the International Conifer Conservation Programme. Reserves at Nasampulli and Namuncahue have been established under its aegis and that of other Chilean authorities. The native Chilean species is now listed in the Convention on International Trade in Endangered Species (CITES) and is on the World Conservation Union (IUCN) 'Red List' as 'vulnerable'.

There is a certain sad irony that the genus is named after a native Indian tribe, the Araucas from southern Chile, whom Bernardo O'Higgins helped to extinguish in the campaigns which elevated him to supreme military commander of Chile, and now only the trees remain. The name 'Monkey Puzzle' may derive from the practice of using trained monkeys to gather the fruits from tropical trees, selecting, for example, only the ripe fruit from coconut palm. Early botanists used to rent a monkey locally to help gather leaves, flowers and fruits in tropical areas, and it would have been a problem for these animals to traverse the very sharp pointed leaves of *Araucaria* to reach the fruits at the tip – not that this would have been required, since the large fruits or cones of this genus, which take two years to develop, fall to the ground when ripe.

Menzies would have been fascinated by the chance finding of the 'Wollemi Pine' (*Wollemia nobilis*), a so-called living fossil and one of the world's oldest and rarest trees. Previously thought to be extinct, it was found in a rain forest gorge near Sydney, Australia in 1994 and appears to be a genus intermediate between *Araucaria* and the New Zealand Kauri Pine (*Agathis australis*).[32]

NOTES

1. Groves (2001), 26
2. Justice (2000), 21
3. Ibid., 22
4. Musgrave, Gardner and Musgrave (1998), 56
5. Cowan (1954), 219–22
6. Musgrave, Gardner and Musgrave (1998), 146–7
7. Harris (2003), 405–6
8. A huge cross-section of this species dominates the second floor of the British Museum (Natural History), London.
9. Olson (1993), 14–15
10. Galloway and Groves (1987), 3
11. King (1994), 35
12. Walker (2006), 315
13. Ibid., 316
14. Ibid., 317
15. Ibid., 319
16. RBGE mss. Folder 2, Edinburgh
17. Newcombe, xix, in Groves (2001), 106
18. Jepson, W. L., 'The Botanical Explorers of California – vi Archibald Menzies', in Lamb (1993), 331
19. Ibid., 242
20. Ibid., 244

21. Justice (2000), 101 *et seq.*
22. Ibid., 108
23. Balfour (1924), 22–3
24. McCarthy (2006), 59
25. Justice (2000), 67
26. Rodger, Stokes and Ogilvie (2006), 230
27. Groves (2001), 109
28. Groves (1998), 15
29. Smyly (2006), 5–8
30. Bernbaum and Spook (2002), n.p.
31. Lewington and Parker (1999), 51
32. Justice (2000), 32

18

The Puzzle Resolved

In several of the published articles on the life and accomplishments of Archibald Menzies, doubt has been cast on the tale (referred to in an earlier chapter) of his pocketing the *Araucaria* nuts from the table of the Irish Captain-General of Chile, Captain-General Bernardo O'Higgins. Menzies himself never recorded the banquet or secreting the nuts. Marks suggests, in an article dedicated to investigating the story, that it is apocryphal.[1] He considers that the story has been confused with another, in which Menzies, while on one of the *Discovery's* visits to California, was given a flowering branch by a priest at the mission of San Diego. Menzies recorded in his journal:

> … he sent me also a quantity of fruit in kernels which he said were the natural produce of the country. They were about the size of small kidney beans and in their taste somewhat like bitter almonds; to these he ascribed many virtues by taking them internally or by external application in the form of cataplasms … but what was most pleasant to me, he sent along with them some of the plants that produced them which were immediately planted in the frame on the quarterdeck and I have the pleasure to add were brought back alive to England and placed in his Majesty's Royal Garden at Kew.

This however was almost certainly the Jojoba or Goatnut, *Simmondsia californica*, according to Groves.[2]

Marks considers the tale of the introduction of the Monkey Puzzle a 'long shot' and states that 'at no point in his journal does Menzies mention those other kernels, the edible seeds of the monkey puzzle – conical, three centimetres long and two centimetres wide, tasting of sweet chestnuts'. However, the matter may be laid to rest from a very authoritative source. Eric Groves, the foremost scholarly authority on Menzies, in his comprehensive article on the botanist, states quite categorically: 'That the event was true is not in doubt for it was later recounted by Menzies in old age to Sir Joseph Hooker. Five young trees were brought back, one of which lived on at Kew for nearly a century.'[3]

He supports this in a note in the same article, quoting Elwes and Henry who state that 'Sir Joseph Hooker, who knew Menzies personally, tells me (i.e. Elwes) that he took seeds from the dessert table of the Governor'.[4] Apparently, Menzies was able to bring back five living plants in the plant frame, all of which were given to Banks, who kept one plant for his own collection and gave the remainder to the Royal Botanic Gardens at Kew.[5] According to Marks, within a year of Menzies' death, a Yarmouth nursery was advertising four-year-old Monkey Puzzle plants for £5 per hundred. 'It was told to Elwes by Sir Joseph Hooker, who as a youth had it from Menzies' own lips when he was an old man. Of these trees I have a table made from the last of the five which had been planted out at Kew by Banks; it died in 1892.'[6]

> [Menzies] succeeded in bringing back five of the seedling monkey puzzles for Sir Joseph Banks ... Sir Joseph Banks planted one of the seedlings in his own garden at Spring Grove and sent the remainder to Kew and in 1806 or 1808 at least one tree was considered hardy enough to leave the green house and was planted out, though it was at first protected during the winter months with a temporary frame covered with mats. In 1817 it was reported to have been 'irretrievably injured by its presence at a single gala at Carlton House, owing to the servants having very imprudently attached lamps to the branches of the tree'.[7]

King William presented one of the young trees, when five feet high and growing in a tub, to Lady Granville for her garden at Dropmore, where by 1830 it had reached 60 feet but was said to be rivalled by another at Dropmore, 'the produce of a cutting stolen by a lady from the original plant at Kew nearly fifty years ago'. This original plant was still in 1840

> ... the lion of the gardens. King William, who, in his frequent visits to Kew, never omitted going over the Botanic Gardens, and latterly, when walking became inconvenient, drove through them in a pony phaeton, and at all events looked into every house, delighted to point out the superb tree to such strangers as might be with him.[8]

The final demise of this fine specimen in 1892, when it was almost 100 years old, was recorded in the *Kew Bulletin* early in 1893, where the story of the introduction of the species by Menzies was retold.[9] The same article reminded its readers that it was originally known as 'Sir Joseph Banks's Pine'.[10] The 'Monkey Puzzle Man', if for nothing else, had made his most distinctive mark on the gardens and estates of Britain.[11]

> ... like a heart beating in the crowded restlessness of the towering araucaria.
>
> Pablo Neruda: 'Oh Earth, Wait for Me' in *Memorial de Isla Negra*, 1964

NOTES

1. Marks (1996), 10–13
2. Groves (2001), 100
3. Ibid., 100
4. Elwes and Henry (1906), 1. 46fn. 3
5. Louden (1838), 2432
6. Balfour (1944), 179
7. Neill (1823), 77, quoted in Keevil (1948), 804
8. *Bulletin of Miscellaneous Information*, Royal Botanic Gardens, Kew (1891), 299–300, quoted in Keevil (1948), 805
9. *Kew Bulletin*, 24 February 1824, Miscellaneous Notes, 24
10. Charlotte Geddes of Edinburgh, a great-niece of Menzies, received at her request a section of the Kew tree. She had in her possession not only his honours from Aberdeen and Leipzig universities – as well as the fine oak cases used by the botanist for his collections while on the *Discovery* – but also his original instructions from Banks. (Kew Collectors: Various Collectors, March 1893, Kew Botanic Gardens)
11. In 2004, to celebrate 250 years since Menzies' birth, a young *Araucaria araucana* was planted in the gardens of Castle Menzies.

Appendix 1:

Historical Events during Archibald Menzies' Lifetime (1754–1842)

1744 Britain at war with France discontinuously until 1815
1757 Clive wins Bengal for Britain after victory at Plessey
1759 British defeat French at Quebec
1763 End of Seven Years War: Canada ceded to Britain by French
1769 Cook charts east coast of Australia and reaches New Zealand
1770 James Bruce discovers source of Blue Nile in Abyssinia
1774 James Watt makes first steam engine
1775–83 American War of Independence
1784 British Government controls India under India Act
1788 Colony of Australia founded
1789 French Revolution
1791 HMS *Discovery* sets sail for survey of Northwest of America
1792 France proclaimed a republic
1793 War with Revolutionary France
1793 Alexander Mackenzie is the first person to traverse North America, reaching Bella Coola just weeks before Menzies reached this inlet
1795 HMS *Discovery* returns to England from North America
1796 Mungo Park reaches Niger
1799 British take control of South India after Battle of Seringpatam
1799 Napoleon proclaims himself First Consul of France
1801 Mathew Flinders circumnavigates Australia
1801 Union of Great Britain and Ireland
1804 Lewis and Clark complete crossing of America
1804 Napoleon crowned Emperor of France
1805 Battle of Trafalgar
1806 Britain re-occupies Cape of Good Hope in South Africa
1807 Abolition of slave trade in British Empire
1808–14 Britain fights France in Spain during Peninsular War
1815 Battle of Waterloo
1828–29 Russo-Turkish War
1830 Belgium becomes independent from Holland
1832 First Parliamentary Reform Act in Britain
1840 First Opium War between Britain and China
1841 Britain annexes Hong Kong

Appendix 2:

Outline Biography of Archibald Menzies (1754–1842)

1754–68 Early life and education at Aberfeldy.

1768 Training in horticulture at Royal Botanic Garden Edinburgh under Professor John Hope and first plant collecting in Scottish Highlands.

1778 Qualifies as surgeon, University of Edinburgh.

1782 First naval appointment to Caribbean as assistant surgeon.

1784 Appointed to Halifax, Nova Scotia – first correspondence with Sir Joseph Banks and despatch of plant material.

1786–89 Voyage on the *Prince of Wales* to Pacific Northwest on fur-trading expedition. Sea otter trade and first encounters with native peoples.

1789 Returns to England, works in Sir Joseph Banks' library and prepares for next major voyage with George Vancouver aboard HMS *Discovery* to carry out five-year survey of North American coast. Instructions from Banks on collecting and recording, and first difficulties with Vancouver.

1791 With *Discovery en route* to Northwest coast, visiting/collecting in South Africa, Western Australia, New Zealand and Tahiti.

1791–94 Surveying the Northwest coast from California to Alaska – plant collecting, relations with Spanish in California and with native peoples, etc. Three winter visits to Hawaii and first recorded ascent of Wha-ra-rai and Mauna Loa.

1795 The journey home and rift between Vancouver and Menzies and its aftermath.

1796–1803 Later naval career in Caribbean, Mediterranean, etc. Awarded honorary degrees from universities of Aberdeen and Leipzig.

1798 Following return to England, elected Fellow of the Linnean Society.

1803–42 Marriage and establishment of medical practice in London, developing connections with botanical world and Kew, and advising younger botanical explorers especially on proposed American expeditions.

Appendix 3:

Instructions to Archibald Menzies from Sir Joseph Banks prior to the Voyage of HMS *Discovery* 1791–95

Soho Square
22 February 1791

Sir,

The business on which you are employed being of an extensive nature, as it includes an investigation of the whole of the Natural History of the Countries you are to visit, as well as an enquiry into the present state & comparative degree of civilization of the Inhabitants you will meet with, the utmost degree of diligence and perseverance on your part will be necessary to enable you to do justice to your Employers and gain credit to yourself.

The following Instructions you will consider as a guide to the outline of your conduct, but, as many particulars will doubtless occur in the investigation of unknown Countries that are not noticed in them, all such are left to your discretion & good sense; and you are hereby directed to act in them as you judge most likely to promote the interest of Science, & contribute to the increase of human knowledge.

In all places where the Ship in which you are embarked shall touch, and the Commander shall make sufficient stay, you are to pay a particular regard to the nature of the soil, & to note down its quality, whether Clay, Sand, Gravel, Loam &c. &c., and how it is circumstanced in regard to water. You are to remark particularly [on] the size of the Trees that grow upon it, whether they stand in thick close Groves, or separate and distinct from each other. You are to consider also, as far as you are enabled to do by the productions, the probable Climate, and whether, should it any time hereafter be deemed expedient to send out settlers from England, the Grains, Pulse and Fruits cultivated in Europe [that] are likely to thrive, and if not what kind of produce would in your opinion be the most suitable.

As far as you find yourself able, you are to enumerate all the Trees, Shrubs, Plants, Grasses, Ferns and Mosses you shall meet with in each Country you visit by their scientific names as well as those used in the language of the Natives, noting particularly the places where each is found, especially those that are new or particularly curious. You are also to dry specimens of all such as you shall judge worthy of being brought home, particularly those of which you shall procure either living Plants or Seeds, in order that the Persons who are employed in examining the Plants you furnish to his Majesty's Gardens at Kew may be assisted in ascertaining their names and qualities.

Whenever you meet with ripe seeds of Plants, you are carefully to collect them, and, having dried them properly, to put them up in paper packages, writing on the outside, or in a corresponding List, such particulars relative to the soil and climate where each was found, and the mode of culture in your opinion likely to succeed with it as you may think necessary to be communicated to His Majesty's Gardeners; and you are to forward these packages directed to me for His Majesty's use by every convenient opportunity that shall occur, dividing them for safety's sake into duplicates as often as you shall judge needful.

When you meet with curious or valuable Plants which you do not think likely to be propagated from seeds in His Majesty's Garden, you are to dig up proper Specimens of them, plant them in the Glass Frame provided for that purpose, and use your utmost endeavours to preserve them alive till your return. You are to consider every one of them, as well as all Seeds of Plants which you shall collect during the voyage, as wholly and entirely the property of His Majesty, and on no account whatever to part with any of them, or any cuttings, slips, or parts of any of them for any purpose whatever but for His Majesty's use.

As soon as you shall have provided yourself with living plants, and planted them in the Glass frame before mentioned, you are at all times, when the Ship shall be watered, to acquaint the Commanding Officer what quantity of water you judge necessary for their support and preservation, by the week or month, in order that he may be enabled to make a competent provision of that article for their future maintenance & nourishment.

In all your excursions on shore, you are to examine with care and attention the Beds of Brooks and Torrents, the steep sides of Cliffs, and all other places where the interior Strata of the Earth are laid bare by water, or otherwise to remark [on] the nature of the Earth and Stones of which they are composed; & if among them you discover Ores or Metals, or any Mineral substances which bear a resemblance to such things, or any Beds of Coal, Limestones, or other matters likely in your opinion to prove useful to mankind, you are to collect and preserve specimens of them, carefully noting the exact spot on which each was found. You are also to examine the Pebbles and Sand brought down by the Rivers and Brooks from the Inland Country, and to collect and bring home samples of such as you suspect to contain Mineral substances, even though so minute as not to be discoverable but by a Microscope.

At each place where you land, you are to inform yourself as well as you are able what sort of Beasts, Birds and Fishes likely to prove useful either for food or in Commerce are to be found; and pay particular attention to the various ways of catching them in Traps, or otherways used by the Natives. You are to pay particular attention to every part of the natural History of the Sea Otter, and to learn all you are able concerning wild Sheep said to be found in the Inland Countries, and, if in your power, to procure a Skin of one of them for your Employers. You are also to note particularly all places where Whales or Seals are found in abundance. At all places where a friendly intercourse with the Natives is established, you are to make diligent inquiry into their manners, Customs, Language and Religion, if to obtain all the information in your power concerning their Manufactures, particularly the Art of dying, in which

Savages have frequently been found to excel; and if any part of their conduct, civil or religious, should appear to you unreasonable as not to be likely to meet with credit when related in Europe, you are, if you can do it with safety and propriety, to make yourself an eye witness of it in order that the fact of it's existence may be established on as firm a basis as the nature of the Enquiry will permit. You are to keep a regular journal of all occurrences that happen in the execution of the several Duties you are entrusted to perform, and enter in it all the observations you shall make on every subject you are employed to investigate; which journal, together with a complete collection of specimens of Animals, Vegetables & Minerals you shall have obtained, as well as such curious articles of the Cloths, Arms, Implements and manufactures of the Indians as you shall deem worthy of particular notice, you are on your return to deliver to His Majesty's Secretary of State for the Home Department, or to such person as he shall appoint to receive them from you.

I am, Sir,
Your most obedient
humble Servant,

Jos: Banks.

Appendix 4:

Plant Species Collected by Archibald Menzies 1791–94 as listed (simplified) by E. W. Groves (2001) excluding California (see Appendix 5)

Abronia latifolia	Yellow Sand Verbena
umbellata	Sand Verbena
Acer circinatum	Vine Maple
glabrum	Douglas Maple
macrophyllum	Bigleaf Maple
Allium acuminatum	Hooker's Onion
cernuum	Nodding Onion
Alnus incana	Thin-leaved Alder
rubra	Red Alder
viridis	Sitka Alder
Amelanchier alnifolia	Saskatoon
Amerorchis rotundifolia	Small-leaved Orchis
Andromeda polifolia	Bog Rosemary
Araucaria araucana	Chile Pine
Arbutus menziesii	Pacific Madrone
Arctostaphylos columbiana	Northern Manzanita
tomentosa	Shaggy Bark Manzanita
uva-ursi	Kinnikinnik
Astragalus trichopodus	Rattleweed
Atriplex gmelini	Narrow Orache
Baccharis pilularis	Chaparral Broom
Betula occidentalis	White Birch
papyrifera	Paper Birch
papyrifera var. *kenaica*	Alaskan Coastal Birch
Caltha leptosepala	Broad-leaved Marsh Marigold
leptosepala subsp. *leptosepala*	Alpine White Marsh Marigold
Calypso bulbosa	Fairy Slipper Orchid
Carpobrotus aequilateralis	Sea Fig
Ceanothus thrysiflorus	Blue Blossom
Chimaphila menziesii	Little Pipsissewa
umbellata	Princes Pine
Cladothamnus pyroliflorus	Copper-bush
Clintonia uniflora	Queen's Cup

Colutea arborescens	Bladder Senna
Coptis asplenifolia	Spleenwort-leaved Golden Thread
Corallorhiza mertensiana	Western Coralroot
Cornus canadensis	Bunchberry or Dwarf Dogwood
nuttalli	Western Flowering Dogwood
sericea	Red Osier Dogwood
Corylus cornuta	Beaked or California Hazel
Crataegus douglasii	Black Hawthorn
Dodecatheon pulchellum	Few-flowered Shooting Star
Drosera rotundifolia	Round-leaved Sundew
Dryas drummondii	Yellow Mountain Aven
Empetrum nigrum	Crowberry
Epilobium minutum	Small-flowered Willowherb
Erysimum menziesii	Menzies Wallflower
Euphorbia misera	Cliff Spurge
Fraxinus latifolia	Oregon Ash
Garrya elliptica	Coast Silktassel
Gaultheria shallon	Salal
Gentiana douglasiana	Swamp Gentian
sceptrum	King Gentian
Heliotropium curassavicum	Seaside Heliotrope
Heuchera parviflora	Alpine Arrowroot
Holodiscus discolor	Creambush Ocean Spray
Juniperus scopulorum	Rocky Mountain Juniper
Kalmia microphylla	Western Bog Laurel
Ledum groenlandicum	Labrador Tea
palustre	Northern or Narrow-leaved Labrador Tea
Ligusticum scoticum	Beach Lovage
Lilium columbianum	Tiger Lily
Linnaea borealis	Twinflower
Listera caurina	North-Western Twayblade
cordata	Heart-leaved Twayblade
Loiseleuria procumbens	Alpine Azalea
Lonicera ciliosa	Western Trumpet Honeysuckle
Lysichiton americanus	Skunk Cabbage
Mahonia aquifolium	Tall Oregon Grape
nervosa	Dull Oregon Grape
Malus fusca	Western Crabapple
Menyanthes trifoliata	Buckbean
Mertensia maritima	Sea Lungwort
Mespilus germanica	Medlar

Mimulus aurantiacus	Sticky Monkeyflower
Nemophila menziesii	Baby Blue-eyes
parviflora	The Grove Lover
Nothofagus menziesii	Silver Beech
Orthilia secunda	One-sided Wintergreen or Side Bells
Oxalis albicans	Hairy Wood Sorrel
Parkinsonia aculeata	Mexican Palo Verde
Parnassia fimbriata	Fringed Grass of Parnassus
Pedicularis menziesii	Menzies Lousewort
parviflora	Small-flowered Lousewort
Penstemon menziesii	Menzies Penstemon
serrulatus	Coast Penstemon
Philadelphus lewisii var. *gordonianus*	Mock Orange
Phyllodoce empetriformis	Red Mountain Heath
Picea abies	Norway Spruce
glauca	White Spruce
glauca var. *albertiana*	Western White Pine
mariana	Black Spruce
sitchensis	Sitka Spruce
Plantago macrocarpa	Alaskan Plantain
Plectris congesta	Sea Blush
Populus tremuloides	Quaking Aspen
tremuloides var. *aurea*	Western Trembling Poplar
Pyrola aphylla	Leafless Wintergreen
asarifolia	Pink-flowered Wintergreen
dentata	Nootka Wintergreen
picta	White-veined Wintergreen
Quercus garryana	Garry Oak
Ranunculus californicus	Californian Buttercup
Rhododendron macrophyllum	Pacific Rhododendron
Rhynchospora alba	White Beaked Rush
Ribes bracteosum	Stink Currant
divaricatum	Wild Gooseberry
hudsonianum	Northern Blackcurrant
lacustre	Prickly Currant
laxiflorum	Trailing Blackcurrant
lobbii	Gummy Gooseberry
malvaceum	Chaparral Currant
menziesii	Menzies Gooseberry
speciosum	Fuschia-flowered Gooseberry
Romanzoffia californica	California Misat-Maiden

Rosa gymnocarpa	Baldhip Rose
nutkana	Nootka Rose
Rubus parviflorus	Thimbleberry
pedatus	Five-leaved Bramble
spectabilis	Salmonberry
Salicornia maritima	European Glasswort
virginica	American Pickleweed
Salix alaxensis	Alaska Willow
barclayi	Barclay's Willow
bebbiana	Bebb Willow
sitchensis	Sitka Willow
Sanguisorba menziesii	Menzies Burnet
Saxifraga caespitosa	Tufted Saxifrage
Schiedea menziesii	—
Sedum rosea	Roseroot
Silene acaulis	Moss Campion
Spiraea menziesii	Menzies Spiraea
Tellima grandiflora	Fringe Cup
Thuja plicata	Western Red Cedar or Arbor Vitae
Tofieldia glutinosa	Sticky False Asphodel
Tolmiea menziesii	Youth-on-age
Triteleia hyacinthina	White Brodiæa or Fool's Onion
Tsuga heterophylla	Western Hemlock
Vaccinium alaskense	Alaska Blueberry
caespitosum	Dwarf Huckleberry
membranaceum	Thin-leaved Blueberry
ovalifolium	Black Huckleberry
ovatum	Evergreen Huckleberry
oxycoccus	Bog Cranberry
parvifolium	Red Huckleberry
uliginosum	Bog Blueberry
vitis-idaea	Lingonberry or Mountain Cranberry
Vancouveria hexandra	Inside-out Flower
Verbena lasiostachys	Western Vervain
Viola epipsila	Marsh Violet
langsdorfii	Alaska Violet
Zigadenus venenosus	Death Camus

Appendix 5:

Plants found by Archibald Menzies in California in 1792 and 1793*

Abronia latifolia	Yellow Sand Verbena
umbellata	Sand Verbena
Aesculus californica	Californian Buckeye
Arctostaphylos tomentosa	Shaggy Bark Manzanita
Artemisia californica	California Sagebrush
douglasiana	Mugwort
Astragalus trichopodus	Rattleweed
Ceanothus thrysiflorus	Blue Blossom
Cleome isomeris	Bladder Pod
Epilobium ciliatum	Fireweed, Willow Herb
Ericameria ericoides	Goldenbush
Eschscholzia californica	California Beach Poppy
Euphorbia misera	Cliff Spurge
Ferocactus viridescens	Coast Barrel Cactus
Gaultheria shallon	Salal
Heliotropium curassavicum	Seaside Heliotrope
Heteromeles arbutifolia	Christmas Berry
Lonicera ledebourii	Honeysucklc
Macrocystis pyrifera	Common Long Kelp
Mammillaria dioica	Nipple Cactus
Mesembryanthemum chilense	Ice Plant
Mimulus longiflorus	Musk Flower
Opuntia engelmannii	Engelmann's Prickly Pear
prolifera	Cholla
serpentina (parryi)	Cane Cholla, Snake Cholla
Oxalis californica	Californian Wood Sorrel
Parkinsonia aculeata	Mexican Palo Verde
Pinus radiata	Monterey Pine
Platanus racemosa	Western Sycamore
Polygonum paronychia	Knotweed
Populus balsamifera	Black Cottonwood
Quercus agrifolia	Coast Live Oak, Encina
lobata	Valley Oak, Roble
Ranunculus californicus	Californian Buttercup

Salicornia virginica	Pickleweed
Salix lasiandra	Shining Willow
lasiolepis	Arroyo Willow
Sequoia sempervirens	Coast Redwood
Simmondsia californica	Jojoba, Goatnut, Pignut
Sisyrinchium californicum	Yellow-eyed Grass
Solidago spathulata	Coast Goldenrod
Verbena lasiostachys	Vervain

* As listed by Alice Eastwood (1924) and brought in line with Munz, P. A. (1959), *A California Flora*, with several additions from other sources.

Bibliography

Unpublished Sources

British Columbia Archives and Records Service, Victoria. Archibald Menzies: correspondence and papers

British Library. Archibald Menzies' *Journal of the Voyage in the Discovery*, Add. MS. 32641

British Museum (Natural History) Botany Library. Banks Correspondence, Dawson Turner Transcripts

Linnean Society, London. Menzies, *A Journal of Vancouver's Voyage for December 1790 to February 1794* (5 vols). Transcript ms 418

Mitchell Library, Sydney. Brabourne Papers

National Archives, London. *A Voyage to the NW Side of America. Journal of the Prince of Wales*. ADM 55/146

National Archives of Scotland. John Hope Collection GD 253/146/2/12/2

National Library of Australia. Archibald Menzies' *Journal of the Voyage in the Discovery*

RBGE mss. Menzies, Sir Robert and Castle Menzies. Miscellaneous Papers 1700–1833. Accounts, records, journal, etc.

Robertson, J. I. *pers. comm.*

Royal Botanic Gardens, Kew. Banks Correspondence; W. J. Hooker Correspondence

Trinity College Library, Cambridge. Dawson Turner Correspondence

Trolle Ljungby Castle, Bäckaskog, Sweden. Carl Gustav von Brinkman Collection, Swartz Correspondence

University of Edinburgh New College. Archibald Menzies Journal relating to Sandwich Islands

University of Washington Library. A. Menzies Papers

Published Sources

Aitken, J. J., 1988. 'Archibald Menzies 1754–1842.' *Newsletter of the Friends of St. Andrews University Botanic Garden*, 36.

Allen, D. E., 1977. 'Archibald Menzies in Nova Scotia.' *Journal of the Society for the Bibliography of Natural History*, 8.

Anderson, B., 1939. 'The Vancouver Expedition: Peter Puget's Journal of the Expl-oration of Puget Sound May 7–June 11, 1792.' *Pacific North West Quarterly*, 30.

Anderson, B., 1960. *Surveyor of the Sea: The Life and Voyages of Capt. George Vancouver.* Toronto: University of Toronto Press.

Anon., 1891. *Bulletin of Miscellaneous Information.* Surrey: Royal Botanic Gardens, Kew.

Anon., *1842. Gentleman's Magazine*, 2nd Series, 17.

Badè, W. F., 1924. *The Life and Letters of John Muir.* Boston: Houghton Mifflen.

Baglin, D. and Mullins, B., 1970. *Australian Banksias.* Sydney: Horwitz Publications.

Baigent, E., 2004. 'Archibald Menzies.' *New Oxford Dictionary of National Biography*, 30, p. 826 (61 vols).

Balfour, F. R. S., 1924. 'Review of Menzies's Journal of Vancouver's voyage, April to October 1792.' *Transactions of the Royal Scottish Arboricultural Society,* 38.

Balfour, F. R. S., 1944. 'Archibald Menzies, 1754–1842: Botanist, zoologist, medico, and explorer.' *Proceedings of the Linnean Society*, 156th session.
Bance, P., 2004. *The Duleep Singhs: The Photograph Album of Queen Victoria's Maharajah*. Stroud: Sutton Publishing.
Bernbaum, E., and Spook, J. D., 2002. *Seasonal Interpreters' Handbook.* The Mountain Institute.
Bown, D., 1992. *4 Gardens in One: The Royal Botanic Garden Edinburgh.* Edinburgh: HMSO.
Breen, K., 1994. 'Rodney: Les Saintes, 1782' in E. J. Grove, ed. *Great Battles of the Royal Navy.* London: Arms & Armour.
Britten, J., 1924. 'Review of 1923: Menzies's Journal of Vancouver's Voyage, April to October 1792 (qv).' *Journal of Botany*, 62.
Cavanah, T., 1990. 'Australian Plants cultivated in England, 1771–1800' in P. S. Short, ed. *History of Systematic Botany in Australasia*. Melbourne: Australian Systematic Botany Society.
Clark, A., 1965. 'Titus Smith, Junior, and the Geography of Nova Scotia in 1801 and 1802.' *Annals of the Association of American Geographers*, 54 (4).
Clowes, W. L., 1901. *The Royal Navy: A History.* Vol. 4. London: Sampson Low.
Coleman, E. C., 1988. *Captain Vancouver, North West Navigator.* Whitby: Caedmon.
Colnett, J., 1940. *The Journal of Capt. James Colnett aboard the 'Argonaut' from April 26 1789 to November 1791.* Toronto: The Champlain Society.
Comrie, J. D., 1932. *History of Scottish Medicine.* London: Bailliere, Tindall & Cox.
Cowan, J. M., 1954. 'Some Information on the Menzies and Jack Collections in the Herbarium, Royal Botanic Garden, Edinburgh.' *Notes from the Royal Botanic Garden Edinburgh*, 21.
Dawson, W. R., 1934. *The Smith Papers.* London: Linnean Society of London.
Desmond, R., 1995. *Kew: The History of the Royal Botanic Gardens.* London: Harvill Press.
Dillon, R. H., 1951. 'Archibald Menzies.' *British Columbia Historical Society*, 15.
Eastwood, A. ed., 1924. 'Menzies California Journal.' *California Historical Society Quarterly*, 2(4).
Eastwood, A., 1950. 'Charles Vancouver's Plan.' *Pacific North West Quarterly*, 41.
Elwes, H. J. and Henry, A., 1972. *Trees of Great Britain and Ireland* (7 vol.). Edinburgh: S. C. Wakefield for Royal Forestry Society.
Fisher, R., 1992. *Vancouver's Voyage: Charting the North West Coast, 1791–1795.* Seattle: Douglas & MacIntyre.
Fletcher, H. R. and Brown, W. H., 1970. *The Royal Botanic Garden Edinburgh 1670–1970.* Edinburgh: HMSO.
Friedenberg, Z. B., 2002. *Medicine Under Sail.* Annapolis: Naval Institute Press.
Fry, M., 2001. *The Scottish Empire.* Edinburgh: Tuckwell Press & Birlinn.
Galloway, D. J. and Groves, E. W., 1987. 'Archibald Menzies M.D., F.L.S. (1754–1842) Aspects of his life, travels, and collections.' *Archives of Natural History*, 14.
Galois, R. ed., 2004. *A Voyage to the North West side of America: The Journals of James Colnett.* Vancouver: University of British Columbia Press.
Gascoigne, J., 2004. 'Sir Joseph Banks.' *New Oxford Dictionary of National Biography*, 3 (61 vols).
George, A. S., 1987, *The Banksias Book.* Kenthurst: Kangaroo Press.
Gillies, W. A., 1938. *In Famed Breadalbane.* Perth: Strathtay Clunie Press.
Godley, E. J., 1960. 'A note on Archibald Menzies.' *Transactions of the Royal Society of New Zealand,* 88.
Godwin, G., 1930. *Vancouver, A Life 1757–1798.* London: Philip Allan.

Gorsline, J. ed., 1992. 'Rainshadow: Archibald Menzies and the Botanical Exploration of the Olympic Peninsula.' *Jefferson Historical Society International Maritime Bicentennial.*

Graham, G. S., 1971. *A Concise History of the British Empire.* London: Thames & Hudson.

Gray, J. ed., 1893. *Letters of Asa Gray* (2 vols). London: Macmillan & Co.

Grinnel, J. N., 1932. 'Archibald Menzies, first collector of California Birds.' *The Condor,* 34.

Groves, E. W., 1998. 'Archibald Menzies: An early plant collector on the Pacific north and west coast of America.' *Menziesia,* Vol. 3 Part 1. (Spring).

Groves, E. W., 2001. 'Archibald Menzies (1754–1842), An early plant collector on the Pacific north and west coast of North America.' *Archives of Natural History,* 28.

Harlow, V. T., 1952. *The Founding of the Second British Empire 1763–1793* (Vol. 1).London: Longmans, Green & Co.

Harris, M., 2003. *Botanica North America: the illustrated guide to our native plants, their botany, history, and the way they have shaped our world.* New York: Harper Resources.

Harvey, W. H., 1852–53. *Nereis Boreali Americana* (Parts II and III). Washington & London: John van Voorst.

Hedge, I. and Lamond, J. M., 1970. *Index of Collectors in the Edinburgh Herbarium.* Edinburgh.

Hepper, F. N., (ed.)1989. *Plant Hunting for Kew.* London: HMSO.

Hoare, M. E. ed., 1982. *The Resolution Journal of Johann Reinbold Forster.* London: The Hakluyt Society.

Hollingsworth, S., 1876. *An Account of the Present State of Nova Scotia.* Edinburgh: William Creech & T. Longman.

Home, E. and Menzies, A., 1796. 'A description of the anatomy of the Sea Otter from a dissection made November 15th, 1795.' *Philosophical Transactions of the Royal Society,* 86.

Hull, G., 2001. 'Archibald Menzies (1754–1842) A respected surgeon-naturalist.' *Journal of Medical Biography,* 9.

Hunter, T., 1883. *Woods, Forests and Estates in Perthshire.* Perth: Henderson, Robertson & Hunter.

Jeffery, R. W., 1907. *Dyott's Diary 1781–1845.* London: Constable.

Joestring, E., 1964. *An Introduction to Hawaii.* San Francisco: 5 Associates.

Johnston, J., 1792. *A Guide for Gentlemen Studying Medicine at the University of Edinburgh.* London: printed for G.G.J. and J. Robinson; Bell & Bradfute; Mudie.

Justice, C. L., 1991a. 'Archibald Menzies and the discovery of *Rhododendron macrophyllum.*' *Journal of the American Rhododendron Society,* 45.

Justice, C. L. 1991b. 'Some trees discovered by Archibald Menzies on the shores of the east coast of the Pacific Ocean.' *International Dendrology Society Yearbook.*

Justice, C. L., 2000. *Mr Menzies' Garden Legacy: Plant Collecting along British Columbia's Coast.* Vancouver: Cavendish Books.

Keevil, J. J., 1948. 'Archibald Menzies, 1754–1842.' *Bulletin of the History of Medicine,* 22.

Keevil, J. J. (1957), *Medicine and the Navy 1200–1900* (Vols III and IV), eds. C. Lloyd and J. L. S. Coulter. Edinburgh: E & S Livingstone.

King, J. C. H., 1981. *Artificial Curiosities from the Northwest Coast of America.* King, J. C. H., 1994. 'Vancouver's Ethnography: A preliminary description of five inventories from the voyage of 1791–95.' *Journal of the History of Collections,* 6(1). London: British Museum Publications.

Lamb, W. K. ed., 1984. *A Voyage of Discovery to the North Pacific Ocean and Around the World 1791–1795 by George Vancouver.* London: The Hakluyt Society.

Lamb, W. K., 1993. 'Banks and Menzies: Evolution of a Journal' in R. Fisher and H. Johnson, eds. *From Maps to Metaphors: the Pacific World of George Vancouver.* Vancouver: University of British Columbia Press.

Lane, C. and Leigh, R. 1842. 'Archibald Menzies, Esq. (Obit.).' *Proceedings of the Linnean Society of London,* 1.

Lewington, A. and Parker, E., 1999. *Ancient Trees.* London: Collins & Brown.

Lewis, M., 1960. *A Social History of the Navy 1793–1875.* London: Chatham Publishers.

Lindsay, A., 2005. *Seeds of Blood and Beauty: Scottish Plant Explorers.* Edinburgh: Birlinn.

Louden, J., 1838. 'Genus VI Araucaria.' *Arboretum et Fruticetum Britannicum,* 4.

Lysacht, A. M., 1971. *Joseph Banks in Newfoundland & Labrador 1766: His Diary,*

Manuscripts, & Collection. London: Faber and Faber

Lyte, C., 1980. *Sir Joseph Banks, 18*th *Century explorer, botanist and entrepreneur.* Vermont: David & Charles.

McCarthy, J., 2006. *Wild Scotland.* Edinburgh: Luath Press.

McDiarmed, Rev. J., 1791. *Statistical Account of 1791, Parish of Weem,* 12.

McKay, M. D., 1954. *Aberfeldy Past and Present.* Aberfeldy: Aberfeldy Town Council.

McNab, R. ed., 1908. *Historical Records of New Zealand* (Vol. 1). Wellington: J. Mackay, Govt. Printer.

McNab, R. ed., 1914. *Historical Records of New Zealand* (Vol. 2). Wellington: J. Mackay, Govt. Printer.

Marks, B., 1996. 'Menzies and the Kidnapped Kernels' *Kew.* No. 17 Summer.1996.

Marshall, J., 1823–28. *Royal Naval Biography.* London: Longman, Hurst, Rees, Orme and Brown.

Marshall, J. S. and Marshall, C., 1967. *Vancouver's Voyage.* Vancouver: Mitchell Press.

Masefield, J., 1971. *Sea life in Nelson's time.* 3rd ed. New York: Maynard, C., 2003. *A Nelson Companion: A Guide to the Navy of Jack Aubrey.* London: Conway Maritime Press.

Meany, E. S., 1907. *Vancouver's Discovery of Puget Sound.* New York and London: Macmillan.

Menzies, A., 1828–29. 'An account of the ascent and barometrical measurement of Wha-ra-rai.' *Magazine of Natural History,* 1(2).

Minter, S., 2000. *The Apothecaries' Garden: A New History of Chelsea Physic Garden.* Stroud: Sutton Publishing.

Moll, E., 2006. 'The Cape Floral Kingdom.' *Alpine Gardener: The Bulletin of the Alpine Garden Society,* 74.

Morton, A. G., 1986. *John Hope 1725–1786: Scottish Botanist.* Edinburgh: Edinburgh Botanic Garden (Sibbald) Trust.

Musgrave, T., Gardner, C. & Musgrave, W., 1998. *The Plant Hunters: Two Hundred Years of Adventure & Discovery around the World.* London: Ward Lock.

Naish, J., 1988. 'Archibald Menzies: Surgeon and Botanist.' *International Dendrology Society Yearbook.*

Naish, J. M., 1996. *The Interwoven Lives of George Vancouver, Archibald Menzies, Joseph Whidbey, and Peter Puget.* New York: Edwin Mellen Press.

Neill, P., 1823. *Journal of a Horticultural Tour.* Edinburgh: Bell & Bradfute.

Newcombe, C. F. ed., 1923. *Menzies' Journal of Vancouver's Voyage, April to October 1792,* Archives of British Columbia, Victoria. Memoir 5.

O'Brian, P., 1987. *Joseph Banks: A Life.* London: Collins Harvill.

Olson, W. M., 1993. *The Alaska Travel Journal of Archibald Menzies 1793–1794*. Fairbanks, Alaska: University of Alaska Press.

Raban, J., 1999. *Passage to Juneau: A Sea and its Meanings.* London: Picador.

Raddall, T. H., 1950. *Halifax: Warden of the North.* London: J. M. Dent& Son.

Risse, G. B., 1986. *Hospital Life in Enlightenment Scotland.* Cambridge: Cambridge University Press.

Rodger, D., Stokes, J. & Ogilvie, J., 2006. *Heritage Trees of Scotland* . Edinburgh: Forestry Commission Scotland.

Rosner, L., 1991. *Medical Education in the Age of Improvement: Edinburgh Students and Apprentices.* Edinburgh: Edinburgh University Press.

Schultes, J. A., 1829. 'Schultes's botanical visit to England.' *Botanical Miscellany,* 1.

Scouler, J., 1826. 'Account of a voyage to Madeira, Brazil, Juan Fernandez and the Galapagos Islands performed in 1824 and 1825.' *Edinburgh Journal of Science,* 5.

Sharp, A., 1963. *The Discovery of Australia.* Oxford: Clarendon Press.

Short, P. S. ed., 1990. *History of Systematic Botany in Australasia.* National Library of Australia. SouthYarra, Victoria: Australian Systematic Botany Society.

Small, A. C., 1972. 'Archibald Menzies, MD, FLS (1754–1842).' *Journal of the Scottish Rock Garden Club,* 13.

Smiles, S., 1861. *Lives of the Engineers* (vol. 2), (abridged from 5 vol. 1874 edition by C. J. Shepherd 2006) pp. 275–6. London: Folio Society

Smyly, M., 2006. 'My Favourite Tree'. *Holfordiana,* No. 60.

Stewart, A., 1928. *A Highland Parish or the History of Fortingall.* Glasgow: A Maclaran & Sons.

Thomas, N., 2004. *Discoveries: The Voyages of Captain Cook.* London: Penguin Books.

Turnbull, F., 1954. 'Vancouver and Menzies *or* Medicine on the QuarterDeck.' *Bulletin of the Vancouver Medical Association,* 30(7). pp.277-285

Twain, M., 1938. *Letters from the Sandwich Islands.* Stanford: Stanford University Press.

Villiers, A., 1967. *Captain Cook, the Seamen's Seaman.* London: Hodder & Stoughton.

Walker, M., 2006. 'The Weather Observations of Surgeon Menzies.' *Weather,* 61.

Wilson, W. F. ed., 1920. *Archibald Menzies: Hawaii Nei 128 Years Ago.* Honolulu: New Freedom.

Index